ENGLISH RECUSANT LITERATURE
1558—1640

Selected and Edited by
D. M. ROGERS

Volume 207

How True Christiane Libertie . . .
1614

ST. ROBERT BELLARMINE
Of the Seaven Wordes Spoken
by Christ upon the Crosse
1638

How True Christiane Libertie
Consisteth in the True
Service of God . . .
1614

The Scolar Press
1974

ISBN o 85967 190 9

Published and printed in Great Britain by
The Scolar Press Limited, 59-61 East Parade,
Ilkley, Yorkshire and
39 Great Russell Street,
London WC1

1819630

The following works are reproduced (original size), with permission:

1) *How true Christiane libertie* . . ., [anon.], 1614, from the incomplete unique copy in the library of Prinknash Abbey, by permission of the Librarian.

Not in Allison and Rogers; not in STC.

2) St. Robert Bellarmine, *Of the seaven wordes spoken by Christ upon the crosse*, 1638, from a copy in the library of Ushaw College, by permission of the President.

References: Allison and Rogers 99; STC 1842.

HOVV TRVE CHRISTIANE

LIBERFIE CONSISTETH
IN THE TRVE SERVICE
OF GOD, AND NOT TO
DOE VVHAT EACH ONE
lifteth, as our carnall Gofpellers
would have it be.

A ROVEN,

PRENTET IN THE PRENT HOVS
OF MARIN MICHEL

1614,

HO VV TRVE CHRISTI-
ANE LIBERTIE CONSITETH
*in the true seruice of god, and not to doe
vvhat each one lifteth as our earnall
Gofpellers vvold haue it to be.*

 O the end wee moy the
better vnderftand the carnall libertie of our Gofpellers (which is no other
thing in deed, but the fer-
uice of Sathan (wee fhall deelaire pref-
entlie wherein confifteteth true chriftiã
libertie, which is no other thing Indeede but the true feruice of God, as wee
fhall proofe hereafter.

Before all the things wee muft vnderftand that oure Chriftian libertie carieth
with it felfe tow things, the firft is to be
made freie from the feruile yoke of
Iudaicall cerimonies.

The fecound is to be made free from
deadly finne tirrany of Sathan & gylt-
inffc of eternall damnation, which thrie
things are fo linked to gether that non
of them can be feuered from the other.

As concerning the fiirst point of our Chriſtian Libertie, which is to be free from the ſeruile yoke of Iudaicall cerimonies, it is prooued by theſe authorities of the holy Scriptoure which enſue hereaſter.

Act. 15.

This it is writtene in the Acts of the Apoſtles: why tempt you God, (ſayeth S. Peter) to put a yoke vpon the necks of the Diſciples which neither your ſelues nor yet your Fathers could beare before.

Gal. 4. 9
Gal. 5. 1.
1. Heb. 7.
32. 1.
bid. 18.

But how will you tourne ageine to the weak and poore Eliments, which you will ſerue againe ſtand and be not holden againe with the yoke of ſeruitde, the Prieſthoode: being tranſlated it is neceſſarie that there be alſo a tranſlation of the Lawe. (infra) reprobation being made of the former Commandement, becauſe of the weakneſſe and vnprofitableneſſe thereof for the Lawe brought no thing to perfection.

You ſee by all theſe Authorities of the holy ſcriptoure how theſe rits and cerimonies of the Iewes were troubleſome to be kept becauſe of the greate multitude thereof, they were werke and beggarly Eliments, for ſo much as the could giue

giue no grace at all, as our Sacraments doe to the worthie receiuers. Therfore reprobation was made of them at the cuming of Chtift, which was the time of correction, fo wee were made free from the feruill yoke of all thefe Iudaicall cerimonies. This much concerning the firft point of of Chriftian Libertie.

The feeound point of Chriftian Libertie is to be made free from flauerie of finne Tyrranie of Sathan and gyltineffe of Eternall dantion which thrie things ar fo linked to gether that non of them can be feuered from the other.

For Sathan in the begining of the world did fo fubdue the whole world to his obedience be originall finne when he did withdrawe our firft parents from the obedience of God to his fubieftion, that all thier pofteritie are borne the Children of wraith & indigation in the curfe and malediction of God, fubiect to deadly finne, corporali death and damnaion Eternaall.

Therfore Chrifti calleth Sathan the Prince of this world. S. paul calleth Sathan the God of this world, which hath blinded the minds of Infidells and worketh in the children of difobedience.

ephef. 2 3.

1hon 12 3 1. 2.

cor. 4. 4

ephef. 2. 2.

Chr-

Chriſt compareth him to aſtrong armed man, which keepeth his paliee by ſtrong hand that is the Dominion which he hath ouer the ſoules of men by ſinne, for as the kingdome of Chriſt is Eſtablliſhed in the ſoules of men by grace ſo the kingdome of Sathan is ſtrenthned in the ſoules of men by deadly ſinne.

Act. 2.
33.

Threfore it was decreed in the concell of the holy Erinitie that the ſonne of God ſhould inueſt him ſelfe with humãe nature and ſuffer death vpon the Croſſe for many reſpects, firſt to ſatiſſie the Iuſtice of God, for the offence done to God by Adame and his poſteritie, ſecondly to redeeme the man from the painis of hell, deadly ſinne and Tyrrany of Sathan thirdly to purchaſſe to man the fauoure and grace of God in this world and glorie in the other world to cume.

As concerning Sathan he hade no right to vſurpt any Dominion aboue the ſinnes of men, Becauſe they are creaturs of God and doe nowiſe belong to him, bot the Iuſtice of God for the offence done to God did permite him to take dominion ouer the ſonnes of Adame and to

2. *cor.* 4.
4 *epheſ.*
2. 2.

vſe his Tyrranie againſte them, to deceiue and blind their minds with falſe

Imaginatons

& points of Infidalitie & to ſtirre them
vp to all kind of ſinne and chiefly to
Idolarie.

Sathans Dominion is to greate ouer
the ſonne of men, that there is no humaine power, that may deliuer them from
his Tyrraie, without the ſpeciall vertue *Iob.* 41.
and aſſiſtance of God, for there is no
power ſayeth God vpon earth that may 24 *Tit.*
be compared to his power. 3. 12.

This Dominion and Tyrranie of Sat-
han is taken away from the ſonnes of *epheſ.* 6.
men, by the Sacrameut of penitence, but 12.
chiefly by the vertue of Baptiſme. where
in the mereits of Chriſts paſſ.ō are fully
applyed to them, where they obtaine
remiſſione of all their ſinnes Iuſtified &
made the ſonnes of God, & ſo tranſlated
from the power & Dominion of Sathan
to the Kingdome of Chriſt.

So in that conſiſteth chiefely Chriſtian
Libertie, to be déliuered from the gilt
of Eternall damnation deadly ſinne. & *chiefe*
Tyrranie of ſathan; for theſe thrie things *fruun* of
are ſo linked to gether that non of them *C hʳyi*
can be ſeueered from the othere, for the *paſſſt*
chiefe fruits of Chriſts paſſion conſiſt in
that, men ſhould be dcliuered from the
ſlarerie of ſinne, Tyrtanie of ſathan, &
giltineſſe

giltineſſe of Eternall death, that (ſo being reſtored to the grace and fauour of
God) wee may from hencefourth ſerus
God by Chriſtian Iuſtiee and holyneſſe
of Life, as S. Luke wriett without feare
being deliuered from the hands of our
enimis wee may ſerue ham in holyneſſe
and Iuſtiee all the dayes of our Life

luc. 1.
74.

Ihon 8.
34.

Chriſt did deliuer his faitfull floxe frõ
the ſeruitud and bondage of dedly ſinne
as he ſayeth in the Euangell of S. Ihon
verely I ſay vnto you that whoſeuer co-
miteth ſinne is ſeruant vnto ſinne, but
yf the ſonne ſhall deliuere you form ſinne, you ſhall be free Indeede.

Youe ſee here how Chriſtian Libertie
conſiſteth in that wee by the grace of
Chriſt ſhould be deliuered from the ſeruitud and bondage of deadly ſinne.

Rom. 6.
16.

S. paul likewiſe ſayeth to this purpoſe,
knowe you not that to whom ſoeuer you
giue your ſelues as ſeurnts to obey. that
you are ſeurnts to him whõ to you obey
whether it be to ſinne, vnto death, or
obedience vnto Iuſtice, and when you
were the ſeruants of ſinne, you were voide of Iuſtiee.

Here you ſee that the ſeruitude and
bondage of men, is to ſinne vnto deảtd,
                                        and

Christian libertie to liue in Iustice and holynosse of life.

As concering our deliuerie from the tyrranie of Sathan, Chrst sayeth: the prince of this world shall be cast fourth, that is out of the Dominon ouer mens soules.

Ihon 2. 23.

Colloss. 1. 23.

S. Paul sayeth likewese to the collossians who hath deliuered vs from the power of darknesse and hath translated vs in the Kingdome of his deare sonne. You see here how our Christion libertie consisteth in that point, that is to be deliuered from the power and tyrrany of sathan and since translated to the Kingdom of heaun, by the grace of Christ giuen vnto vs in the Sacramsnt of Baptisme and penitence by the merits of his passion.

1. Ihon.

S. Ihon in his cànonicall Epistle writeth to the same purpose saying: he that sinneth is of the Deuill, for this purpose the sonne of God was made manifest that he might disolue and driue away the workes of cf Deuill.

Marke here that as the seruitud and bondags of man consisteth in deadly sinne which is the seruice of the Diuill so our Christiã libertie côsisteth in Iustice and

& holyneſſe of life, which is the ſeruice
of God, for this cauſe the ſonne of God
did come in this world to diſolue and
driue away ſinne, which is the woeke &
ſeruice of Sathan, to make men worke
the workes of iuſtice. which is the ſeruice of God and true Chriſtian libertie of
the ſoule.

Therefore S. Paul ſayeth: being made
free from ſinne you are made ſeruants
vnto Iuſtice. (againe) the Lawe of the
ſpirit of life by Chriſt Ieſus hath fredde
me from the Lawe of ſinne and death
that is as much as yf he wold ſay. as the
Lawe of God written in the tables of
ſtones did condeme all ſuch to the death
as did not keepe the ſame, ſo the lawe of
ſpirit of grace graffed and written in the
hearts of the faithfull, deluereth them
from ſuch ſinne and death in making
them to keepe the ſame, according to
the ordinance of God.

That this Lawe of the ſpirit of grace
which deliuereth men from the ſlauerie
of deadly, Tyrranie of Sathan, & giltineſſe of Eternall death. is graffed and
written in the ſoules of the faithfull of
the New Teſtament S. Paul writteth againe expreſly to the Hebrewes ſeying
for

Ephel.
1. 4.
Ephel. 2.
10.
Rom. 6.
18.

hebr. 8.
10.

for this is the Newe Testament which I will dispose to the House of Israell, after these dayes sayeth our Lord, giuen my lawes in their minds and in their herrts, I will writt them,

Thus as the breach of the written lawe of God maketh men slaues to sinne. to Sathan, and giltie of Eternall damntion: Rightso the Lawe of grace graffed and written in the hearts of the faithfull maketh them to keee the written Lawe, and consequently deiuereth them from the Curse of the written Lawe, that is from the slauerie of deadly. sinne Tyrraie of Stahan and giltinesse of Eternall death, as S. paul writteth to the Romams: so our Christion libertie consisteth in that point, that the faithfull by the Lawe of grace graffed in their hearts by the merits of Iestis Christ are truely made free from the slauerie of deadly sinne Tyrrany of Sathan and giltinesse of Eternall death, and inableth them to serue God freely & glaidly, by Christian Iustce, and holynesse of life, as S. Luke writteth in his Euangell. **Rom. 8. 2.**

This freedome from sinne the Angell of God did promise, when he said to S. Iosephe: Iesus shall saue his people from their **Jae. 74. mat. 1. 21. tit. 2. 14.**

thair sinnes S. paul also sayeth: Christ
gaue him selfe for vs that he might redeeme vs from all Iniquitie.

So yf wee were not made free from
deadly sinne and Iniquite, Tyrrauie of
Sathan and giltinesse of Eeternall deatd,
Chrst can nowrse be called our sauiour
and redemptour, because our freedeme,
Christian libertie, and redemption consisteth chiefely in that point (according
to the former Scriptours) that Christ
redemed vs from our sinnes and Iniqui-
ties, Tyrranie of Sathan, and giltinesse
of Eternall death, and yf wee abyde still
in deadly sinne (as the protestants will
haue all men to doe (then they must
also grant that they doe not only abid in
slauerie of deadly sinne, but also in the
Tyrranie of Sathan, and giltinesse of
Eternall damnation, without true Christian libertie, because deadly sinne,
Tyrranie of Sathan, and giltinesse of
of Eetrnall dath are so linked together
(as is mentioned aboue) that it is impossible to any of them to be seuered fró
the other.

Rom. 8.
11.   S. Paul writteth againe: the creature
shall be deliueaed from the seruitud and
bondago of corruptió in to the glorious
libertie

libertie of the sonnes of God.

Here S. Paul opposeth the libertie of the sonnes of God to the seruitude and bondage of corruption. the corruption of man is deuyded in tow kinds, in the corruption of the qualitiee of the sonne, which man did contract by our mortalitie of the Bodie.

This corruption of the facultie of the soule is an habituall auer sion from God, which is deuided in tow pairts in the auer sion of the mind from God, & corruption of the concupissance.

The auer sion of the mind from God is formalli originall sinne, and corruption of the concupissence an effect therof

This auer sion of the mind is taken away by Baptismant grace. when the Children of Adame are made the sonnes of God. and also by the Sacrment of Penitence when the man tourneth from deadly sinne to the fauour and grace of God againe.

S. Paul speaking of this renouation of the mind, which is our first iustification thus writteth to the Ephesians renued in the spirit of your mind and put on the new man which according to God is created in the Iustice and holynesse of
trueth

D. Tom
Q. 82.
art. 1.3.

Mat·
28. 16.
Mar c.
16. 16.
Eze ch
18. 21.
Ihon 2
20. 0 2.
Ephes.
4. 23.
Ephes.
6. 14

trueth: (againe) ſtand therfore hauing
your loynes girded in truth and clothed
with the briſtplate of Iuſtice.

Thus as the man did looſe originall
Iuſtice in his ſoule by the fall of Adame:
ſo his mind is rernued & clothed agane
by the grace of Iuſtification, which he
obtaineth in the Sactament of Penitence
by the mirits of Chriſts Paſſion; ſo the
corruption of the mind is taken away
by the grace of Iuſtificatiõ in thes world

As concering the corrption of the
concuſpiſſeuce which is an effect of
originall ſinne, it is litle and litle taken
away by the mortificaton of the fleſh &
worthie recption of the holy Sacrament
for the diſordained affectious of the
concupiſſence, are ſo bond by the grace
of God receiued in the holy Sacrament
that the Spirituall man hath full Dominion ouer them, although they be not
altogether extinguiſhe in him.

Thus when the mind of man is conuerted to God, and the diſordained affections of the concupiſſence ſubdued to
the obedience of reaſon by the grace
of God, then the coruption ſett at libertie from the Dominion of the diſor-
daind affections of the concnpiſſence
which

*howv
reaſn is
ſett at
libeytie*

which is true Christian libertie.

As contrariwse when the disordained affections of the concupissance ouer throw reason and stirre vp men to deadly sinne, then the man is drawen away frō his true Christian libertie, (which consisteth in the Iustice of the soule and holynesse of life) and reason is made seruant to the concupissance, & the man slaue to-sinne, drudge to Sathan, & also giltie of Eternall damnatione.

For as deadly sinne, Tyrraie of Sathan, and giltinesse of Eternall damnation are properly the curse of the writtē Lawe, which euery man doe incurre by transgression of the same, so the lawe of the spirit of life is grafted in the soules of the faitfifull, which deliuereth them from such a curse of the written lawe in making them to keepe the same by the vertue of Christian Iustice & holynesse of life giuen by the grace of God as S. Paule writteth to tbe Romains saying: the lawe of the spirit of life by Christ Iesus hath freedde me from the lawe of *Rom 8.* sinne and death. againe Christ hath re- *2.* deemed vs from the curse of the lawe, *Galat.* that is when he did purchase such abou- *3 ᵵ3.* ndance of gracc to his Elect by his deatd

vpon

vpon the Croſſe, as enableth them tõ keepe the lawe, and ſo ſaue them from the curſſe of the ſame.

Thus as the corruption of the mind is taken away by theſe gifes of grace in this world, rightſo the corruption and mortalitie of the Bodie ſhall be taken away by the gifts of giorie in the other world to come.

Therifore it flloweth by good conſequence that the libertie of the ſonnes of God conſiſteth in the gifts of grace which make the faithfull free from deadly finne, Tyrranie of Sathan, and gilthíeſſe of eternall death in this world, & in the gifts of glorie, which inueſt the corruptible Bodie of man with Incorruption in the world to come.

VVherefore S. Paul ſpeaking of the libertie of the ſonnes of God by grace in this world, he thus writteth to the Galatians ſaying: for Bretheré you haue been called vnto libertie only vſe not your lebertie in occaſion of the fleeſh, but by Charitie ſerue on an other. ſo our Chriſtian libertie is not to Liue according to the fleeſh and to doe what wee liſt without ſubiection to any lawe, as the Protiſtante wol haue it to be, but

Gelat. 5. 13.

to

to serue one an other by Christian Charitie and holynesse of lite.

S. Iames in his canonicall Epistle doth
confirme the same thus writting but he
that looketh in the lawe of perfect liber- *Iacob.* 1.
tie and hath remained in it not made
a foregetfull hearer but a doer of the 25.
same, the worker shall be blessed in his
deede.

Here you see how Iames in this sente-
tce calleth the lawe of perfect liberte; so
that Christian libertie and hapinesse of
man is to abyd constantly in the lawe of
God and so he shall be bleessed in his
workes & deeds when he faitfully doth
keepe the same. *2.cor.* 3.

S. Paul likewise sayeth: where the 17.
spirit of onr Lard is there is libertie, this *Rom.* 5.
is the spirit of life of grace (as S. Paul 5.
writteth to the Romains) powred in
the hearts of the faithfull, which deliuereth thē not only from the seruile yoke
of the olde lawe but also from the slauerie of deadly sinne & seruitud of Sathan.

Therefore as true Christian libertie
and hapinesse of man stand in the keeping of Gods Cōmandemrth, which is
no other thing but to loue God and our
Nightbour faithfully by Charitable
aficction

C

affection. ſo the boūdardge ſeructde and vnhapineſſe of man, coſiſiſt in the breach and tranſgreſſion of Gods cōmandements, whereby the tranſgreſſour maketh him ſelfe bound ſlaue to deadly ſinne, and gratfull ſeruant to Sathan and giltie of eternall damnation.

Now good reader to conclude this purpoſe, you may ſee moſt euidently by theſe former authoritites of the holy ſcriprour, how true Chriſtian libertie conſiſteth in the ſeruoce of god, whereby the fathfull doe ſerue god by true Iue. 2. 74. Chriſtian libertie and holyneſſe of life (as S. Luke writteth) and not to liue acording to the fleeſh and to doē what eatch on deſireth without ſubiection to any lawe, eitheir diuine or humaine, as our Proteſtants wold haue their Chriſtian libert e to be, according to their goſpell.

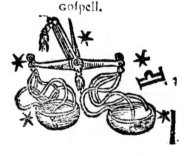

HOVV THE LIBERTIE
VVHICH THE PROTE-
STANTS CHALLENGE VN-

to them selues by their Gospell, is not
true Christian libertie. vvhich confi-
steth in the true seruice of God
and holynesse of life.

(As is prooued abue) but bodage
anc flauerie of finne and damnable feruice mad to Sathan.

WE haue prooued aboue in the
Chapter before how true Chriftian libertie confifteth in the
true feruice of God, Chriftian Iuftice
and holyneffe of life.

Now it refteth to prooue that the
libertie of the Gofpell which the Proteftants challenge to the them felues, is
not true Chriftian liberie, but flauerie
of finne, and damnble feruice of Sathan.

For probation of this point, you
moft vnderftan that the chiefeft point of
the Proteftants libertie (which they call
falfly Chriftian libertie) is to be exempt
and

and made free in their conſciecs from
the keeping of the Lawe of God, ſo that
it hath no power to accuſe or condemne
them before the Iudgement of God,
when they tranſgreſſe the ſame.

For Luther, writeth in his comentaries to the Galatians.

Luth
cap 2 n̄
Galath: t
only fad r
is neceſſa
to ſaluat-
ion all
vvorkes
are indiff
erentibid
Luther
bath no
thing to
doe vvith
the lavy

Sola fides neceſſaria eſt, vt Iuſti ſimus,
cætera omniæ liberrima, neque præcepta amplius
neque, prohibita. that is, only faith is neceſſarie that wee be iuſt, all other things
are free, neither Cõmanded, nor yet
forbiden.

He writteth againe in that ſame place:
Si conſcientia dictat peccaſti, Reſponde peccaui.
Ergo Deus punietet damnabit, non, at lex hoc
docet, nihil mihi cum lege, quare quia habeo
Libertaem: that is, yf thy conſcience accuſe the that thou haſt ſinned anſwere
I haue ſinned then God will puniſh and
condamne this, nor yet the Lawe of firm-
eth the ſame but I haue no thing to doe
with the Lawe wherefore; becauſe I haue
libertie.

Here Luther oppoſeth their Chriſtian
libertie, ſo to the Lawe of God, that the
on can not ſtand with the other, wherefore ſuch as are ſubiect to keepe the
Lawe of God haue no Chriſtian libertie,
and likewiſe ſuch as haue Chriſtian libe-
libertie

libertie haue no thing to due with the Lawe of God. thus ne make h all Proteſtants free frome keeping of the Lawe of God, the by their Chriſtian libertie, ſo they may doe what they pleaſe contrarie to the Lawe of God, withont ſcruple of conſcience, becauſe it hath no power to occuſe or condemne them before the Iuhment of God, according to this doctrine of Luthers.

Luther writteth againe in his Booke of Chriſtian libertie *Nullo opere, Nulla. lege homini Chriſtiano opus eſt cum per fidom fit Liber ab omni lege.* that is as yf he wold ſay the Chriſtian man hath on need of any worke or of any Lawe becauſe he is made free from all Lawes, by faith in Chriſt.

Thus you ſee good riader how Luther maketh all his proteſtants free in their conſciencer from keeping of rhe Lawe of God, ſo that they may doe what they pleaſe without damnation prouiding they beleeue to be ſaue in the blood of Chriſt.

Caluin taixeth Luther by the hand in this point of Chriſtian libertie, thus writting in his Inſtitutions of the Lawe of God, which are the ten morall cōmandements

Col. lib. 2 Inſt. cap 7. ſect 14

andementes: *Nunc Ergo quomam &c.* Now
therefore becaufe the Lawe hath a
power towards the faithfull not fuch a
power as may bind their confciences
with a curfe (Infra) or to make them
offrayed confounding their côfcences
with a curfe deftroy the tranfgreffours
therof.

Thrie things are to be confidered in
thefe worde of Caluins: the firft is that
the Lawe hath no power to condemne
the trnfgreffour, or malefactour, with
D. Tom. a curfe that is (as much as yf he wold
in cap. 3. fay) that the Lawe of God hath no
ad Galat. power to condemne the tranfgreffour,
as gilty of death, for the curfe of the
Lawe is not only priuation of grace
which is the death of the foule, in this
life, punition likewife by corporall
Mat. 25. deatd, but alfo damnation eternall as
Chrift fayeth: go you accurfed to euer
lafting fire.

The fecound poent dependeth vpon
the firft that is eôfidering that the Lawe
of God hath no power to condemen the
tranfgreffour with a curfe, or giltineffe
of death, the tranfgreffour or malefactour, needeth not to be affrayed for any
punition, when he tranfgreffeth the fam
                                        this

This is the libertie they challenge to
them lelues to doe all kind of euill, without all feare of Gods Iudgement or
damnation eternall,

The third point not vnlike tow formé,
is that the Lawe of God hatd no power
to confoúd or deftroy the tranfgreffour,
that is as yf he wold fay, the Lawe of
God hath no power to confound the
tranfgaeffour or malefactor in the Iudgement of God nor yet power to condemne, or deftroy him by eternll damnation, aginft that fentetnce of S. Paul
writtlng to the Hebrewes: a man defpyfing the Lawe of Moyfes without any
mercie daith vnder tow or therie witne-
ffis. how much more thinke you doth he
deferue worfe punifhment. which hath
troden the fonne of God vnder foote
that is in defpyfing his Lawe and cómandements.

heb. 10.
18.

Caluin writteth againe: for fith the
Lawe Leaueth no man righieous, either
wee are execluded from all hope of 'ufti-
fication, or wee moft be loofed from the
Lawe, and fo that there be no regaird at
all hade of workes, (Infra) therefore
taiking away all mention of the the
Lawes, and laying afide all thinking

lib. 3.
Inft. cap.
16. *fect*
2.

vpon

vpon workes, wee muſt embrace the only mercie of God, when wee entreat of Iuſtication.

Here good reader you ſhall obſerue that Caluin,, to eſtabliſh his Iuſtifieatiō by only faith in the blood of Chriſt, and merice of God hee maketh him ſelfe free from the Lawe of God, and all good workes as ſeruing to no purpoſe, for their Iuſtification and ſaluation.

Ibidem. *ſeʄt.* 4. Caluin writteth againe our conſcience being free from the voke of the Lawe it ſelfe, of their owen aceord let them obey the will of God.

This is as much as yf he wold ſay the conſciekes of the proteſtants and purit-ans, will not be conſtrained by any Lawe, to obey the will of God, or to doe any good workes, but yf they pleaſe to obey the will of God, and worke good workes of their awen accored & good will they may doe the ſame, and yf in caſe they doe otherwiſe, they are ſo free from the yoke of the lawe, that it hath no power to condemne them with *Cal. lib.* a curſe affray, confound, or deſtroy thē *2. Inſt.* when they tranſgreſſe the ſame, as Cal-*cap.* 7. uin writteth in the ſecond bookes of his *ſeʄt.* 14. Inſt.

This much concering the firſt point
of the Proteſtants libertie. whereby they
make them ſelues free from keeping of
the Lawe of God, with freedome to doe
what they pleaſe, either good or euil
without ſcruple of conſcience, feare of
Gods Iudgements, or eternall domnatō

The ſecound point of their Chriſtiā
libertie, is to be made free in their conſciences from the Lawes of temporall
Princes and Magiſtrats, ſo that they
ſtieke not for feare of conſciences to,
tranſgreſſe the Lawes of their Prince
when the they may doe it ſecreetly without ſlander or punition of Magiſtrate.

For Luther writteth in his booke Int-
iuled of the capiutie of Babilon. *quo iure*
Papa. &c. by what right doth the pope
ordaine Lawes vpon vs, who gaue him
power to thruſt in captiuitie the libertie
which is giuen vs by Baptiſme, neither.
the Pope Biſhope or any other mortall
man hath powere to bind any Chriſtian
man with the ſyllabe, of any Lawe vnleſſe it be the mans conſent.

luth. lib.
de capti-
uit. Bab-
ilna cap
de Bapti-
ſmo.

Thus you ſee good reader, how no
mortall man hath power to bind the
conſciencs of the Protſtants, whether
he be a ſpirituall or tempoarall prnce
vnleſſe

D

vnleſſe it bemade by the mans owen
conſent, for Baptiſme ſayeth, Luther,
hath made them all free in conſceinces
from the Lawes of mortall men, ſo the
P. oteſtáts without ſcruple of conſcieces
may tranſgreſſe the Kings Lawe, when
they may doe the ſame quyetly without
ſlander and punition of the Mahiſtrate
Luther againe writteth the ſame erroour
in his booke of Chriſtian libertie.

Caluin agreeth with Luther in this
point of doctrine of the libertie from
Lawes of princes thos writting: *Iam vero*
com &c. Now therefore ſith faithfull
conſciences, hauing receiued ſuch prerogatiue of libertie, as wee haue aboue
ſette foorth (Infra) wee conclude that
they are exempt from all power of men
(Infre) Paull declaireth, that Chriſt is
deſtroyed vnleſſe our conſciences ſtand
faſt in their libertie, which verely they
haue loſt, yſ they may at the will of man
be ſnared with their bounds of Lawes &
ordinances.

Here you ſe good reader, according
to this doctrins of Caluins, how the
conſciences of the Proteſtants, can not
be bound by any power of Lawes or
ordinances of men.

Ther

Belarm.
lib 4 de
ſum mo
pont fice,
cap. 15

Therefore what euer the King or temporall Prince, command the Protestants to doe by their Lawes, the Protestants are not bound in consciece to keepe the Kings Lawes, but may transgresse them when they please without scruple of conscience, and chiefely when they doe it quyetly without slaunder or punitiō of the magistrat, so thes libertie which the Proteltants challaunge to thē selues is to be free from keeping of all Lawes (as much of God as of man) this is no other thing but to haue libertie to cōmite all kind of sinnes which are forebidden by the Lawes of God and man. *lib.* 4.

Caluin writteth againe: moreour this encresseth the difficultie that Paul teacheth that the Magistrat ought to be obeyed not only for feare of punishment but also for consciences saixe, wher vpō follouth that consicints are also bound with the politique Lawes, but yf it were so then all should fall that wee haue spxen in the laft chapter, and Intend now to speaxe concerning the spirituall gouernment.

Inst cap. 10. *sect.* 3.

S. Paul Rom. 13. 1.

Here you fee good reader how *Caluin* reasoneth againft the truth when he sayith: that the consciences were bound by politique Lawes (as S. Paul sayeth) thē

all

all that he hath said aginst this opiaion should fall and that also which he is to speake of spirituall gouerament thereafter: so he thinketh no shame to dispute against the expresse words of S. Paul, which sayeth that the magistrat ougt to be obeyed not only for feare of punitiõ, but also for conscience siake, which sentence the Protestans deny, to establish their Iustification by only faith, without all good workes cõmanded by the lawe of God and man.

'Rhm31
I.
libertie to
sinne as
Caluin
teacheth
Ibid. sect

Caluin writteth againe that althought the Bishops of the Romaine Chnrch were true Bishops (as they are) yet I deny that they are therefore apointed Lawe makers ouer the faithfull.

Ibid. sect

Caluin writtetd againe thus saying our consciences haue on thing to doe with men, but with God only.

Thus you see euere where, how Caluin denyetd flatly, that consciences of the faithfnll be bound by the Lawes of men, whether they be spiriual or temporall. so that is the libertie of their Gospell, is to doe what they pleafe without controlling of any Lawe, either of God or man, as prooued aboue.

The third point of their libertie, is
to

to be mad free from the working of all good workes, and not bound in conscience before God to worke them, but to esteme of them as things indifferent, so that the faithfull shall nowise be touched in his conscience to vse indifferently all outward actions. at some times, and some time leaue theme vnused, as it pleaseth him to doe.

For proofe of this point of their libertie they affirme that difference which is betwene the Lawe of Moyses in the old Testament and the Euangell of Christ in the nowe Testament, is that the Lawe of Moyses promised Iustification and saluation to only such as did keepe the Lawe: but the Euangell of Christ (say they promiseth Iustification and saluation by only haith in Christ, without any condition to keepe the Lawe of God or yet to worke good workes. *Luth. in cap. 2 t. ad gaplan philiti. de locis lege ett euangelioi*

This is the very ground of their Religion and libertie of their gospell, to obtaine both Iustification & saluuation by only faith in Christ, without any condition to keepe the ten comandements of God, or to worke any good workes at all,

For Luther writeth thus in his comentaries

cōmentaries to the Galatians: *Sola fides*
neceſſaria eſt. vt Iuſti ſimus, cætera omnia libe-
rina, neque precepta amplius n°q, prohibita.
That is only faith is neceſſarie to make
vs iuſt. all other thengs are free or Indifferent, neither cōmanded nor yet fore-
biden.

You ſee by theſe words of Luthers
that only faith is neceſſarie to ſaluation
all other things (as good workes are fre
and Indifferent, neither cōmanded nor
yet forebidden: ſo the Proteſtants are
not bound in conſeience, before God
to worke good workes but they may
worke them, or not worke them Inde-
fferenetly, as they pleaſe, becauſe they
are neither cōmanded nor yet forebidd-
en, according to this doctrine of luthers
Luther writteth againe in the argument
of the Epiſtle to the Cialatians: *Summa*
ars et ſapientia Chriſtiano eſt, neſcire Legem,
Ignorare opera, et totam Iuſtitiam actinam
that is, the higheſt arte and Chriſtian
wiſdome, is to miſknow the Lawe, for-
eget all good workes, and all actuall
Iuſtice.

You ſee how he baniſheth Cleane
away all good workes, which are the
actuall Iuſtice of Godlie Chriſtians
with the Lawe of God it ſelfe.

Luther

Luther writteth againe in his booke of Christian libertie: *Null opere. Nulla lege homini Christiano opus est, cum per sit liber ab omni lege.*

That is the Christian man hath no neede of any worke or of any lawe. sith by faith in Christ he is made free from all lawes.

You see here how they are not bound in conscience to workes before God, but make them selues free from working of all good workes by their faith in Christ only. thus when they are not bound to worke no good workes in their côscence before God, they must haue libertie to liue in 'sinne and doe what they please.

Luther writteth againe in his booke of christian libertie: *Bona opera non faciunt vnum bonum. nec mala malum.* that is, good workes makes not a man good, nor euill workes make not a man euill.

So according to this doctrine the Christian man needeth neuer to paine him selfe to doe good worke, because he is neuer better to doe the same, and like-wsehe needeth neuer to feare to doe any euill workes or any sinne that may plea-sour him, because it will not make him worse in doing the same.

luther

lib. de lib Christ.

no laure or good vvorke needfull to the protestants.

Luther writteth againe: *vbi fides est nullum peccatum noccre potest;* where faith is no sinne can harme the man.

Here he trketh the feare of God cleane away, and teacheth the man that he may com't all kind of sinnes he pleaseth, without hurt of his conscccnce & saluation prouyding he beleeue in Christ.

*Luth. lib.
de capte-
uit babi-
lonica.
cap. Bap-
tismo.*

He writteth againe: *vidi quame dines sit homo Christianus, vell Baptisatus. vt etiam volens, non posset perdere saluem suam, quantiscunq peccatis, nisi uolet credere, nullaenim peccata possunt Illum dammare nisi sela Incredulitas.* Thou seest how rich the Baptised Christian is, that euen willingly he can not loose his saluation, howsoeuer great his sinnes be vnlesse he will not beleeue, for no sinne can condemne him but only Incredulitie.

VVhat malitious spirir of hell could haue giuen greater libertie to man to comet all crymes of the world, to satisfie his concupssance & disordaed appetite, without all feare of conscience, then Luther hath giuen here to his Protestants when he sayeth that the Christiants, man can not loose his saluation howsoner great his sinnes be, vnlesse he wile not beleeue, & that no sinne can harme him

him or condemne, but only Incredulitie.

This is the libertie of their gospell to
be made free from the working of all
good workes with libertie to cõmit all
the sinnes of the world, for bidden by
the lawes of God and man, wherefore
this libertie of theirs is not true Chriſtian
libertie, which is the true ſeruice of
God to worke good workes, but the
damnable ſeruice to Sahan.

Now yf you will aſke at Ihon Caluin
what he beleeueth concerning the working of good workes, he will ſay to you,
that the faithfull are not bound in con-
ſcince before God to worke good workes
but to hold them as things Indifferent,
to be vſed, or left vnuſed according to
the will of man.

For thus he writteth in the third booke
of his Inſtitutions: either wee are exclu-
ded from the hope of Iuſtication or wee
muſt be looſed from the lawe & ſo that
there be no regarde at all head of good
workes (Infra) therefore taiking away
all maution of the lawe and laying aſide
all thinking vpon workes, wee muſt
embrace the only merele of God, when
wee Intreat of Iuſtification.

Caluin in theſe words maketh him
ſelf e

Cal. libr.
3 Inſt.
cap. 19.
ſeſt. 2.

selfe and all his disciples free from keeping of the Lawe of God, and working of good workes, to establish his Iustification by only faith.

Ibidl sest
6.

Caluin writteth agiane speaking of their Christian libertie: the third pairt (of Christian libertie) is that wee be bound with no conscience before God of any outward things, which are by them selues Indifferent, but that wee may indifferently some time vse them, and some time leaue them vnused.

Caluin in these words holdeth all the outward actions of the bodie, and good of the faithfull, as things Indifferent to be vsed or left vnused according to the will of man prouyding he hold fast the inward action of the soule, which is to beleeue to Iustified in Christ, setting asid the Lawe of God and all good workes as is mentioned before.

An other proofe wherefore the Protestants hold them selues free in conscience before God, from the working of all good workes, is that they esteeme all the good workes of iust man to be but deadly sines weighted in the Iudgement a God, and because God will not Cómand a man to cómit deadly sinne, thence

thence is that they are free in confcience
before God from the warking of all
good workes, which are no other thing
but dedly finnes, as they all rme them
felues. weighated in the Iudgemena of
God.

For Luthet thus writteth in his affert-
ions: that no mon is, which fhould not
perfuad him felfe to finne deadly at all
times, yf his life be compared to the
Iugement of God.

Caluin likewife agreeth with Luther
thus writtig: that which is amongft the
comoune people accounted righteoune-
effe it before God meere wickedneffe.

All the Proteftants and Puriains agree
in this point of Religion, that there beft
workes weighted in the Iudgemen, of
God are but deadly finnes, or then Infected with the poyfon of deadly finne,
therefore they affirme that they are not
bound in confcience to worke them.

This is the libertie of their gofpell to
be free in confcience before God from
the worxing of good worxes with librtie
to doe what they pleafe, prouyding they
beleue to be faue in the Blood of Chrift,
without the workes of the Lawe,

VVhat other thing is this libertie of

*lib. 3.
Inft. cap.
22. fect.
4.*

*libertie to
cõmit all
kind of
finnes.*

our

our gofpellers but only (as S. Peter fayed) a veale or Cookft of malice to doe what they pleafe, vnder pretence of their libertie, and faith in the blood of Chrift.

1. pet. 2. 18. Protestants are feruauts to their owen corcupiffance and bune flauees to finue and Saran. 2. Pet. 2. 18.

And in an other place they fpeaking proud prefumptàous words of vanitie they allure in defires to with drawe the felues from finne and errour promitting them libertie (that is to performe without feruple of confcience their owen carnall defires (where as they them felues are the feruants of corruption, that is of their owen corrupted concupiffance difordained appetite, vitious affections for of whome a man is ouercome, of that he is the flaue; alfo confidering therefore, that they are ouercome by theire owen vitious defires and likewife by Sathan, they are flaues to their owen vitious defires and feruants to Sathan, which holdeth them (as S. Paul faveth) in his fnares and captiuit. at his owen will·

2, Tim 2. 26.

Althought wee haue fuffie’ently prouued (as much by the holy Scripturs as by their owen doctrine) how the libertie of their gofpell is no other thing but to be exeemed and made free in their consciences from the workin̄g of all good workes to establiſh their Iuſtification by only faith in the blood of Chriſt neuer the leſſe for the better Inſtructiō of theſe that are ſemple and In gnorant. I thougt good to make their libertie (which is but a veale of malice) mere euident to the whole worlde by ſuch exampels as eſſue hereafter.

The firſt example is yf a Proteſtant̄ Merchrtn which is to paſſe to on cuntrey where Idolatrie is profeſſed, wold aſke at hie Miniſter yf he minght with ſaue conſcience goe to the Idolater Church and there adore the Idolls of the cuntrey with ſaue conſcience, for the ſauetie of his life, and free traficking in the contrey, the Miniſter could anſwere to him no other wiſe (according to the former doctrine of the Proteſttants and libertie of their Goſpell) but that he might goe in to the Idolater Church, & there adore Idolls, becauſe he is not bound in conſcience to keepe the Lawe of God where ti is ſaid: The Lord thy God thou ſhalt ador and him alone ſerue *Deut. 6. 13.*

The ſecound example is: yf a man which can not be reuenged of an other by force, for the diſpight and Inuy he

carieth

carieth againſt his enimie, wold demãd
at his Miniſter yf he might Inpoyſon
him with ſaue conſcience, and ſo beraue
his enmie of his life the Miniſter muſt
ſay (accordind to the libertie of their
Goſpell) that he might kill his enimie
any way that lyth in the reach of his
power without hurt of his conſciece,
becauſe he is not bound in conſcence to
keepe the lawe of God where it is ſaid:
thou ſhalt not kill or ſlay the nightbour.

The third example is: yf a genlle
woman which were adected wantoeſſe,
wold aſke quyetly at her Miniſter, yf
ſhe with ſaue conſcience might play the
wanton with a young ſtrgpeling by her
huſband, the Miniſter muſt anſwere to
her, that ſhe may paſſe hir time with any
young man ſhe likеth beſt prouiding
ſhe doe the tourne quyetly without ſlã-
under, becauſe ſhe is not bound in conſcience to keepe the comandement of
God where it is ſaid: Thou ſhalt not
cõmit adultriee, by reaſon of the libertie
of the their Goſpell, and faith in the
blood of Chriſt & likwiſe that ſhe hath
not freewill to reſiſt ther temptaion, but
that ſhe muſt yeelde vnto the ſame for
that is their doctrine.

The

The fourth example is yf a feruant Proteftante which hade the handling of his Maifters filuer wold afke at his Minifter, yf he might take any of his maifters goods or guere quyetly with faue confcience, the Minifter muft anfwere to him that the feruent Proteftant may take his Maifters guere with faue confcience puouiding he doe the fame quyetly without flaunder, becaufe he is not bound in confcience (by reafon of the libertre of their Gofpelle) to keepe the cómandements of God, where it is faid: thou fhalt not fteelle, and likewife becaufe he hath not freewill to refift the temptation but that he muft yeeld vnto the fame according to their doctrine.

The fift example is yf a man wold Inqire of his Minifter yf he might with faue confcience be a fals witneffe and fore fweare him felfe to pleafour his friend in any action of Iuftice, becaufe he may gaine twantie crounes of the funne fo to doe, the Minifter con anfwere no otherwife, but he may doe the fame with faue cenfience, prouiding he doe his tourne fecreetly, becaufe the liberte of their Gofpell faith in the Blood of Chrift haue deliuered and him

end

and made him free in conſcience from the keeping of that Lawe where it is ſaid:thou ſhalt not beare falſe witnenſſe againſt thy nighbour.

The ſext example is: yf aproteſtant will demand of his Miniſter whether he is bound in conſcience, to faſt, pray, or to giue almes to the poore or not, the Miniſter muſt anſwere him, that he is not, bound in conſcience ſo to doe becauſe that yf he wold giue all his ſubſtance to the poore that wold not helpe his ſoule to heauen nor yet by faſting or praying,for ſo much that the Iuſtfieation and ſaluation of man is by only faith in the bloode of Chriſt, and not by faſting praying almes deeds, or any other good workes, which in the Iudgment of God are no other thing but deadly ſinnes althought they apeare to be good workes in the fight of the world.

The ſeauinth example is: yf a Theefe were condemned to death by a lawefull Iudge, the Theefe may ſay to the Iughe that he doth him wrong to doe ſo becauſe that he condemnith an Innocent man, yf you will ſpeare why ſo, he will anſwere you & ſay that he is not bound in in conscience to keepe that comandëent of God, where it is said; thou shalt not steele, becaufe he is made free from the keeping of all lawes, both of God and man and working of all good workes, by libertie of their Gofpell and faith in the blood of Chrift, which is the only meane whereby he obteuinth Iuftification and faluation without all good workes cömanded by the lawes as much of God as man.

And for defence of this eraour they alledge the autboritie of S. Paul which writting to the Romains fayeth: for wee account a man to be Iuftified by faith, without the workes of the Lawe: (Againe) whofoeuer are of the workes of Lawe are vnder a curfe (Againe) & that in the Lawe no man is Iuftified in the of God, it is manifeft becaufe the Iuft liueth by faith. (againe) Chrift hath deliuered vs from the curfe of the Lawe (as they fay) can neither accufe or condemne the tranfgreffour or mal- ectour becaufe Chrift hath deliuered the faithfull from all curfes and punition of Lawes and craueth no thing of them but to beleeue that they fhall be faue by his blood without workes of the Lawe.

Rom. ℈. 28.

Galat 3. 2. 6,

Galat. 3. 22.

Scriptu- res falflee Innerpre- ted.

this

F

This is the chiefe ground of their religion which coſiſteth in thrie things: the firſt is that a Proteſtant ſhould neur paine him ſelfe to doe a good worke, becauſe it is but a deadly ſinne in the ſight of God, which deſerueth rather damnation, thon any rewerd of iife, as Luther and Caluinin writteth in werdes expreſſe.

Luth. in aſſertart. 36. cal. in antido. coueil. trident.

The ſecond is that a Proteſtant ſhonld nowiſe feare the Iudgment of God or eternall damnotion in comieting any ſinne where in he delighteth: beeauſe that ſinne can not hurt the mans ſaluation (as they ſay) which beleeueth to be ſaue in the blood of Chriſt,

ſecs. 6. et lib. 3. Inſt. cap. 12. ſeſtioue. 4.

The third point is that a proteſtant obtaineth his Iuſtificati on and ſaluation without all good workes cōmanded by the Lawe by only faith in Chriſt, as Luther writteth in his comentaries to the Galtians when they ſay that a true liuely faith can not be without good workes.

Iath. lib. de capti. uit. Babilon. cap. de baptiſ. cul. lib. 2 Inſt. cap. 8 ſeĉt. 56.

wee anſwere that their faith can not be a quicke liuing faith, but a dead damnable faith becauſe all the beſt fruits and good workes which ſpring out from their faith are but deadly ſinnes in the Iud

Inth. in cap. 2. ad galat.

Iudgment of God as all the proteſtants
affirme them ſelues, and chiefely Luther & Caluin in the places aboue quoted.
therefore the Proteſtants con not be
ſaue neither by their faith in Chtiſt,
nor yet by their good workes: becauſe
their faith is but a dead haith cõdemned
by the apoſtle S, Iames, and all their
good workes deadly ſinnes condemned
in the Iudgment of God.

S. *Iame,*
the 2. cap.

Now to drawe neere an end concerning the Chiſtian libertie of the Proteſtants, wee affirme their Chriſtiã libertie
which they challenge to them ſeules (according to their doctrine) no other
theng, but to be made free in their con-
ſciens from keeping of all Lawe, both
of God aud man, and likwiſe to be free
from working of all good workes cõmanded by the Lawes, for the one dependeth from the other, and ſo conſequen-
tly to doe what they pleaſe in all ſinn-
efull deſires without feare of the Iudgment of God or of eternall damnation
prouyding they beleue to be ſaue by the
blood of (Chirſt.

Therefore wee conclude moſt truyl
that ſuch a libertie (to be made frec
from all Lawes and good workes cõmanded

cõmanded by God & man & to doe what
they pleafe in all finnefull defires without fear of Gods Iudgments or damnation) is not Chriftian libartie, which
confifteth in Chriftian Iuftice and holyneffe of life, but the very feruice of Sathan done to him by deadly finne and
damnable workes worthie of eternall
damnaion.

S. Ihon.
3. 8,

For as S. Ihon fayeth: he that comit?
teth finne is of the Deuill. but all the
workes of the proteftants and all the
actions of their Religion are deadly
finnes, and meere malice in the fight of
God. ergo all the workes of the proteftants and all the actions of their Religion, are no other thing, but the damnable feruice of Sathan.

S. Ihon.
2. 4.
S. Ihon.
calleth
m
thers.

Moroouer S. Ihon fayeth againe: he
that faeth he knoweth God keepeth not
his cõmandements, he is a lyer and the
truth is not in him.

But the Proteftants fay they know
God by faith and keepe not his cõmandements.

Ergo all the Proteftants are but lyeres
and the truth is not in them.

This I. fpeake chiefly of the Pillars
of the Proteftant Chruch, (which gaue
them

them selues out most Impudently for
reformers of the truth) as of Luther,
Caluin, and such like, and not of
Ignorant Ptoestants deceiued
by them, which know not
Indeed well what they
should beleeue.

FINIS

LVTHERS LOVING EPISTLE
TO KATARINE BORA
NVNE

VVHEN I to writte doe take my penne in hand
 To make thy mind the truth to vnderstand
My katharine ſwet my Ioy my richſt Treaſure
 Belou'd by me, loue without all meaſure
I doe not know what pairt I ſhall beginnie
 To ſhewe the loue that ly my breſt within
VVhich I doe beare to the my only life
 In wiſhing the to be my wedded wyfe
ʒf in thy lappe by death ſhould fall a ſleepē
  ſt happie I ſhould Goe to acherones kipē
   ere I ſhould ſiing with Muſes myne anonē
   hy praiſes in the campe Heliſion
   y happie life I ſhould eſteeme to be
   ʒf it were ſpent in thy ſociete
   ny pretnce wold bring me ſuch Earthly Ioy
 As ſhould preſerue my ſoule from all anoy
 ∧ whit I doe not caire of heauen or hell
   Prouydiing in thy fauour I may duell
This only thou which phenixe is to me
 which may me bleſſe with thy ſweet looking Eye
Mv life my death doe in thy power ſtand
 To liue or die as thou wilt me cōmand
Therefore my Bore I praie the not to kill

ST. ROBERT BELLARMINE
Of the Seaven Wordes Spoken
by Christ upon the Crosse
1638

OF THE
SEAVEN
VVORDES
SPOKEN BY CHRIST
vpon the Croſſe,

Two Bookes.

Written in Latin by the moſt Illuſtrious *Cardinall Bellarmine*, of
the Society of *Ieſus*.
And tranſlated into Engliſh by A. B.

Foderunt manus meas & pedes meos.
Pſal. 21.
They haue digged my hands & my feet.

Permiſſu Superiorum, 1 6 3 8.

The Translatour to the Reader.

Ood Reader, in place of a Ceremonious and formall Dedicatory Epistle, I send thee these few lines. The worke heere translated is one the spirituall Treatises of the most Learned, and Vertuous *Bellarmine* of Blessed Memory; being entituled, *Of the seauen VVords spoken by Christ vpon the Crosse.* Prize the Contents of these words, as thou prizest thy owne soule; they being in number few, in force and weight many. Take them, as so many rich Legacies, left by our charitable Testatour, immediatly before his death, to mankind, And who is he that neglecteth the Legacies of his dying Lord and Friend?

Most men do much regard & ponder the last words of a dying man, at that tyme hauing his senses and memory vnperished, who during the whole course of his life had gained among others a great name, & reputation of VVisdome. Of what estimate

A 2   then

then ought we to make the VVords of *Chriſt*, vttered in his dying ſtate, who was not only wiſe, but *VViſdome it ſelfe*; VVho is the *VVord it ſelfe:* VVho is *God himſelfe.* Theſe *VVords* hereafter following in this Treatiſe, Chriſt ſpake being nayled vpon the Tree of the Croſſe, a Tree infinitly more high (as reaching from Earth to Heauen) then the higheſt Cedar *in Libanus.* Taſt of the fruits, which may be gathered from thence ; *ſince arbor bona fructus bonos facit, Matth. 7.*

Vpon *this Tree* death became dead vvhen life thereon did dye. This *Tree* was the *Chayre*, from whence our ſpiritual Doctour dictated his Precepts to vs Chriſtians; It was the *Pulpit*, out of which our Heauenly *Eccleſiaſtes* preached to mankind; Briefly it was, and is the true *Ladder of Iacob* (adumbrated and ſhadowed by that Ladder ſpoken of in *Geneſis*) by which the ſoule of Man aſcendeth vp to Heauen. Thus not enlarging my ſelfe further, and humbly intreating the charitable remembrance of all good Catholiks in their Deuotions, I leaue thee to the peruſing of what followeth.

Thine in *Chriſt* crucifyed,

A. B.

The Preface of the Authour.

Ehould now the fourth yeare is paffed, when as preparing my felfe to my End, I retire to a place of quietnes and reft, exempt from negotiations, and throng of Bufines; but not exempt from the meditation of the facred Scriptures, and from the writing of fuch things, which to me in tyme of meditation do occur; That if I be not able to profit others either by my owne fpeaches, or by compofing of any large and voluminous Booke; at leaft that I may be of power to ad-uance my Brethren in their fpirituall Good, by fome fmall deuout Treatife.

Now calling to mind, of what fub-ieckt I might chiefly make choyce, which might difpofe me towards dying well, & might profit my Brethren towards liuing well; *The death of our Lord* prefented it felfe to me, and that laft *Sermon* of his, which confifting of *feauen moft fhort* (but moft graue)*fen-tences,*the *Redeemer of the World* from

A 3   the

the Croffe, as from a high and eminent
Chayre, deliuered to all Mākind: Since
in that Sermon, or in thofe *feauen*
Words, all thofe Points are contained,
of which the faid Lord thus fpeaketh.
Luc. 18. *Behould, we go vp to Ierufa-*
lem, and all things shalbe confummate,
which were written by the Prophets, of
the fonne of Man.

Thofe things, which the Prophets
did foretell of Chrift, are reduced to
foure Heads, or branches. To wit,
to his *Preaching* and Sermons made
to the People; To his *Prayer* directed
to his Father; To the moft *grieuous*
Euills which he was to fuffer; To fublime and *admirable* Works performed by him. All which feuerall Points
did admirably fhine in the life of
Chrift. For firft, our Lord did moft frequently preach in the Temple, in the
Synagogues, in the fields, in defert &
folitary places, in priuate Houfes, and
to conclude euen out of the fhip, to
the People ftanding vpon the fhore.

Furthermore, He fpent for the
moft part, whole nights in Prayer to
God; for thus the Euangelift fpeaketh:
Luc. 6. *He paffed the whole night in*
Prayer to God, Now his admirable and
afto-

astonishing working of *Wonders*, of which the holy Gospells are very full, doth concerne the expelling of the Deuils, curing the sicke, multiplying of bread, and in appeasing or allaying tempests or stormes all sea. To conclude, the *Euills* that, in recompence of the Good which he had done, were perpetrated against him, were many, not only in contumely of Words, but also in stoning of him, and in endeauoring to cast him headlong dovvne from a fearefull Precipice.

But all these seuerall Points were consummated and perfected most truly vpon the Crosse. For first, He so mouingly & persuadingly preached from the Crosse, as that many returned from thence, *knocking their Breasts.* And further, not only the harts of men (but euen the stones, as it were, through a secret compassion) were riuen and torne a sunder. He in like manner so prayed vpon the Crosse, as that the Apostle sayth thereof, *Heb* 5. *Cum clamore valido, & lachrimis, exauditus est pro sua reuerentia*, With a strong Crye, and teares, he was heard for his reuerence. Now what he suffered vpon the Crosse, was of so high a

A 4   nature,

nature, in reference to thofe things which he had fuffered through the reft of the life; as that they alone may be thought peculiarly to belong to the *Pafsion*.

To conclude, He neuer wrought greater Prodigies and fignes, then when lying vpon the Croffe, he was brought to extreme imbecillity and weaknes. For at that time, he did not only exhibite Miracles from Heauen: (the which the Iewes had before importunely demaunded of him) but alfo a litle after, he wrought the greateft Miracle of all; When being dead and buried, by his owne proper force and Vertue, he returned from Hell, and refuming his Body, reftored it againe to life; yea to an immortall life. Therfore we may conclude, that vpō the Croffe all things were truly performed and accomplifhed, which were written by the Prophets of the Sonne of Man.

But before we defcend to write of the particular **Words** of our Lord, I hold it conducing to our purpofe, to fpeake fome thing of the *Croffe* it felf, which was the Chayre or Pulpit of the Preacher, the Altar of the Prieft facrifizing; the race, or place of him that
did

did combat and feight, the fhop (as it
were) of working miraculous things.
Firſt then, touching the forme of the
Croſſe, the more common Opinion of
the Ancients is , that it confiſted of
three ſeuerall parcels of Wood; One
long, vpon the which the Body of our
Lord crucified , was laid or extended;
another ouerthwart, in which the hãds
were faſtened ; the third was affixed
and ioined to the lower part, vpon the
which the feet did reſt, but fo nailed
thereto, that they could not be moued
from thence . This is the Opinion of
the two moſt ancient Fathers, *S. Iuſti-*
nus, & *S. Irenæus*: Who clearely ſhew,
that both his feete did reſt vpon the
Wood, & that the one foote was not
lying vpon the other . From which
poſture of our Lords Body it followeth, that there were foure nayles of
Chriſt, and not only three , as many do
imagine , who out of that conceit do
paint Chriſt our Lord , fo vpon the
Croſſe, as if he had the one foot vpon
the other. But *Gregorius Turonenſis*
(*i. de glo. mart. c. 6.*)moſt euidently im-
pugneth this, and fortifieth his Opinion from ancient Pictures of Chriſt
crucified . And I my felfe did fee at

Paris in the Kings Library, certaine moſt ancient *Manuſcripts* of the Goſpells, in diuers places wherof Chriſt was painted Crucified, but euer with foure Nayles.

Furthermore, the long Wood did ſomwhat appeare aboue that parcell of Wood, which was ouerthwart, as *S. Auſtin*, and S. *Gregory Nyſſenus* do write; And this ſeemeth alſo to be gathered from the words of the Apoſtle, who writing to the *Epheſians, c. 3.* thus ſayth : *That you may be able to comprehend with all the Saintes, what is the breadth, and length, and height, and depth* , (to wit of the Croſſe of Chriſt.) By which wordes he clearly deſcribeth the figure of the Croſſe, which hath foure extremities; to wit, *Latitude* in the ouerthwart or traſuerſe Wood; *Longitude* in the long Wood ; *Altitude*, in that part of the log Wood which appeared aboue the ouerthwart; and *Profundity* in that part of the long Wood, which was ſtucke into the ground.

Our Lord did not vndergoe this kind of Torment by chance, or vnwillingly; but made ſpeciall choice and election of it euen from all Eternity, as

S. *Au-*

S. *Auſtin* teacheth from that Apoſtolicall teſtimony of the Acts *c. 2. Him, by the determinate counſell and preſcience of God, being deliuered, by the hands of wicked men you haue crucified & ſlaine.* And accordingly Chriſt himſelfe in the beginning of his preaching ſaid to *Nicodemus Ioan. 3. As Moyſes exalted the ſerpent in the deſert, ſo muſt the Sonne of Man be exalted; that euery one, which belieueth in him, periſh not, but may haue life euerlaſting.* In like ſort our Lord often ſpeaking to his diſciples of his *Croſſe*, did counſell them to imitation, ſaying: *Matt. 16. He, that will come after me, let him deny himſelfe, and take vp his Croſſe, and follow me.*

Why our Lord did chooſe this kind of puniſhment, he only knoweth, who choſe it: Notwithſtanding there are not wanting ſome Miſteries therof, the which the holy Fathers haue left to vs in Writing. *Saint Irenæus* writeth, that the two armes of the *Croſſe* do agree vnder one Title, in the which was written, *Ieſus Nazarenus Rex Iudeorum*, that we might vnderſtand thereby, the two People (to wit the *Iewes* and the *Gentils*) which before

fore vvere deuided, in the end were to be ioyned togeather into one Body, vnder one Head which is Chrift. *S. Gregory Nyffene* writeth, that part of the Croffe, vvhich looketh towards Heauen, to fignify, that by the Croffe, as by a key, Heauen is opened to man; and that part of it, which declineth towards the Center of the World, to denote that Hel was fpoiled by Chrift, when he defcended thither. The two armes of the Croffe, which are ftretched towards the Eaft, and Weft, to fhaddow, that the repurging of the whole World was after to be performed by the Bloud of Chrift.

But *S. Ierome, S. Auftin,* and *S. Bernard* do teach, that the chiefe Miftery of the Croffe is briefly touched in thofe vvords of the Apoftle: *Quæ fit latitudo, longitudo, fublimitas, & profundum;* Since (fay thefe Fathers) that firft the Attributs of God are fignified in thefe Word, to wit, Power in height; In depth wifdome; in Latitude goodnes; in Longitude Eternity. Againe the Vertues of Chrift fuffering, are adumbrated and *Typically* figured therein; As in Latitude *Charity*; in Longitude Patience; in Altitude Obedience;

dience, in Profuudity Humility. Laftly the Vertues, vvhich are neceffary to thofe, who are faued by Chrift, are alfo here fignified: In depth Faith, in height Hope ; in breadth *Charity*, in length Perfeuerance. From the which we are to be inftructed, that *Charity* (vvhich deferuedly is called the Queene of Vertue) euery where hath place in God, in Chrift, and in vs. But touching other Vertues, fome of them are in God, others in Chrift, and others in vs. And therefore it is leffe to be admired, if in thofe laft Words of Chrift, which vve now vndertake to explaine, *Charity* do obtaiue the firft Place.

Firft therefore we will explicate the three firft *Words or Sentences*, which were fpoken by Chrift about the fixt houre, before the Sunne was obfcured, and darknes couered the whole Eartb. Next we will difcourfe of the then defect of the Sunne. That done, we vvill explaine & vnfould the reft of the Words of our Lord, which were fpoken about the ninth houre , as *S. Mathew* writeth; to wit, when the darknes did depart , and the death of Chrift drew neare, or rather was euen at hand.

O F

OF THE
THREE FIRST WORDS
ſpoken by Chriſt vpon
the Croſſe.

THE FISRT BOOKE.

The firſt Word, to wit, Father,
forgiue them, for they know
not what they do, *is literally
explicated.*

CHAP. I.

Hriſt Ieſus, being the Word
of his Eternall Father, and of
whom the Father himſelfe
thus clearly ſpeaketh: *Ip-
ſum audite, heare him, Matth.* 17. and
vvho of himſelfe manifeſtly pronounceth, *One is your Maiſter, Chriſt, Math.*
23. to the end that he might fully performe

forme the office taken vpon him, not
only liuing, neuer ceased from teaching; but euen dying from the Chaire
of his Crosse, preached and deliuered
certaine few vvords, but those most
fiery, most profitable, and most efficacious; and such as are truly vvorthy to
be imprinted in the depth of the
Hart of all Christians, that there they
being reserued & meditated on, might
answuerably in their actions be put in
execution. The first Sentence is this. *Luc.*
23. *Father forgiue them, for they know*
not what they do. Which sentence as
being truly new & vnaccustomed, the
Holy Ghost would haue it foretould
by the Prophet Esay, *c.* 53. in these
words: *He hath prayed for the Transf-*
gressours. Now hovv diuinely S. **Paul**
said, 1. *Cor.* 13. *Charity seeketh not her*
owne, may easely be euicted enen from
the order of these Sentences of our
Lord: since of these Sentences, three
of them belong to the good of others;
Other three to a peculiar and proper
Good; and one of them is promiscuous
or common. Thus the first care & sol-
licitude of our Lord vvas touching o-
thers, the last touching himselfe.

Novv, so far forth, as concernes the
three

three first Sentences, vvhich belong to
others; the first is directed to our
Lords Enemies , the second to his
friends, the last to those of his kinred
and affinity. The reason of this Order
or Method is this : *Charity* first relie-
ueth and helpeth such as be in want;
And those, who at that tyme suffered
most spirituall war, were his Enemies;
and we also as being the disciples of
so great a Maister vvere in want, as
standing in neede of being instructed
hovv to loue our Enemies. Which precept is far more difficult, thē to know
how to loue our friends or allies; since
this is most easy, being (after a sort) begotten with vs , and increaseth with
vs, and doth often preuaile more then
reason requireth. Therefore the Euangelist saith: *Iesus autem dicebat* , where
the word *(autem)* designeth the time
and occasion of praying for his Enemies , and implyeth an *Antithesis* , or
opposition of words with words, and
vvorkes with workes. As if the Euangelist would haue said : *They did crucify our Lord, and deuided* his garments
in his ovvne sight; and others derided,
traduced, and defamed him, as a seducer and Lyar, But he seing and hearing
these

these passages, and suffering most vehement paines, by reason of his hands & feete most cruelly pierced through vvith nailes, did render good for euill, and said: *Pater dimitte eis*, Father forgiue them.

He heere calleth him *Father*, not *God*, nor *Lord*; as vvell knowing, there vvas need of the benignity of a Father in this busines, but not of the seuerity of a Iudge. And becaufe to appeafe God (doubtlefly offended through such perpetrated impieties) it was conuenient to interpofe the comfortable Name of a *Father*; Therefore that vvord, *Father*, feemeth thus much in this place to signify: I am thy Sonne, vvho now suffer; I pardon them, pardon them alfo O Father. For my fake remit them this their offence, though they do not deferue it. Remember alfo, that thou art a Father vnto them by Creation, through the which thou haft made them to thy owne likenes and similitude; therefore impart to them thy paternall Charity; fince though they be wicked, yet are they thy fons. *Dimitte*, forgiue them: This word comprehendeth the summe of the Petition, vvhich the Sonne of God,

B

as an Aduocate for his Enemies, doth exhibite to his Father. Novv this VVord, *Forgiue*, may be referred both to the Punishment and to the offence. Yf it be referred to the punishment, then his prayer was presently heard : because whereas the Ievves through this vvicked Crime, deserued to be instantly penished, as either to be consumed vvith fire falling from Heauen, or to be ouervvhelmed vvith Water, or to perish through ivvord and famine; yet was the Punishment due for this offence and sinne, prolonged and delayed for the space of forty yeares, vvithin vvhich compasse of time, if that Nation had done Pennance, it had remained safe and in security. But because it negiected all performance of Pennance; God did send against them the Army of the Romans, *Vespasian* then being Emperour; vvho ouerturovving the chiefe Citty, destroyed the Ievvish Nation, partly through famine in releiging the City, partly in putting to the ivvord many after the Citty vvas taken; partly by selling and leading them Captiues; and partly by dispersing and relegating them into **seuerall Countries and Places.** VVhich

very

very point firſt by the Parable of the
Vine, of the *King* cauſing a Mariage to
be ſolemnized for his Sonne, and of
the barren and vnfruitfull *fig tree*; and
after in moſt expreſſie words our Lord
vpon Palme-ſunday by his owne weeping and lamentation did foretell.

Now ſo far as belongs to the fault
and offence, his prayer was alſo heard;
becauſe through the merit and vertue
of his Prayer, Grace of Compunction
was giuen to many from God. Among
whom thoſe were, *Who returned
knocking their breaſts*; as alſo the *Centurion*, who ſaid: *In very deed this was
the Sonne of God:* And many others
more, who after the preaching of the
Apoſtles were conuerted, and there-
vpon confeſſed him, whom afore they
had denied, & worſhipped him whom
they had deſpiſed, The Reaſon, why
Grace of Conuerſion was not giuen to
all, is, becauſe the Prayer of Chriſt was
conformable to the Wiſdome and
Will of God; VVhich point S. *Luke*
writeth in other VVords, in the Acts
of the Apoſtles, *c.* 13. ſaying: *As many
belieued, as were preordinate to life
euerlaſting.*

Illis, them: By this word thoſe are

vnderstood, for whom Christ prayed,
that they might obtaine Pardon, And
truly they seeme to be the first, who
actually nayled Christ vnto the Crosse,
and who deuided his garments among
themselues, and then all those are vnderstood, who were the Cause of our
Lords Passion, for example *Pilat*, who
pronounced sentence against Christ,
The *People* who cryed, *tolle, tolle, cru-
cifige eum*, 2Way, away with him, crucify him; The chiefe of the Priests and
the Scribes, who falsly accused him;
And to ascend higher, euen the *First
Man* himselfe, and all his Posterity,
who through sinne, gaue occasion of
Christ his Passion. Therefore our Lord
prayed for pardon, from the Crosse,
for all his Enemies. All of vs were in
the number of his Enemies, according
to that of the Apostle. *Rom.* 5. When
*we were Enemies, we were reconciled to
God, by the death of his Sonne.* Therefore euery one of vs, euen before we
were borne, are numbred in that most
sacred *Memento* (so to speake) in the
which Christ (the supreme Bishop)
prayed in that most holy *Masse*, which
he performed vpon the Altar of the
Crosse. VVhat retribution therefore, O
my

*my Soule,*wilt thou giue to him, for all
thofe Benefits,which he gaue to thee,
before thou hadſt Being ? Our Bleſſed
Lord did fee , that thou once waſt in
the number of his Enemies, neuertheleſſe he prayed to his Father for thee
(neither feeking after him , nor defi-
ring him fo to pray)that this thy madnes fhould not be imputed to thee. Is it
r   then thy duty , euer to haue euer
imprinted in thy hart , the remembrance of fo benigne and louing a Pa-
trone, and not to let flip any occaſion
of feruing of him? And is it not in like
fort reaſonable, that thou,as being inſtructed by fo great an example, fhouldeſt not only learne to pardon thy enemies and to pray for them , but alfo
that thou fhouldeſt perfwade all o-
thers to do the fame? Say therefore,
O *my Soule* , this is moſt iuſt and fitting, and I do much couet and determine to accomplifh the fame, and the
rather , feing he, who hath left this
moſt remarkable Exãple , is ready out
of his goodnes to affoard his efficacious hand and help , to the effecting
of fo great a VVorke.

   Non enim fciunt , quid faciunt, For
they know not what they do. That

this Intercession of Chrift may feeme
more reafonable, he doth extenuate
& excufe the Offence of his Enemies,
in fuch fort as he can. Certainly he
could not excufe the Iniuftice of *Pilate*,
neither the Cruelty of the fouldiers,
nor the malice of the Chiefe of
the Priefts, nor the fooliſhnes and vn-
thankfulnes of the Common People;
nor finally the falfe teftimonies of
thofe, who fwore againft him. Only
this remained, that he did excufe-the
Ignorance of them all; For truly (as
the Apoftle fpeaketh 1. *Cor.2.*) *If they
had knowne, they neuer would haue
crucified the Lord of glory.* But although
neither *Pilate*, nor the Chiefe Priefts,
nor the People, nor the Minifters of
his Paſsion, did know *Chrift* to be the
Lord of Glory; yet did *Pilate* know,
that Chrift was a iuft and holy man,
and deliuered ouer to him through the
malice of the Chiefe Priefts; As alfo
thofe high Priefts did know, that he
was the true Chrift which was promifed in the Law, as S. *Thomas* teacheth; becaufe they could not deny,
neither did they deny, but that he did
worke many miracles, which the Prophets foretould the true *Mefsias* was
a ſ̃eꝛ to doe;   To

To conclude, the People did know, that Chrift was condemned without iuft caufe, fince *Pilate* openly cried out, faying: *I find no caufe in this Man; I am innocent of the Bloud of this iuft man.* And although the Iewes, or the Chiefe of them, or the People did not know, that *Chrift* was the Lord of Glory; Yet they might well haue knowne the fame, had not Malice blinded their Harts; For thus S. Iohn fpeaketh, *cap.* 12. *VVhereas he had donne fo many miracles before them, they belieued not in him, becaufe Efay the Prophet faid: He hath blinded their eyes, and hardned their Heart, that they may not fee with their eyes, nor vnderftand with their Heart, and be conuerted &c.* But yet this blinding doth not excufe the man blinded, fince it is Voluntary, though not precedent; euen as thofe, who do finne of malice, do labour indeed with fome Ignorace, which Ignorance doth not excufe them; in that it doth not precede, or goe before but only accompany the finne. For the *VVifeman* truly fayth, *Prou.* 24. *They do erre, who worke Euill;* And the *Philofopher* accordeth therto, teaching, that, *Omnis malus, ignorans,* And vpon this ground

it

it may be truly said of all sinners : *Non sciunt, quid faciunt*. For it is impossible to desire or will *Euill*, with reference to *Euill*; since the Obiect of the will, is not a thing either good or Euil, but only that which is good ; VVherefore those, who choose what *is* euill, do euer choose it , as it is represented vnder the shew of Good; yea vnder the colour of the chiefest good, that then can be obtained.

The reason hereof is the perturbation of the inferiour part of the soule, which doth darken reason, and causeth it to discerne that seming Good only, which is in the thing, that is desired . For who chooseth to commit Adultery or Theft, vvould neuer chuse the same , except his mind were bent vpon the Good of the delight or gaine, which is in Adultery or Theft, as also except he had shut his eyes against the euill of Turpitude or Iniustice , vvhich *is* in Adulterie or Theft. Therefore euery sinner is like vnto a man , who desiring to cast himselfe dovvne from a great height into a Riuer, doth first shut his eyes, and then after cast himselfe into the Riuer. In like sort, vvho doth Euill, doth hate

the

the light, and laboureth with voluntary Ignorance, vvhich Ignorance doth not excuse, in that it is Voluntary. But heere it may be demanded, if this Ignorance doth not excuse, why then doth our Lord say; *Forgiue them, for they know not what they do?* To this it may be answered, that the words of our Lord may be vnderstood chiefly & first of them, who crucified him; whome it is probable to haue beene then ignorant not only of the *Diuinity* of Christ, but also of his Innocency, and that they simply performed the worke or charge imposed vpon them. Therefore for these Men our Lord did most truly say: *Father, forgiue them, for they know not what they do.*

Furthermore, if the Words be vnderstood of vs, before we had a *Being,* or of many sinners absent, which truly were ignorant of what was then done at *Ierusalem,* our Lord with iust reason said: *They know not what they doe.* To conclude, if the words be vnderstood of those, who were present, and were not ignorant, that *Christ* was the *Messias,* or an innocent Man; then it is to be said, that the Charity of Christ was so great, as that he was

C   willing

willing to leffen the finne of his Enemies, in fuch manner as he could. For
although that Ignorance doth not
fimply and abfolutely excufe, yet it
feemeth to pretēd fome reafon (though
weake) of excufe; becaufe they had
more grieuoufly finned, if they had
wholy wanted all Ignorance. And although our Lord was not ignorant,
that that excufe was not a reall excufe,
but only a fhaddow of an excufe, yet it
pleafed him to alledge it for an excufe; that from thence we might be inftructed of the good Will and difpofition of our Lord towards finners; &
how defirous he would haue beene to
haue taken and alledged a better excufe euen for *Caiphas* and *Pilate*, if a
better and more warrantable could
haue been found, or pretended.

Of the firſt fruite of the firſt
Word, ſpoken vpon the Croſſe.

CHAP. II.

VVE haue explicated & vnfoul-
ded the conftruction & Sentence of the *firſt* *Word* pronounced
by

by Chriſt vpon the Croſſe. Now we
will vndertake by way of meditation,
to gather frō the ſaid *VVord*, certaine
fruits , and thoſe moſt holeſome and
profitable to vs All . The firſt then of
theſe ſruits is , that we are inſtructed
from this firſt part of the Sermon or
preaching of Chriſt, from the Chayre
of his Croſſe , that the Charity of
Chriſt was more ardent & fiery , then
we can either vnderſtand or imagine.
And this is that , which the Apoſtle
writing to the Epheſians *cap.* 3. ſayth:
To know the Charity of Chriſt, ſurpaſ-
ſing knowledge. For the Apoſtle doth
intimate in this place , that from the
Miſtery of the Croſſe, we are able to
learne the greatnes of the Charity of
Chriſt to be ſo immenſe , and of that
meaſure, as that it doth ſurpaſſe and
tranſcend our knowledge,ſo as we are
not able to comprehend it in our
thought or cogitation.

When any of vs is afflicted with
any vehement griefe, either of the
Teeth,the Eyes, the Head , or of any
other Member ; our mind is ſo buſied
and fixed in ſuffering that one paine,as
that we cannot extend our thought to
any other thing or negotiation; and

C 2   there-

therefore we cannot then admit Visitation of friends, or entercourse of
men for the dispatch of any busines,
But Christ being crucifyed, did weare
a Crowne of thornes vpon his Head,
as most ancient Fathers(to wit,*Tertullian* of the Latin Church, and *Origen*
of the Greeke) do clearely teach, and
therefore he could not stirre or mooue
his Head without dolour and griefe.
His Hands and Feete were fastened
to the Crosse with nayles, through
the piercing of which our Lord endured most sharpe and intermitted torments. His naked Body being tired &
spent through much whipping, and
long iourneys, and openly exposed to
ignominy and cold, and with its own
weight, enlarging the wounds of his
Hands and feete, with an immane and
incessant dolour, did offer seuerall paines, and (as it were) seuerall Crosses
to our Blessed Lord, Yet neuerthelesse
(O wonderfull Charity and surmoun-
ting our apprehension) all these his afflictions sleighed by him and not wei-
ghed, as if he had suffered nothing, he
was sollicitous and regardfull only of
the health and good of his Enemyes;
and desiring to auert from their heads
the

the impendent danger, cried to his Father: *Father, forgiue them.* VVhat would he haue donne, if those flagitious men had iniustly suffered persecution, and not exercisedit? I meane if those men had beene friends, or of his kidred, or Sonnes, and not Enemies, Traitours, & most wicked Parricides?

Truly, most *mercifull Iesus*, thy Charity hath overcome our Vnderstanding; for I behould thy hart tossed to and fro among the stormes of so many iniuries and griefes (as a rocke beaten vpon with waues on ech side) to remaine immoueable. For thou lookest vpon thy Enemies, who after so many mortall wounds by them inflicted vpon thee, did deride thy Patience,and reioyced at their owne perpetrated iniuries against thee: Thou lookest vpon them (I say) not as an Enemy vpon his cruell Enemies, but as a Father vpon his bewayling Sōnes, or as a Physitian vpon his sicke and languishing Patients: Therefore thou art not offended at them, but thou takest pitty of them, & commends them to thy most powerfull Father, to be cured and made whole. For this is the force and Vertue of true Charity; to

Wit,

wit, to haue peace with all men, to repute not any for *Enemies*, but to liue
peaceably with those who hate peace.

And this is that, which in the *Canticles* is verified of the Vertue of perfect Charity. *Cant.* 8. *Many waters
cannot quench Charity, nor flouds shall
ouerwhelme it*. These many VVaters
are many Passions, which the Spiri-
tuals of wickednes, as so many hellish
stormes by the Iewes and Gentills (as
by cloudes full of hate) haue showred
downe vpon Christ; and notwithstanding, this deluge of VVaters (that is,
of paines and vexations) could not extinguish the fier of Charity, which did
burne in the breast of Christ. Therefore the Charity of Christ did (as it
were) swim aboue that inundation of
many waters, & burning said: *Father,
forgiue them*. Neither only were those
many VVaters not able to extinguish
the Charity of Christ, but also the following flouds of Persecution could
not ouerwhelme & drowne the Charity of the members of Christ. And
therefore a litle after, Christian Charity euen boyling in the breast of *S. Steuen*, could not be extinguished by the
shower of stones cast at him; but increased

creafed its heat, crying: *O Lord, lay not
this finne vnto them.* Act. 7. And after
this the perfect and inuincible Charity of Chrift, being dilated and fpread
in the Harts of many thoufands of
Martyrs and Confeffours, did fo fight
and ftriue againft the flouds both of
inuifible and vifible Perfecutours, as
that it may be truly pronounced: Neuer to the end of the world fhall the
flouds of Perfecution put out, or extinguifh the fyer of Charity.

And that we may afcend from the
Humanity of Chrift to his Diuinity:
Great was the Charity of Chrift, as
being man, towards his Crucifiers;
But the Charity of Chrift, as God, and
of the Father, and of the Holy Ghoft
towards men, was, and euen to the
confummation of the world, fhalbe
far greater; I meane, towards fuch
men, who with God himfelfe did wage
emnity and malice, and who (if it had
layn in their power) would haue de-
truded and thruft him out of Heauen,
and haue killed him. Who therefore
but in thought can conceaue the Charity of God, towards vngratefull and
wicked men? God fpared not the Angels finning, neither gaue he them

place of Repentance: Yet he patiently tolerateth men, who are sinners, Blasphemers, reuolting to the Deuill the Enemy of God. And which is more, he doth not only tolerate them, but in the meane tyme doth maintaine and nourish them; yea sustayneth and supporteth them. For as the Apostle speaketh, *in him we liue, and moue, and be.* *Act.* 17. Neither doth our mercifull Lord only nourish, feed, and sustayne his Enemies; but withall euer heapeth benefits vpō them, graceth them with wit, furnish them with riches, aduanceth them to honours, placeth them in the Throne of Regall Soueraignty; euer expecting in the meane time their returne from the Way of iniquity and perdition.

But to forbeare to wander in that large field of discourse, which manifesteth the Charity of God towardes wicked men, and Enemies of his diuine Maiesty; we will heare consider only the benefit and fauour of Christ. Do we not read, *God so loued the world that he gaue his only begotten Sonne?* *Ioan.* 3. The world is an Enemy to God, *For in maligne positus est*, as S. *Iohn* sayth; and, *He who loueth the*

World,

World, *the Charity of the Father is not in him.* 1. *Ioan.* 2. Againe, as S. *Iames* contesteth, *cap.*4. *The friendship of the world is the Enemy of God;* And againe: *Whosotuer wilbe a friend of this world, is made an Enemy of God.* Therefore God louing the world, did loue his Enemy, thereby to make it his friend. For to that end God did send his Sōne into the world, who is *Princeps pacis,* that by him the world might be reconciled to God. And therefore at the byrth of Christ, the Angels did sing: *Glory in the highest to God, & in earth Peace to men.* Therefore God loued the world (his Enemy) that through Christ he might procure reconciliation and atonement with it, and that it being reconciled, might auoyde the punishment due to his Enemy.

The world did not admit or receaue Christ; It did augment its offence; It became rebellious against the Mediatour; God inspired into the Mediatour, that he should render good for euill, and that he should pray for his Persecutours; He prayed, and, *was heard for his renerence. Heb.* 5. The Patience of God expected, that the world through the preaching of the Apostles,

do pennance, and those who performed pennance, receaued pardon; but
such who would not repent, after lōg
patience of God, were exterminated
by the iust iudgment of God. Therefore we truly learne from the first
word of Christ, *the Charity of Christ
surpassing knowledge*; We also learne
the Charity of God the Father, surpassing knowledge ; *Who so loued the
world , that he gaue his only begotten
Sonne, that euery one, who belieueth in
him, perish not, but may haue life euerlasting. Ioan. 5.*

*Of another fruite of the same
first Word, spoken by Christ
vpon the Crosse.*

CHAP. III.

AN other fruite (and that very
healhfull to all tasting the same)
is, if men will learne to pardon easily
Iniuries offered vnto them, and by this
meanes to make friends of Enemies.
Now for the persuading hereto, the
Example of Christ and God ought to
be a most forcible argument and indu-
cement.

cement: for if Chriſt did pardon his
Crucifiers, and prayed for them, why
ſhould not a Chriſtian man do the like?
Yf God (the Creatour of all)in whoſe
power it is, as being Lord & Iudge, to
take preſent reuenge vpon ſinners,
doth neuertheleſſe expect, that a ſinner ſhould returne to Pennance, and
doth inuite him to peace and reconciliation, and ſtands prepared to pardon
all thoſe, who haue offended his Ma-
ieſty ; Why ſhould not a Creature be
ready and willing to performe the
ſame? Adde hereto, that the pardon-
ning and remitting of an Iniury wan-
teth not a great Reward. It is written
in the hiſtory of the life and death of
Saint *Engelbertus*, Arch-biſhop of
Cullen, that when he was entrapped
by his Enemies in his iourney, and
ſlayne by them, and he then ſaying in
his Hart, *Pater ignoſce illis*, *O Father
pardon them* ; It was reuealed of him,
that for this one act (being in a high
manner gratefull to God) his ſoule was
not only inſtantly taken vp by the
Angels to Heauen; but that being placed in the Quyre of Martyrs, obtained
the Crowne of Martyrs, and after his
death was illuſtrious for many miracles,

O! if Christians did know, how eafily (if themfelues would) they might
be enriched with ineftimable Trea-
fure, and might be aduanced to high
Titles of Honour and glory, if fo they
would fuppreffe and curbe the pertur-
bations and pafsions of their mind
& with a true fortitude would fpurne
at fmall Iniuries againft them committed, they would not be of fuch a flinty
and inexorable difpofition, to remit, or
fuffer wrongs and offences. But they
will reply ; It femeth to be aduerfe &
euen incōpatible with the law & right
of Nature, that a man fhould fuffer
himfelfe to be betrampled and trod-
den vpon by other men, offered wrōgs
and difgraces, either in word or deed :
For we fee euen brute Beafts, who are
carryed only by the inftinct of Nature,
to affault other Beafts their Enemyes,
with great fierfnes , and do labour to
kill them. In like fort, we haue experience in our felfes, that if vnexpectedly we meete or fall vpon our Enemy,
inftantly our Choler is inflamed, our
Bloud begins to rife and boyle , and
that we haue a defire euen naturally
of Reuenge.

Bue

But he is greatly deceaued, who thus disputeth, and he doth promiscuously confound a iust defence, with an iniust reuenge. A iust defence is not subiect to reprehension; and this is that, which euen nature instructeth vs; to wit, *vim vi repellere*, to repell and withstand force by force; but she teacheth vs not, to reuenge an iniury receaued. No man is forbidden to resist, that a wrong be not offered him; But to reuenge an Iniury already committed, the diuine Law prohibiteth: since this belongeth not to any priuate Man, but to the publike Magistrate. And because God is the King of kings, therefore he crieth out, & sayth: *Reuenge to me, and I will reward. Deut.* 32. Now that Beasts with a maine fiercenes rush vpon other Beasts their Enemies, this proceedeth, in that Beasts cannot discerne betwene Nature, and the Vice, or imperfection of Nature; but men, who are endued with Reason, ought to make a distinction betweene Nature or the Person which is created good by God, and the Vice or sinne which is euill, and proceedeth not from God. Therefore a man receauing an Iniury, ought to loue the person,

son, but to hate the Iniury, and not so much to be offended with his Enemy, as to communicate and pity him ; imitating herein Physitians , who loue their sicke Patients, and therefore endeauour to cure them ; But de hate their disease and sicknes, laboring with all their skill and art to expell it.

And this is that which our Maister and Physitian of our Soules, *Christ Iesus*, did teach, when he said: *Loue your Enemies, do good to them, that hate you, and pray for them that persecute and abuse you, Matth. 5.* Neither was our Maister Christ like vnto the Scribes & Pharisees, who sitting vpõ the Chaire of *Moyses*, did teach, but did not answerably thereunto ; But he sitting in the Chaire of the Holy *Crosse* , did accordingly as he taught and preached. For he loued his Enemies , and he prayed for them, saying : Father forgiue them, *for they know not what they dos.* Now whereas the Bloud beginneth to rise and boyle in men, when they see them of whom they haue receaued an iniurie ; the reason of this, is, because such men are *Homines animales*, and haue not yet learned to restraine with the bridle of Reason the

motions

motions of the (inferiour Part of the Soule, which is common to them with Beasts. But such men, as are *Spirituales*, to wit, spirituall, and know how not to yeald to their owne Passions, but to maiſter and ouerule them, are not offended at their Enemies; but pitying them, do labour by curtesies and benefits to reduce them to peace and concord.

But this (many men say) is ouer harſh and vngratefull, especially to such, as being nobly borne, are solicitous (and so ought to be) of their Honour. To this I answere, that the point here enioyned is easy, for the yoake of Chriſt, who imposed this Law to his Diſciples and followers, is sweet, and his burden easy, as we read in the Goſpell; and his Commandements are not heauy, as *S. Iohn* affirmeth; Now if they seeme more difficult and burdensome to vs, then we expect, this falleth out through our owne default, in that there is but litle Charity of God in vs, or none at all. For nothing is difficult to Charity, according to that of the Apoſtle. 1. *Cor.* 13. *Charity is patient, is benigne, suffereth all things, belieueth all things, hopeth all things, beareth all things.*

things . Neither did Christ alone loue
his Enemies (though he did in a far
more eminent degree, then any other)
for euen in the Law of Nature, holy
Ioseph the Patriarch, did wonderfully
loue his Enemies, by whom he was
sold. And in the written Law, *Dauid*
did patiently beare his Enemy *Saul*,
who sought his death a long tyme;
And yet when *Dauid* had oportunity
to kill *Saul*, he euer did forbeare the
same. Againe in the law of Grace; *S.*
Stauen, the *Protomartyr*, did follow the
example of Christ, who, when he was
stoned, prayed saying: *Lord, lay not this*
sinne vnto them. Act. 7. In like sort, S.
Iames, who was cast downe from a
great height, by the Iewes, and being
most neare to his death, cried out : O
Lord, pardon them , for they know not
what they doe. And the Apostle *S. Paul*,
speaking of himselfe and of his fellow Apostles, thus sayth: 1. *Cor.* 4. *We*
are cursed, and we do blesse; we are per-
secuted, and we sustaine it, we are blaf-
phemed, and we beseech. To conclude,
many Martyrs and infinite others following the Example of Christ, haue
easily fulfilled this Precept.

But some others do further vrge,
saying.

saying; I grant, we are to pardon our
Enemies, but this is to be performed
in due tyme; to wit, vvhen the memory of the receaued iniury is partly for-
gotten, and the mind returneth to it
felfe, as voyde of Pafsion. But what, if
it fall out, that in the meane tyme,
thou be fnatched out of this life, and
happen to dye, and thou art found
without the veftment of Charity, and
it be faid vnto thee, *How camest thou
in hither, not hauing a wedding garment? Matt.* 22. Wilt thou not be then
dumbe, when thou fhalt heare the
Sentence of the Lord, faying: *Bind him
hand and foot, and caft him into vtter
darknes; there fhalbe weeping & gna-
fhing of teeth?* Therefore I wifh thee
to be diligent and attent, and to imitate the Example of thy Lord, vvho in
that very inftant, wherein he had receaued the iniurie, and vvhen his
hands and feete did yet diftill dovvne
abundance of Bloud, and when his
whole Body was tormēted with moft
bitter paines, faid vnto his Father, *Father forgiue them.* This is the true and
only Maifter, whom all men ought to
heare, vvho vvill not be drawne into
any Errour. Of this our Maifter, God

D   the

the Father thus pronounced from Heauen; *Ipsum audite, Heare him. In him are all the Treasures of Wisdome, and knowledge of God.* Certainly if thou vvouldest take counsell of *Salomon,* thou mightest securely inough anker thy selfe vpon his aduice or iudgment: *Et ecce plus quam Salomon, hic; And behould, more then Salomon, heere.* Math. 12.

But yet I heare some refractory man or other, still impugning this doctrine, and saying: If we should render good for euill, benefits for iniuries, & louing words for Contumelies; the Wicked by this meanes would grovv insolent, and the Transgressours more bold, the iust should be oppressed, & Vertue betrampled vpon, and contemned. But the matter standeth not so. For often, as the wiseman speaketh: *Prou.* 15. *A soft answere breaketh anger*; and very often the Persecutour doth so admire the patience of the iust man by him wronged, as that thereby of an Enemy he becomes his friend. Neither are there wanting here vpon earth Politike magistrates, Kings, and Princes, vvhose office and charge is, to chastize according to the seuerity of
the

the Lavves, the procacity and insolency of the Wicked, that so the Iust and Vertuous may lead a quiet and peaceable life. And if Humane Iustice should sometimes conniue, or winke at such euill deportment; yet the Prouidence of God is euer vigilant, which vvill not leaue any Iniustice vnpunished, nor any good varewarded; and vvhich by a vvounderfull course procureth, that the Wicked whiles they thinke to oppresse the Iust, do therein exalt them, and make them more resplendent and glorious. For thus S. Leo speaketh, *Serm. de S. Laurentio.* O *persecutour, thou hast byn cruell against the Martyr, thou hast beene cruell, I say, but thou hast increased his Palme, whilest thou increasest his paines; for what hath not thy wit inuented for the greater glory of the Victour, when both the Triumphs, and the very Instruments of his Punishments do proclaime his Honour!* The which sentence may be iustifyed of all Martyrs, as also of the ancient Saints. For nothing hath made *Ioseph* the Patriarch, more celebrious & famous, then his Persecution comming from his owne Brethren; for whiles through enuy they sould him

to

to the *Madianits*, they were thereby
become the Cause, that he was made
Prince of all *Egypt*, & of his Brethren.

But passing ouer these points with
a gentill touch ; Let vs briefly gather
togeather the many and great detriments, which men suffer, who, that in
the eye of man they may decline but
the shadovv of disgrace, do endeauour
with all stifnesse, and resolution of
mind, to reuenge the Iniuries receaued from their Enemies . First , they
discouer and betray their owne folly,
whiles they seeke to cure a lesser Euill
by a greater. For it is a Principle acknowledged by all, and taught by the
Apostle. *Rom.* 3. *That Euill is not to be
done* , *that Good from thence may rise* ;
Euen as greater Euills are not to be
perpetrated, for the preuention of lesser. Who receaueth an Inirzy, falleth
into *Malum Pœna :* Who reuengeth
an Iniury, falleth into *malum Culpa:*
But *malum Culpa* is incomparably
for greater, then *malum Pœna* . seing
this later maketh a man miserable but
not wicked; the other maketh one
both miserable and wicked, This *malum pœna* depriueth a man of a temporall Good, but *malum Culpa*, depriueth

ueth him both of temporall and Eternall Good. Therefore that man who to be freed of the Euill of Punishmēt, falleth into the Euill of Offence, may well resemble him, who to make his shoo (being ouer short) fitting to his foote, is content to cut of part of his foote, which is euident madnesse.

But there is not any man to be found so grosly exceeding the limits euen of naturall Reason in temporall matters, Neuerthelesse many are to be found so blinded, & seeled vp in iudgment, as that they feare not most heinously to offend God, that thereby they may auoyd the shaddow (as aboue I said) of disgrace among men, or that they may conserue the smoake of Honour with them. These men do fall into the indignation and hate of God, and if they do not recall and make a serious introuersion of their owne state in tyme, and performe great Pennance, they shalbe punished with sempiternall shame and disgrace, & shall lose all eternall Honour and renowne. Furthermore such men by their reuengefull proceedings, do a most gratefull office to the Deuill and his Angels; who incite and stirre vp their

Enemies

Enemies to offer to them Wrongs &
Iniuries, to the end that Emnity, and
want of Charity may rise amõg them.
Now how foule and vnworthy a thing
is it to seeke rather to gratify the most
cruell Enemy of mankind, then Christ
Iesus, I leaue to the iudgment & consideration of all pious men.

But to proceed : it often falleth
out, that he who hath receaued an iniurie, and seeketh reuenge, doth dan-
gerously wound or kill his Enemy, and
then by the sentence of the Prince, all
his goods being confiscated, he is either to suffer death, or forced to fly
his Country, to the vtter ruine & de-
struction of himselfe, his Children, and
his whole House, and Family. Thus
doth the Deuill play with, and delude
such men, who couet more to be Ves-
salls and slaues to false Honour, then
to become seruants and brethren to
Christ, our supreme King, and Cohe-
ryes with him in his most ample and
euerlasting Kingdome. Wherefore
since so great and heauy a losse doth
expect, and waite for those foolish
men, who contrary to the Precept of
our Lord, refuse to be reconciled to
their Enemies, let all others, who haue
true

true Iudgment, heare & follow Chrift
(the Maiſter of vs all) teaching in his
Goſpell, and confirming this his doctrine in workes , euen from the
Croſſe .

The ſecond Word , which is :
Amen, *I ſay to thee , this day
thou ſhalt be with me in Paradiſe.* Luc. 23.

CHAP. IV.

AN other Word, or rather another Sentence ſpoken by Chriſt
vpon the Croſſe , as *S. Luke* witneſ-
ſeth, was that bountifull and magnificall promiſe to the Thiefe, hanging v-
pon the Croſſe with him: *This day thou
ſhalt be with me in Paradiſe.*The occaſion of this ſpeech of Chriſt was, thet
when two theeues vvere crucified
with him (the one on his right hand,
the other on his left) the one of them
increaſed the heape of his former ſinnes by blaſpheming of Chriſt, and vpbrayding him with imbecillity and
weaknes, ſaying: *Yf thou be Chriſt, ſaue
thy ſelfe and vs.* I grant *S. Mathew* and
                                         S. Marke

S. *Marke* do write, that the **Theeues** crucifyed with Chrift, did exprobrate to him his weaknes, But it is moft probable, that S. *Mathew* and S. *Marke* did take the plurall number for the fingular number; Which manner of fpeach is frequent in the facred Scriptures, as S. *Auſtin* obſerued in his booke *of the Confent of the Euangelifts.l.3.c.*16. For the Apoftle writing to the Hebrews, fayth : *They ſtopped the mouthes of Lyons, they were ſtoned, they were heweḍ, they went about in ſheepskins, in Goate-skins;* and yet whe ſtopped the mouths of Lyons, was but one *Daniell,* and who was ſtoned, was but one *Ieremy,* and vvho was hewed in peces vvas but one *Eſay;* Add hereto, that S. *Mathew* and S. *Marke* do not fo exprefly fay, that both the Theeues did braid Chrift, as we find S. *Luke* exprefly to vvrite: *Vnus autem de his &c. One of the theeues, that were hanged, blafphemed him.*

For the greater probability of truth, we may further fay, that there cã be no reafon alledged, why the fame theefe ſhould both blafpheme, and praife Chrift. And whreas fome do reply, that this theefe, who afore did
blafphemȩ

blaſpheme, did after change his Iudgement, and prayſed Chriſt, when he heard him ſay : *Father forgiue them, for they know not what they do :* is euidétly repugnant to the Goſpell; for *S. Luke* relateth, that Chriſt prayed for his Perſecutours to his Father, before the wicked Theeſe begunne to blaſpheme. Therefore the iudgements of *S. Ambroſe* and *S. Auſtine* are to be imbraced heerin, who mantaine, that of the two theeues, the one did blaſpheme, the other did prayſe and defend Chriſt. Therfore the other thieſe did anſwere to the thieſe blaſpheming, thus : *Neyther doſt thou feare God, whereas thou art in the ſame dā̄nation?* *Luc.* 23. This good and happy thieſe, partly from the vertue of the *Croſſe* of Chriſt, and partly from diuine light and inſpirarion, which then did begin to ſhyne to him, vndertooke to correct his Brother, and to draw him to a more ſafe mynd & iudment. The meaning of whoſe words is this: Thou wouldeſt imitate the blaſpheming Iewes; but they as yet haue not learned to feare the iudgment of God, becauſe they are perſuaded they haue ouercome; and they do vaunt &

E   glory

glory of their Victory, when they see
Christ nayled to the Crosse, and themselfes to be free and at liberty, suffering no euill. But thou, who for thy
offences, hangest vpon the Crosse, and
hastest towards death, why dost thou
not begin to feare God? Why heapest
thou sinne to sinne ? And further, this
happy Thiefe increasing in his good
VVorke, and seconded vvith the light
of the Grace of God, confesseth his
sinnes, and preacheth the Innocency
of Christ: saying : *Et nos quidem iustè,*
and vve are iustly (to vvit condemned
to the Crosse) *but this man hath done
no Euill.* *Luc.* 23.

Lastly, the light of Grace more
resplendently shining, he addeth: *Domine memento mei &c. Lord remember me, when thou shalt come into thy
kingdome.* Certainly the Grace of the
Holy Ghost, which vvas in the hart of
this Thiefe, is most wonderfull. *S. Peter* the Apostle denieth Christ ; the
Thiefe nayled to the Crosse confesseth
him: The disciples going to *Emaus,* say,
But we did Hope ; the Thiefe confidently speaketh, saying : *Remember me,
when thou shalt come into thy kingdome.* S. *Thomas* the Apostle denied
to

to belieue in Chriſt, except he ſaw that
Chriſt had riſen frō death; The Thiefe
being vpon a Croſſe and ſeing Chriſt
faſtened to the Croſſe, doubteth not
to acknowledge, that after he was to
be a King. But who had taught this
theefe ſo high Myſteries? He calleth
that man *Lord*, whom he did behould
naked, wounded, lamenting, openly
derided and contemned, and hanging
with him. He further ſayth, that *Ieſus*
after his death, was to come into his
kingdome. From which point we vnderſtand, that the Theefe did not
dreame of any future temporall kingdome of Chriſt here vpon earth. (ſuch
as the Iewes do expect) but belieued
that Chriſt after his death, was to be
an *Eternall King* in Heauen. Who had
inſtructed him in ſuch ſublime Sacraments? Certainly only the ſpirit of
Truth, which did preuent him in the
benedictions of ſweetnes . . Chriſt after
his Reſurrection ſaid to his Apoſtles:
*Chriſt ought to ſuffer theſe things, and
ſo to enter into his glory*. But the *Theife*
did foreknow this after a wounderfull
manner, and did confeſſe it at that
tyme, when there appeared no likely-
hood in Chriſt to raigne, Kings do

reigne vvhen they liue, and when they ceaie to liue, they ceaie to reigne. But the *Theefe* openly affirmed, that Chrift by death was to come into his Kingdome.

The vvhich point our Lord did explaine in one of his Parables, vvhen he faid: *Luc.* 19. *A certaine Noble man went into a farre Country, to take vnto himfelfe a kingdome, and to returne.* This our Lord faid, being moft neare vnto his Paffion; fignifying that by death, himfelfe was to goe into a far diftant Country or Region, that is, to an other life, or vnto Heauen, which is moft remote from the Earth; and to goe, to the end to receaue a moft large and euerlafting kingdome; and after to returne at the day of iudgment, that he might make retribution either of reward or punifhment to all men, according as they had deferued in this lyfe. Therefore of this kingdome of Chrift, which prefently after his death he was to receaue, the wvfe *Theefe* faid: *Remember me, when thou fhalt come into thy kingdome.* But was not Chrift a king before his death? Certainly he was; and therefore the *Magi* cryed out; *Vbi eft, qui natus eft,*
                                        Rex

Rex Iudæorum ? Where is he that is borne king of the Iewes ? *Math. 2.* And Chrift himfelfe faid to Pilate : *Thou faift, that I am a King ; For this was I borne, and for this came I into the world, that I fhould giue teftimony to the Truth. Ioan. 18.* Neuerthclefle he was a king in this world, as a ftranger among his Enemies, and therefore he was acknowledged as a king only of few, but contemned and badly entreated by many. And in regard thereof he faid in the Parable aboue cited, *that he was to goe into a far Country, to take vnto himfelfe a kingdome*; He faid not, to feeke , or to gaine a Kingdome which did not belong to him , but to receaue his owne kingdome , and to returne; therefore the Theefe wifely faid : *VVhen thou fhalt ceme into thy kingdome.*

To proceede ; The kingdome of Chrift fignifieth not in this place any Regall Potency or Soueraignty : For this euen from the beginning he had, according to that of the Pfalme 2. *I am appointed king by him ouer Sion, his Holy Hill*; And in another place : *He fhall rule from fea to fea , and from the Riuer euen to the ends of the world.*

E 3 *Pfal.*

*Pſal.*71. And Eſay ſayth: *cap.*9. *A litle one is horne to vs, and a ſonne is giuen to vs, whoſe Principality is vpon his ſhoulder.* And Ieremy, *cap.* 23. *I will rayſe vp Dauid, a luſt branch, and he ſhall reigne a king, and ſhalbe wiſe, and he ſhall do iudgement and iuſtice vpon the earth.* And Zacharias *cap.*9. *Reioyce greatly O daughter of Sion, make iubilation O daughter of Ieruſalem: Behold thy king will come to thee, the iuſt and Sauiour, himſelfe poore, and riding vpon an Aſſe, and vpon a Coult the foale of an Aſſe.* Therefore of this kingdome Chriſt did not ſpeake in the Parable aboue, neither the good *thiefe,* when he ſaid, *Remember me, when thou ſhalt come into thy kingdome:* but both did ſpeake of perfect Beatitude, by the which a man is exempted and freed from all ſeruitude and ſubiection of things created, and only is become ſubiect to God, whom to ſerue is to reigne, and he is conſtitured by God himſelfe ouer all his Workes,

This Kingdome, ſo farre forth as it concerned the Beatitude of the Soule, Chriſt receaued euen from the beginning of his Conception; but as it concerned his Body, he had it not
actually,

actually , but only by right , vntill after his Resurrection . For whiles he
was a Pilgrime or stranger heer vpon
Earth , he was subiect to wearines, famine, thirst, iniuries, wounds, and to
death it selfe : yet because the glory
of the Body was due to him , therfore
after his death he did enter into his
glory , as due to him . For thus our
Lord himselfe speaketh after his resurrection : *Ought not Christ to haue
suffered these things , and so to enter
into his glory ?* Which glory is called
his glory , because he is of power to
communicate it to others , and in this
respect he is said to be , *Rex gloria, Dominus gloria* , and, *Rex Regum* : And
he himselfe saith to his disciples : *I
dispose for you a Kingdome.* It is in our
power to receaue glory, or a Kingdom,
but not to giue ; and accordingly it is
said to vs : *Matth. 25. Enter into the
ioy of thy Lord* , and not into thy owne
ioy . Therefore this is that Kingdome,
of which the good *Thiefe* sayd : *when
thou shalt come into thy Kingdome.*

But heer the great Vertues, which
shine in the prayer of this *Holy Thiefe,*
are not to be passed ouer in silence ;
that therby we may the lesse wonder

at

at the anſwere which Chriſt our Lord
made to him : he ſaith , *Lord remem-*
ber me , when thou ſhalt come into thy
Kingdome. He calleth Chriſt *Lord* ; by
which title he acknowledgeth himſelfe to be his ſeruant , or rather his
redeemed bondſlaue , and confeſſeth
him to be his *Sauiour*. He adioyneth :
Remember me , which is a word full of
hope, Fayth, Loue, Deuotion , & Humility. He ſayth not, *remember me , if*
thou canſt , becauſe he belieued Chriſt
could doe all things ; neither ſaith he ,
if it pleaſeth thee , becauſe he was con-
fident of Chriſts charity and goodnes.
He ſaith not , *I deſire the conſort and*
participation of thy Kingdome , becauſe
his Humility would not beare this
kind of ſpeach ; to conclude, he deſireth nothing in particular , but onely
ſaith , *rmember me,* which is as much,
if he had ſaid , *If thou wilt vouchſafe*
only to remember me ; if thou wilt be
pleaſed to turne the Eye of thy Benignity towards me , it is ſufficient for
me ; becauſe I am aſſured of thy Power
and Wiſdome, and vpon thy goodnes
and Charity I wholy anker and ſtay
my ſelfe . He laſtly addeth this , *when*
thou ſhalt come into thy Kingdome ; to
ſhew

shew that his desire was not fixed vpõ
any weake and temporary benefit, but
that it afpired to thinges fublime and
eternall.

Heere it followeth , that we confider the Anfwere of Chrift : he fayth ;
*Amen , I fay vnto thee , this day thou
shalt be with me in Paradise.* That par-
ticle , *Amen*, is a word graue and fo-
lemne with Chrift , the which he was
occuftomed to vfe , when he would
affirme any thing earneftly and vehemently. S. *Auftin* was not afraid to
fay , that this word *Amen*, was (as it
were) the oath of Chrift , *tract. 41. in
Ioan.* Properly it is no oath, fince when
our Lord faid in S. *Mathew* ; *I fay to
you, not to fwere at all.* And a litle after:
*Let your fpeach be, yea, yea, no, no : And
that, which is ouer and aboue thefe, is of
Euill. Mat. 5.* Novv it is no way probable , that our Lord fhould haue
fworne fo often , as he pronounted
Amen, fince he vfed this word , *Amen*
many tymes; And in S. *Iohn,* he fayth
not only , *Amen* , but *Amen , Amen.*
Therefore S. *Auftin* truly faid , that
Amen, was *as it were an Oath,* but he
faid not, that *it was an Oath.* For this
word , *Amen*, fignifieth *Truly* ; And
when

when one sayth, I say truly to thee, he affirmeth earnestly, and an earnest affirmation is peculiar to an Oath Therfore Chrift with good reason said to the Thiefe, *Amen* I say to thee; that is; I truly do affirme, but do not fweare.

And indeed there were three emergent Reasons, which might cause the Thiefe to wauer and rest doubtfull of the Promise of Chrift, except he had auerred it with so earneft an afseueration. The first may be drawne from the person of the *Thiefe*, who seemed not in any sort worthy of so great a Reward, or so great a guift. For who would imagine, that a *Theife* fhould from the Crosse prefently pasle to a kingdome? The second Reason is taken from *Chrift* promising, who at that instant seemed to be reduced & brought to extremity of want, weaknes, & calamity. For the *Thiefe* might probably thus reason and difcourse with himfelfe: Yf this man during his life tyme, was not able to performe any thing in behalfe of his friends, fhall not he be lefse able, being dead? The third reason may haue reference to the thing *promifed*. For here *Paradife* is promifed: but *Paradife* (as then all men tooke

tooke notice) did belong not to the
Soule, but to the Body ; since by the
Word, *Paradise*, a terreitriali Paradise
was vnderstood by the Iewes. It had
beene more credible to the *Thiefe*, and
subiect to his beliefe, if our Lord had
answered : *To day thou shalt be with
me in the place of repose and refreshment with Abraham, Isaac, and Iacob.*
For these Reasons therefore did our
Lord premise those words: *Amen, Dico tibi.*

Hodie, to day. Our Lord sayth not,
In the day of Iudgment , when I shall
place thee with the Iust vpon my right
hand : Neither sayth he , After some
yeares of thy being in Purgatory, will
I bring thee to a place of rest ; Nor
doth he say: I will comfort thee after
certaine Months, or Dayes ; but he
sayth, *This very day* , before the sunne
shall set, thou shalt passe with me from
the gibbet of the Crosse, to the delights
of Paradise. A wonderfull Liberality
or Bounty of Christ, and a wonderfull
happines of the sinner. With iust reason therefore *S. Austin* (following *S.
Cyprian* herein) is of Opinion , that
this good *Thiefe* might be reputed a
Martyr, and therefore escaping Purgatory,

tory, did passe from this World immediatly to Heauen. The Reason, why
the good *Thiefe* might be called a
Martyr, is, in that he publikly confessed Christ, at such tyme, when his Disciples were afraid to speake a word in
Honour of him; therefore in regard of
this his free and ready Confession, his
death with Christ, was reputed with
God, as if he had suffered for Christ.

Those words : *Mecum eris*, *Thou
shalt be with me* ; though no other
thing should be promised, then what
these words only import, yet had it
bene a great benefit and reward vnto
the Thiefe: For as S. *Austin* writeth:
*tract. 5. in Ioan. Vbi malè poterat esse
cum illo, & vbi bene esse poterat sine illo? VVhere could the good thiefe be euill
being with Christ ; and where could he
be well being without Christ* ? For no
smal! reward and remuneration hath
Christ promised to those that follow
him, when he said, *Ioan. 12. Yf any man
minister to me, let him follow me ; and
where I am, there also shall my minister
be.* But our Lord promised to the thiefe
not only his presence or company, but
further added, that the *Thiefe* should
be in Paradise,

What

What the word *Paradise*, in this p'ace may signify (notwithstanding the different opinions of some) needeth not be disputed of. For it is certaine, that Christ the same day after his death, was with his Body in the Sepulcher, with his Soule in Hell : for thus much the Creede of our Fayth deliuereth to vs. It is also no lesse certaine, that the Name either of Celestiall or Terrestriall *Paradise* cannot be ascribed either to the Graue, or to Hell. Not to the Graue ; because that was a most narrow & strait place, only fitting to receaue and containe dead Bodies (to omit, that the Body of Christ & the Body of the good Thiefe were not put in one and the same graue;) Therefore it followeth, that if the *Graue* had beene vnderstood in this place, that promise had not bene fulfilled, *To day thou shalt be with me.* Neither can the Name of *Paradise* be aptly applyed to *Hell*; seing *Paradise* doth signify a garden of delights. And certainly in the terrestriall Paradise, there were trees, bearing fruite and flowers; there were also most cleare Waters, and an incredible sweetnes of Ayre. And in the celestiall Paradise there

there were, and are immortall pleasures, an inextinguible Light, and the
seates of the Blessed. But in Hell, euen
in that place, where the soules of the
holy Fathers did stay, there was no
light, no sweetnes, no delight. True it
is, that those soules were not tormented, but rather contrariwise, seeing the
hope of their future Redemption, and
the Visitation of Christ to come to
them, did exhilerate & comfort them:
yet notwithstanding this, they were
detayned (as Captiues) in an obscure
and darke Prison. For thus doth the A-
postle (expouding the Prophet) speak:
*Ephes. 4. Christ ascending en high, led
Captiuity captiue.* And *Zachary* sayth,
*cap. 9. Thou in the bloud of thy Testá-
ment, hast let forth thy Prisoners out of
the Lake wherein is no Water.* Where
those words, *thy Prisoners*, and, *out of
the lake in which there is no water*, do
not intimate any sweetnes of Paradise,
but the darknes of a Prison. Therefore
the name of *Paradise* signifieth no o-
ther thing, then the Beatitude of the
Soule, which is placed in the Vision of
God: for that is the true Paradise of
delights; not corporall or locall, but
spirituall and Celestiall.

And

And this is the reason, why the
Theefe beseeching and saying: *Remember me, when thou shalt come into thy
kingdome.* Christ did not answere and
say: *To day thou shalt be with me in my
kingdome,* but, *in Paradise;* For Christ
him'else vvas not to be that day in his
kingdome, that is, in perfect felicity of
Body and soule ; but he was to arriue
thereto vpon the day of his Resurrection, when his Body was to become
immortall, impafsible, glorious, and
not obnoxious or subiect to any seruitude. Neither would Christ haue the
good *Theefe* to be partaker of this
kingdome before the common Resurrection of all Bodies, and the day of
the last Iudgment. Notwithstanding
our Lord most truly-and properly said
to him, *To day thou shalt be with me in
Paradise,* because that very day he was
to communicate to the soule of the
good thiefe, as also to the Soules of all
the Saints in *Limbo Patrum,* the glory
of the sight of God, which himselfe
had receaued from his Conception.
For this glory, or felicity is effentiall,
and it is the supreme Good in the Heauenly Paradise. And certainly the propriety of the words of Christ is to be
admi-

admired. For he said not : *VVe shall be to day in Paradise*, or , *to day we will goe into Paradise*; but, *To day thou shalt be with me in Paradise*; as if he would haue said: Thou art this day with me vpon the Crosse, but thou art not with me in Paradise, in which I am , according to the supreme portion of the soule; but a litle after, yea this very day, thou shalt be with me, not only freed from the Crosse, but euen in *Paradise* .

Of the first fruite of the second Word.

CHAP. V.

FRom the *second Word* spoken vpon the Crosse , we may gather certaine fruits of great worth . The first fruit is, the Consideration of the immense mercy & liberality of Christ, and how behoofull and profitable a thing it is, to serue him. Christ being oppressed with dolours , and paines, might not haue heard the *Theefe* praying to him; but Charity made choyce rather to forget the sharpnes of his tor-

torments, then not to heare a miserable sinner, so confessing himselfe to be. The same Lord, who was altogether silent at the maledictions and exprobrations of the Chiefe Priests, and the souldiers, would not through his Charity be so, to the cryes of a poore and penitent suppliant. He was silent to the reproaches vttered against him, becaufe he is patient; he would not be filent to the confession of the Thiefe, becaufe he is mercifull.

But vvhat shall we may say of the Liberality and Bounty of Chrift? He vvho serueth temporall Lords, doth often take great paines, and gaine but litle. Certainly we may daily see not few, who haue rauelled and spent out many yeares in Princes Courts, and yet in their old age they returne home, almoft Beggars. But Chrift our Prince is truly liberall, truly magnificall; He receaued nothing from the *Thiefe*, but a few good Words, and a prompt desire of seruing and following him; and yet behould, with how great a reward he vvas recompensed. For firft euen that day all his sinnes were fully pardoned, which he had committed during the course of his whole life: Next,

F   he

hevvas adioyned to the Princes of his
People , to vvit, to the Patriarchs and
Prophets : To conclude, he was taken
vp and aduanced to the participation
and. fruition of Chrift his Table , of
his dignity, of his Glory, and finally of
all his Goods. Our Lord faid : *To day
thou fhalt be with me . in Paradife*. And
vvhat our Lord had faid, he prefently
performed: for he d d not defer this
his reward to another tyme ; but that
very day Chrift enriched the *Theefs*
vvith a great reward, an aboundant
Reward, and a Revvard amaffed and
heaped together of all the goods of
Celeftiall Happines.

Neither did Chrift proccede in
this manner of munificence oriy with
this Thiefe . The Apoftles only left
their fmall boates, their places of receauing Tole or Tribute , and their
poore Cottages, that they might ferue
Chrift . But in recompence of this,
Chrift made them , *Princes ouer the
whole Earth*. *Pfal.*44. He alfo fubiected
to their power, the Deuill, Serpents, &
all kind of difeafes. *Matth.* 10. A man
hath giuen to the poore (for the honour and loue he beareth to Chrift) a
litle bread, or but fome old cloaths, or
ragges,

ragges, and yet in recompence hereof he shall heare Christ say at the day of Iudgment: *I was hungry, and you gaue me to eate; I was naked, and you couered me; Therefore take and possesse an euerlasting kingdome. Matth. 25.* To conclude, that I may pretermit all other points of this Nature, Heare, and take notice of the incredible bounty and liberality of our Lord: but we must remember, He was God who thus promised: *Euery one, that hath forsaken house, or Brethren, or sisters, or Father, or Wyfe, or Children, or Lands, for my names sake, shall receaue an hundred fould, and shall possesse life euerlasting. Matt. 19.*

S. Hierome, and other holy Doctours do explicate this promise in this sort; To wit, that who shall suffer losse of any temporall matter for Christ in this present life, shall receaue a double reward, and incomparably greater, then the thing which is left for Christ. For first, he shall receaue spirituall ioy (being a spirituall guift) in this life, which is an hundred fould greater & more precious, then is that which is left for the loue of Christ. So as a man of a cleare and perfect Iudgment,

F 2　　　**would**

would sooner make choyce to retaine
and keep that spirituall good to himselfe, then to change it for an hundred
houses, Lāds, or other such like things.
Againe, as if this reward vvere but
small, and not to be much prized, that
happy Marchant or Negotiatour shall
receaue in the world to come eternall
Life, by vvhich word is signified an immense abundance, or boundles heaping togeather of all goods. But this is
the vnlimited liberality of Christ our
supreme Lord, towards those who are
not afraid, or delay to bynd themselues seriously to his Seruice . Are not
then such men euen distracted and depriued of their Wits , who abandoning Christ, make themselues thral, &
Vassals to *Mammon*, *Epicurisme*, and
Luxurie?

But some men will contest against
what we heere teach, and auer, as neuer hauing tasted of the Riches of
Christ , saying : All which is hitherto
spoken, are but naked Words , since
we daily see many seruants of Christ
to be poore, abiect, contemptible, and
in state deplorable. This *Hundredfould*
vvhich is here so greatly magnified,
vve see not. To this I answere. It is so
indeed;

indeed ; for a Carnall man neuer seeth that *Hūdred fould* promised by Christ; because his eyes are not capable of such a sight; neither doth this man at any time tast that solid and true ioy, which a pure Conscience, and Seraphicall Charity towards, God is accustomed to tast. But here I will produce an Example, from the which Carnality, and Sensuality may in some sort make a cōiecture of spirituall delights, and riches.

We read in the Booke of Examples (*distinct.* 3. *exempl.* 16.) of the most famous men of the *Cistercian Order*, that one *Arnulphus* (noble by byrth, and of great riches) leauing the World, and abandoning from him all temporall cares, became a Monke of the forsaid Order, vnder the famous Abbot S. *Bernard.* This man God did exercise and trye with diuers most sharp scourges of many corporall Infirmities, especially tovvards the later end of his life. But at one time, when his paines began to seize vpon him with greater violence then vsually afore, he cryed out with a great voyce, and said: *Vera sunt omnia, quæ dixisti Domine Iesu.* O Lord Iesu &c, all those

things

things are true , which thou hast said.
And when as those , who were about
him, demaunded why he spake these
Words,he replied : *Dominus in Euan-*
gelio suo dicit , *Qui reliquerit diuitias*
&c. Our Lórd hath said in his Gospell.
He who hath left his riches , and all o-
ther things for Christ ; shall receaue an
hundred sould in this life , and after
wards life euerlasting. *Ego vim huius*
promissionis nunc demum intelligo &c.
I now at length do see and acknowledge
the truth and force of this promise; and
do confesse , that now I do receaue an
hundred sould of all things , or goods,
which I haue left. For the great bitternes of these my paynes is so pleasant
and gratefull to me, through my hope of
Gods good mercy of which these dolours
are a pledge , as that I would not haue
wanted this Hope and Comfort for so
much riches of the world, though a hundred tymes doubled, as I haue left and
forsaken . For certainly the spirituall
ioy,which now is but in hope and expectation, doth a hundred thousand times
exceed al worldly ioy which now actually, and in possession is. Thus far the forsaid *Arnulphus* his words . And I
wouid desire the Reader maturely to
weigh

weigh and confider of them, and then let him iudge, how much is to be efteemed and pryzed a certaine and firme hope (infufed by God) of the prefent obtayning of eternall Beatitude and Felicity.

Of the fecond fruite of the fecond Word.

CHAP. VI.

ANother fruite of the former fecond Word or Sentence, is an acknowledgment of the power of the Grace of *God*, and of the imbecillity and weaknes of mans Will. From the knowledge whereof we may learne, that it is a chiefe matter greatly to confide in the help of God, and greatly to diftruft in our owne proper force and ftrength. Doft thou couet to know the power of the Grace of God? Behould the *good Thiefe*. This man was a notoricus finner, continuing in that moft wicked ftate, till he came to fuffer punifhment vpon a Croffe, that is, almoft till the inftant of his death : And in fo great a perill of Eternall damna-

damnation, there vvas not any who would relieue him either with counsell, or with other help or eafe. For although he was placed neare to our Sauiour; yet he did beare the High Priefts, and the Pharifees, affirming him to be a Seducer, ambitious, and to affect the kingdome of another man. He heard his fellow *Thiefe* vpbrayding Chrift with the fame men. There was not any man in all that Prefence, who would fpeake one word in defence of Chrift; neither did Chrift himfelfe feeke to refute thofe blafphemies and ma'edictions. Yet notwithstanding all this through the moft gracious & admirable fauour of God, whē the *Thiefe* feemed to haue no helpe for his Saluation; and being thus moft neere to Hell, and moft diftant from eternall life, he being in a moment illuftrated, and enlightned from aboue, and loathing his former vvickednes, confeffeth Chrift to be innocent, and to be the king of the future World; And thus being made (as it were) a Preacher, he reprehendeth his fellow, perfuadeth him to repentance, and in the eye of them all doth deuoutely and humbly commend himfelfe to Chrift.

To

To conclude, he did so beare himfelfe herein, as that his penall torments vpon the Croffe, inflicted iuftly vpon him, for his offence, was accepted and taken for his paines due in Purgatory; and thus inftantly vpon his death, he entred into the ioy of his Lord.

From th.s then we may learne, that no man ougnt to defpaire of his Saluation, feing this poore man, who came into the Vineyard almoft at the laft hower, receaued the rewvard vvith thofe who came at the firft. Contrariwife, the other *Thiefe* (that humane infirmity might more appeare) tooke no correption, or admonifhment from that notable Charity of Chrift, who prayed for his Crucifiers in fo louing a manner, neither from his owne proper punifhment; nor from the counfell and example of his fellow; nor from the vnaccuftomed darknes, and cleauing of the ftones, nor from the Example of thofe, who (after Chrift was dead) returned back beating & knocking their Breafts; All vvhich things did fall out after the Conuerfion of the good *Thiefe*, that from thence we might be inftructed, that the one *Thiefe* without thefe helps could be conuerted, the other with all the fam., could not, or rather would not.

But thou wilt heere demaund, why God did infpire and giue the grace of Conuerfion to the one Thiefe, and did not infpire it to the other? I anfwere, that fufficient Grace vvas not wanting to either. And if the one of them did perifh, he perifhed through his owne fault; if the other vvas conuerted, he was conuerted through the Grace of God, but not without the cooperation of his owne free will. But thou will reply; Why did not God giue to both the Theeues that efficacious Grace; which is not refufed, and reiected euen of hard and ftony Harts? This belongeth to the fecrets of God, the which it becommeth vs to admire, but not to fearch into: fince it is fufficient for vs to know, that there is no *Iniquity with God*, as the Apoftle fpeaketh, and that the Iudgments of God may be fecret, but iniuft they cannot be, as *S. Auftin* teacheth. It behoueth vs rather to learne from this proceeding of God, not to deferre or prolong our Conuerfion, till the end of our Life. Since though it happen to one man, to find the Grace of God at the laft howes, hovver, yet to another it falleth out, to find Iudgment.

And if any man will reuolue or looke ouer Hiftories, and obferue the daily euents and chances, he fhall certainly find them to be very few, vvho haue fortunatly and happily paffed out of this World, if fo they liued wickedly throughout the vvhole courfe of their life; but rather after their life negligently led, haue bene fent to euerlafting Punifhment. As on the contrary, moft few can be numbred, who haue liued pioufly and faintly, and yet haue perifhed vnhappily and miferably: but many may be rekoned, who after a vertuous and godly life haue arriued to fempiternall ioyes. Certainly they are ouer bold and ouer rafh, who in a matter fo much importing (to wit, life Euerlafting, or torments euerlafting) dare defer to remaine in deadly and mortall finne but one day; fince they may be receaued and depriued of this prefent life euery moment; and that after death there is no more place left for Pennance, and no Redemption in Hell.

Of the third fruite of the
second *Word.*

CHAP. VII.

THe *third fruit* of the same Sentence of our Lord may be gathered from that , if one will consider, that ther were three Persons crucified in the same place,& at the same houre: One,that was *Innocent*(to wit, *Christ*) an other *Penitent*,the good Thiefe,the third , *obstinate* and obdurate in his sinnes, the bad Thiefe. Or otherwise we may say , There were three Persons crucified at one time; Christ,who was euer excellêtly good,One Thiefe, euer notoriously wicked ; Another Thiefe, who was sometimes wicked, sometymes holy. From this now vve may inferre , that no man in this life can liue without his Crosse , and that those labour in vaine, vvho hope and endeauour to auoyde the same; but those are wise , who receaue their Crosse from the hand of our Lord, & do suffer the same euen till death, not only patiently, but also resignedly and willingly.   That

That all good and Vertuous men
are to haue their Crosses, appeareth
from those words of our Lord: *Math.
16. If any man will come after me, let
him deny himselfe, and take vp his
Crosse, and follow me.* And in another
place: *He that doth not beare his Crosse,
and come after me, cannot be my Disciple. Luc. 14.* The which point the Apostle clearely teacheth, saying, *2. Tim. 3.
All who will liue godly in Christ Iesus,
shall suffer persecution.* To whom are
concordant the holy Fathers, both Latin, and Greeke. For greater breuity I
will insist only in two. *S. Austin* who
writeth: *Vita ista &c. This life is a litle
Tribulation; If it be not a tribulation, it
is not a peregrination; but if it be a peregrination, either thou litle louest thy
Country, or without doubt thou suffe-
rest Tribulation. in Psal. 137.* And the
same Father in another place: *Si putas
te &c. If thou be persuaded, that as yet
thou hast suffered no tribulation, then
thou hast not begun to be a Christian. in
Psal. 11.*

   S. Iohn Chrysostome thus accordeth
with the former Father: *A Christiani
vita &c.* Tribulation is an indissolu-
ble bond from the life of a Christian.
                           G 3   *hom.*

hom 6?. ad ?op. And againe: *Nonpotest dicere &c.* Thou canst not alledge any one, who is exempt from tribulation, because he is Iust. *hom. 29. in Ep. ad Heb.* To conclude, the force of Reason manifestly euicteth this point. Things côtrary without a mutuall concertation and fight cannot stand togeather. Fier and Water, so long as they remayne in seuerall & remote places, rest quiet, and without iarring; But when they meet together, then instantly the Water begins to euaporate and send forth smoke, to leape (as it were) and to make a noyse, vntill either the water be spent and consumed, or the fire extinguished. *Ecclesiasticus* sayth, *cap. 33. Contra malum, bonum est; contra mortem, vita; Sic & contra virum iustum, Peccator.* Against *Euill, is good; against death, Lyfe, so also against a iust man, is a sinner.* Iust men are like to fire, they shyne, they burne, they ascend high, & whatsoeuer they do, they do it efficaciously, vigorously, and sparkily : But the Iniust resemble Water, they are could, they slide vpon the earth, causing in euery place dirt & filth. What wonder then is it, if all good men do suffer persecution at the hands of the **Wicked?**

Wicked? But becaufe euen to the confummation of the World, the wheate and the Darnell fhall grow in the fame fild; the chaffe and the Corne in the fame Barne; good and bad Fifh in the fame Net; that is, Vertuous & wicked men not only in the fame World, but euen in the fame Church, therefore it cannot be otherwife, but that vertuous and holy men fhall receaue from the wicked and impious, Iniuries, and Tribulations.

But neither the wicked do liue in this world, voyde and exempt from the Croffe. For although they do not fuffer perfecution from the Iuft; yet they do fuffer from other wicked men; they fuffer from their owne Vices; they fuffer from a guilty and felfe tormenting Confcience. Certainly the moft wife *Salomon*, who was thought and reputed moft happy (if any man could fo be)could not deny, but that he fuffered his Croffe, when he faid: *Vidi in omnibus &c. I faw in all things Vanity and affliction of mynd.* And a litle after: *I haue beene weary of my lyfe, feing all things vnder the funne to be euill, and all things Vanity, and afflittion of fpirit. Eccl* 3. And *Ecclefiafti-*

cus

cus also *cap.* 40. (a man very wise) hath deliuered this generall Sentence: *Great Busines and trauell is created to all men, and an heauy yoke vpon the children of Adam.* S. *Austin* sayth: *Inter omnes tribulationes &c. Among all Tribulations not any is greater, then the Conscience of a mans sinnes. in Psal.* 45. S. *Chrysostome* in his 2. Homily vpon *Lazarus,* teacheth, that the wicked do not want their Crosses. For if he be poore, Pouerty is to him a Crosse; if Pouerty be absent, then his owne vn-bridled Cōcupiscence doth afflict him more vehemently; Yf he keep his bed for any disease, he lyeth vpon a Crosse; if he be free from diseases and infirmities of the Body, then is he inflamed with anger, which also is a Crosse.

But S. *Cyprian* demonstrateth, that euery man euen from his natiuity is borne to his Crosse, and to tribulation; and that he doth fortell & presage the same by his weeping, as soone as he is borne; For thus that Father writeth, *serm. de patientia. Vnusquisque nostrum &c. Euery one of vs, when he is borne, & receaued into the World, taketh his beginning from teares; And although as yet he be ignorant of all things,*

things, he knoweth no other thing euen at his first birth and natiuity, then to weepe; through a naturall prouidence he bewaileth the anxieties and labours of a mortall life; and the poore ignorant soule presently in the beginning doth protest, and foretell with lamentation and crying, the stormes of the world, into the which he is ready to enter and suffer. Thus **S. Cyprian.** Since then these things are so certaine, who can deny, but that the *Crosse* is common both to good and euill men?

It yet remaineth to make it euidēt, that the Crosse of vertuous men is short, light, and profitable; and continually the Crosse of the wicked, heauy, barren, and continuall. And touching the Crosse of Godly men, That it is short it cannot be denied, seing it cannot be extended beyond the terme or tyme of this lyfe. For iust men dying: *Now sayth the spirit, they rest from their labours. Apoc.* 14. And that, *God shall wype away all teares, from their Eyes. Apoc.* 21. That this present lyfe is most short, though whiles it is flowing avvay, it seemes long and tedious, the sacred Scripture doth not obscurely signify, when it sayth: *Iob.* 14. *Breues*

G 5   *dies*

dies hominis sunt &c. The dayes of man
are short; and man borne of a Woman,
liuing a short tyme. And yet more:
What is your lyfe ? *It is a vopour ap-*
pearing a litle while , and after it shall
vanish away. The Apostle , who may
be thought to haue suffered a most
heauy Crosse, and this for a long time;
to wit , from his youth vnto his old
age, yet doth thus speake hereof: 2.
Cor.4. Our tribulation , which is mo-
mentarie and light, worketh aboue mea-
sure exceedingly an eternall weight of
glory in vs. Where he compareth his
tribulation(suffered aboue thirty yeares)to an indiuisible moment of time;
and he styles it but a small tribulation;
to wit,to be hungry ,to be thirsty, to
be naked, to be stroken and buffeted,
to suffer a daily persecution; to be
thrice beate with roddes by the Roma-
nes; fiue times to be whipped by the
Iewes,to be once stoned,to suffer ship-
wrack thrice; To conclude, to be con-
uersant in many labours , to be much
in prison , subiect aboue measure to
stroks and wounds, and to be often at
the pit-brimme of death.

Now what Tribulations are to be
accounted heauy, if these of the Apostle

ftle be truly light and eafy? But what. If
I fhould add & auer that the Croffe
of luft men it not only light, but fweet
and pleafant, in regard of the fupera-
bundant côfolation of the Holy Ghoft,
accompaning it? Chrift himfelfe thus
pronounceth of his yoake, which may
be faid to be a Croffe: *Matth. 11. My
yoake is fweete, and my burden light.*
And in another place: *You fhall weepe
and lament, but the world fhall reioyce;
you fhalbe made forrowfull, but your
forrow fhalbe turned into ioy; and your
ioy no man fhall take from you. Ioan.*
16. And the Apoftle crieth out: *I am
repleniſhed with all Confolation, I do
exceedingly abound in ioy, in all our
Tribulation. 2. Cor. 7.* To conclude, that
the *Croffe* of the Iuft, is not only ſhort
and light, but alfo fruitfull land moſt
profitable, it cannot be denied, fince
our Lord plainly thus fpeaketh in *S.
Mathew cap. 5. Bleffed are they, that
fuffer perfecution for Iuſtice, for theirs
is the kingdome of Heaven.* And the A-
poſtle in his Epiſtle to the Romans,
*cap. 8. burſteth out, faying: The Paſ-
fions of this tyme, are not condigne to
the glory to come, that fhalbe reuealed
in us.* With whome agreeth his Coa-
poſtle

poſtle *S. Peter*, when he ſayth: *Communicating with the Paſsions of Chriſt, be glad, that in the reuelation alſo of his glory, you may be glad, reioycing.* 1, *Pet.* 6.

Now that the *Croſſe* of the wicked is moſt tedious, moſt heauy, and depriued of all reward or fruit, is eaſily demonſtrated. Certainly the *Croſſe* of the wicked *Theefe* ended not with his temporall life, but continueth euen to this day in Hell, and ſhall continue for all Eternity; for the worme of the Wicked (in Hell) ſhall not dye, and their fire ſhall not be extinguiſhed. And the Croſſe of the *Rich Glutton*, which conſiſted in heaping together of Riches (the which our Lord moſt truly compared to thornes) was not ended in his death, as the *Croſſe* of *Lazarus* the poore beggar was; but accompanying him euen to Hell, doth burne, and torment him, and forceth him to ſay: *I would to God, that a drop of Water might coole my tongue, becauſe I am tormented in this flame.* Thus we ſee, that the *Croſſe* of the wicked neuer findeth end. And in this very time and life, how heauy and ſharpe their *Croſſe* is, the words of
them,

them, whom the Booke of *Wisdome* introduceth as lamenting , do fully witnesse , *Sap. 5.* **We are wearied out** *in the way of iniquity and perdition, & haue walked hard wayes.* What ? Are not Ambition, Couetousnes, Luxury, hard wayes ? Are not those hard wayes , which inseparably attend vpon Vice; to wit, Anger, Dissentions, Enuy ? Are not the workes , which spring from these (that is to say, treacheries reproaches , contumelies, Wounds , and death it selfe) hard wayes? Certainly , these are of that vvorking Nature , at that not seldome they force men (as being desperate) to become their owne Parricides and Butchers; and thus by flying from one *Crosse* , they fall vpon an other farre more insupportable, and dreadfull.

But let vs see , if the *Crosse* of the wicked do bring forth any gayne or fruit . Doubtlesly it cannot produce any thing, that is good ; since *Thornes do not bring forth grapes , nor Thistles figs.* The yoake of our Lord maketh a man quiet , and reposed , according to his owne Words: *Take vp my yoake vpon you , and you shall find rest vnto your Soules. Math. 11.* But the yoake

of

of the Deuill (which is contrary to
the yoake of Chrift) what can it en-
gender, but follicitude and anxiety?
And which ballanceth all other refpects, the *Croffe* of Chrift is a degree
or ftep to euerlafting Happines: *Ought
not Chrift to haue fuffered thefe things,
and fo to enter into his glory?* Luc 24.
Whereas the *Croffe* of the Deuill af-
fordeth a paffage to eternall punifhment : *Goe you into euerlafting fire,
which was prepared for the Deuill and
his Angels. Matth.25.* Such men, who
are carefull of their foules health, let
them not couet to defcend downe
from their *Croffe*, if fo they be crucified with Chrift, as the *Euill Theefe* laboured to doe; but rather let them
with the *good thiefe* adhere, & cleaue
willingly to the fyde of Chrift, and let
them pray to God , that they may
obtaine Patience, but not a defcen-
ding from the *Croffe.* For thus fuffering together with Chrift , they fhall
reigne together with him: *Si compati-
mur, & conglorificabimur. Rom.8.*

Butthey who fuffer the *Croffe* of
the diuell (if they wilbe carefull of
their owne good) let them labour in
all haft & fpeed to change their *Croffe.*
Let

Let them change the fiue yoake of
Oxen , for one yoake of Chrift . The
fiue yoake of Oxen feeme to fignify the
labours and moleftations , which the
wicked vndergo , thereby to fatisfy
the pleafure of the *fiue Senfes* . But
thefe fiue yoakes are changed for that
one fweet and light yoake of Chrift ,
when a man doth turne thofe labours ,
which before he fuffered for the com-
mitting of finne, through the grace of
God , into labours and workes of Pennance . Happy is that foule , which
knoweth how to crucify his flefh frõ
all vice and concupifcence ; and what
riches or charges he hath heeretofore
wafted, in nourifhing and feeding his
fenfuality, fo much to beftow after in
Almes deeds; and what time he hath
loft in attending, or vifiting great Perfons , or in affecting of Ambition , to
redeeme the fame tyme , by fpending
fo much in Prayer , reading of deuout
Bookes , and in feeking the fauour of
God, and of the Princes of the Heauenly Court ; for by this meanes the
Croffe of the euill Theefe, may be chã-
ged for the *Croffe* of Chrift ; I meane ,
a *Croffe* , which is grieuous and bar-
raine , for a *Croffe* which is light and
fruitfull. Moft

Most wisely (as *S Auslin* relateth)
did a noble Commander in the wars,
discourse with his fellow souldier,
touching the commutation & change
of his *Crosse*; his words are these : *Dic
quæso te & c. I pray thee tell me , where
do we intend to arriue by all these our
labours ? VVhat end do we proieƈ in
our thoughts , or seeke after? To what
end do we thus warre and play the souldiers ? Can there be any greater hope for
vs in the Court, then to become the Em-
perours friěds? But what is there,which
is not fragile, vncertaine, and full of
dangers ,and by how many dangers do
men there ascend to greater dangers ?
And how long shall this our state continue? If I wilbe a friend of God, behould
I am so made at this instant.* Thus much
S. *Auslin* recordeth. *Lib.*8.*Confess. c.*6.
Heare we may see , how wisely this
worthy souldier (in accounting the labours spent in seeking the fauour of
the Emperour, to be most trouble-
some, and painfull, and often vnprofi-
table) did proceed ; and in endeauou-
ring to change them into labours more
sweet, more short, and more profita
,ble, for the purchasing of the friendship and loue of God. And thus accordingly

dingly thefe two happy Souldiers did prefently turne the Current of their life; for both of them abandoning their fecufar Warfare, began to be fpirituall fouldiers only to God. And which did more redouble their ioy, was, that both of them had wyues, who hearing of this vnexpected chāge of their Husbands, did themfelues moft willingly and chearefully dedicate their Chaftity to God.

The third Word, to wit, Ecce mater tua, Ecce filius tuus. *Behould thy Mother, Behould thy Sonne.* Ioan. 19. *is litterally explicated.*

CHAP. VIII.

THe laft Sentence of thofe three, which belong to the Charity of our Neighbour is this:*Ecce mater tua, Ecce filius tuus. Behould thy Mother, Behould thy Sonne.*But before we defcend to thefe VVords, certaine precedent words of the Euangelift are to be explicated; for thus *S. Iohn* fpeaketh:

keth: *There stood by side the Crosse of Ie-*
sus his mother , and his mothers sister
Mary of Cleophas , and Mary Magda-
len. VVhen Iesus therefore had seene his
mother, and the disciple standing, whom
he loued , he sayth to his mother : VVo-
man behould thy sonne. After, he sayth
to the disciple: Behould thy Mother; And
from that hower the disciple tooke her
for his owne. Ioan. 19. Of the three women, which stood neere to the *Crosse*
of our Lord, two were most eminent
and well knowne, to wit , *Mary* the
Mother of God, and *Mary Magdalene*;
Touching *Mary* of *Cleophas* , there is
some question or doubt. The common
opinion is, that *Mary of Cleophas* was
German-sister to the *B Virgin* Mother
of God, borne of *S. Anne* by a second
husband : to which *two Maries*, some
do adde a third sister, called *Mary Sa-*
lome. But this last Opinion is wholy to
be reiected, since it is not credible, that
three sisters should be called by one, &
the same name. Againe , the constant
sentence of learned and pious men, is,
that *S. Anne* was the mother only of
the Blessed Virgin; neither is there any
mention of *Mary Salome* in the Gospells . For where *S. Marke* writeth:
Mary

Mary Magdalene, Mary of Iames, *and* Salome bought spices. The word, *Salome*, is not of the second Case, as if it signifi d *Mary of Salome,* as before it is said, *Mary of* Iames ; but it is of the first Case, and of the feminine Gender, as appeareth from the Greeke word σαλωμη·

To conclude, *Salome* was the wife of *Zebedeus,* and mother of S. Iames and S. Iohn the Apoftles, as appeareth out of S. Mathew, and S. Marke: as Mary of Iames, or Cleophas, was the wyfe of Cleophas, and mother of S. Iames the yongar, and of S. Iude, or Thaddeus. Therefore the truth of this point is, that *Mary of Cleophas* was called the fifter of *Mary* the mother of God, because *Cleophas* was the Brother of S. Ioseph, fpoufe to the B. Virgin *Mary:* for the wyues of two Brethren may rightly be called fifters betweene themfelues. In which refpect alfo S. Iames the yonger, is called the Brother of our Lord; to wit, the fifters Sonne, as aboue we faid of S. Ioseph. This History *Eusebius Casariensis* recordeth, and produceth a faythfull and moft credible Authour *Egesippus* who liued in the later end of the dayes of the A-

H 2   poftles.

poftles. The truth alfo of this point is confirmed by *S. Ierome.*

There is alfo an other literall doubt, which here occurreth, to be folued; How *S. Iohn* can fay, that thefe three women did ftand *iuxta crucem Domini*, *by fide, or neare to the Croffe of our Lord*, feing *Marke* and *Luke*, do write, that they did ftand farre of from the *Croffe*. S. *Auftin* reconcileth thefe feeming different teftimonies; faying that thefe holy women might be faid to ftand aloofe from the Croffe, and neare to the Croffe. A farr off, if their ftanding be compared to the fouldiers and other Minifters, who were fo neare to the Croffe, as that they did touch it. Neere to the Croffe they may be faid to ftand, becaufe through their neerenes they might eafely heare the voyce and words of Chrift, the which the common People could not in regard of their greater diftance. It alfo may be further faid, that thofe three holy Women, during the Paffion did ftand farre of the Croffe, as being hindered by the common People and the fouldiers; but a litle after the Crucifixion was accomplifhed, & many departing away, thofe three wome with

                                        S. Iohn

S. *Iohn* did draw more neere vnto the Croſſe. But againſt this may be vrged, that ſuppoſing this conſtruction, how could then the *Bleſſed Virgin* and S. *Iohn* vnderſtand, that thoſe words of our Lord, *This is thy Sonne, This is thy Mother, were ſpoken of them,* ſeing a great company of perſons were there preſent, and Chriſt did not call either the Virgin, or the Diſciple by their proper name, or appellation?

To this I anſwere, that thoſe three Women and S. *Iohn* did ſtand ſo neere vnto the *Croſſe,* as that our Lord might eaſily deſigne and point out with his eyes the perſons, to whom he did ſpeake; eſpecially ſeing it is certaine he directed thoſe words to ſuch as were his friends, and not to ſtrangers. Now among thoſe, who were his owne friends, there was no other man there preſent, to whom he could ſay, *This is thy Mother,* then S. *Iohn;* nor any other VVoman, who through death was depriued of her ſonne, then the B. *Virgin.* Therefore he ſaid to his Mother: *Behould thy Sonne,* and to his Diſciple: *Behould thy Mother;* Of which words this is the ſele & meaning. I now paſſe out of this VVorld to my Father; and

becauſe

because I know thou art my *Mother*,
and that thou haſt neither parents, nor
husband, nor brethren, nor ſiſters;
therefore not to leaue thee deſtitute
of all humane comfort and ayde, I do
commend thee to the charge and care
of *Iohn* my moſt deare Diſciple. He
ſhalbe to thee in place of a Sonne, and
thou to him in place of a Mother .
Which wholſome counſell, or command of Chriſt did greatly pleaſe them
both, and ech of them (as is credible)
accepted thereof with a yealding ſub-
miſſion of head and body. And S. *Iohn*
ſpeaking of himſelfe ſayth. *And from
that houre, the Diſciple tooke her for his
owne : Ioan.* 19. That is, he preſently
obeyed the words of Chriſt , accounting her among thoſe Perſons, whoſe
charge, care, and prouiſion did belong
to him, and ſuch were his Parents being old, *Zebedeus*, and *Salome.*

But now here ariſeth another literall doubt. *S. Iohn* was one of thoſe
who ſaid : *Ecce nos relinquimus omnia
&c.* Behould , we haue left all things,
and haue followed thee, what therefore
ſhall we haue? Matt. 19. Now among
thoſe things, which they had forſaken,
our Lord himſelfe rekoneth Father &
Mother.

Mother, Brethren and sisters, House &
Lands. And of this *S. Iohn* himselfe, &
of his Brother *S. Iames*, S. *Mathew*
thus writeth, *c.* 4. *Illi autem relictis re-*
tibus & patre, secuti sunt eum &c. And
they forthwith left their nets and Fa-
ther, and followed him. What? did he,
who left one Mother, presently receaue another Mother? But the Answere here is obious and facil: For the
Apostles, that they might follow Christ
dimissed and parted with Father and
Mother, so far forth, as they might be
any hinderance to them for the preaching of the Gospell, as also so far
forth, as might concerne any profit or
humane delight, to be taken by con-
uersing with them. But the Apostles
did not shake of the Care, which by
force of Iustice they were bound to
exhibite vnto their Parents, or which
touched the direction and instruction
of their Children, or helpe & succour
of the needy and distressed.

And this is the Reason (as Doctours
generally affirme) why a sonne cannot
enter into a Religious Order, who
hath his Father, or Mother spent or
wasted through old age, or so oppressed with pouerty, as that they be notable

able to maintaine their life without
the suftentation & help of their Sonne. In this fence therefore S. *Iohn* did
leaue Father and Mother, when they
did not ftand in neede of his labour
and care ; But he did vndergoe the
charge and follicitude of the *Bleffed
Virgin* the Mother, at the command of
Chrift, becaufe fhe was depriued of all
humane help and confolation. God indeed could eafily without mans labour, haue prouided by the miniftery
of his Angels, all things which were
neceffary tor maintayning of her life:
(for to *Chrift* himfelfe the Angels did
minifter in the defert) yet it was his
good pleafure thus to proceed with S.
Iohn, that fo he might leaue this meanes of fuccour to the *Bleffed Virgin*, &
alfo thereby honour S. *Iohn*. For God
fent E*lias* to prouide and take care of
the Widow, not that he could not
nourifh and feede her by the Help of
the Crowes, as before he had done;
but that God might thereby more
bleffe the Widow, as *S. Auftin* admonifheth. So it pleafed our Lord to commit the follicitude of his Mother to
his Difciple, thereby to manifeft, that
S. *Iohn* was more beloued of him,
                                    then

then any of the rest of his Difciples.
For in this mutation & change of the
Mother, is fulfilled that Sentence : *He
who hath left his Father and Mother
&c . fhall receaue an hundred fould ,
and fhall poffeffe life euerlasting.* Math.
19. For he truly receaued an hundred
fould, who left his mother, being the
wyfe of a poore fifher, and receaued
to his care, as Mother, the Mother of
the Creatour, the Lady of the World,
being full of Grace, and bleffed among
all Women, and after to be exalted to
the Celeftiall Kingdome, aboue all the
Quyres of Angels.

Of the firft fruit of the third Word.

CHAP. IX.

FRom this *third* Word, or sentence
ſeuerall fruits may be gathered, if
all points thereof be diligently ponde-
red. And firſt is collected and manifeſted from thence Chriſts infinite deſire of ſuffering for our Saluation, that
ſo our Redemption might be made
moſt full and copious. Other men are
I   very

wary in their death, especially in a violent death, being full of dishonour and contumely, that their neerest frieds be not present thereat, for feare that their owne dolour and griefe through their friends sight be augmented. But Christ not content with his owne sufferings (and those most cruell, and attended on with all reproach and contumely) would haue his owne Mother and his Disciple whom he loued, to be present, and to stand neere to the Crosse; that so the griefe of the Compassion of his owne friends, might giue an increase to the griefe of his Passion. Christ being vpon the *Crosse*, resembled (as it were) foure fountaines of Bloud abundantly streaming; For his will and pleasure was, that his owne Bl. Mother, his beloued disciple, *Mary* the sister of his Mother, and *Mary Magdalene*, who most ardently aboue all other VVomen loued him, should be present at his death, that from them, foure foutaines of teares should burst out; so as he should be almost no more troubled at the effusion of his owne bloud, then he was at that copious showre of teares, which the griefe of them then present did extort,

tort, and force from their eyes and Harts.

It seemes to me, that I heare Christ saying: *The sorrowes of death haue compassed me.* Psal. 17. For that sword foretold of good old *Simeon,* which should pierce the soule of my most innocent Mother with incredible griefe and anxiety, doth euen wound my hart. But o bitter death, doest thou separate not only the soule from the body, but also the mother, from such a Sonne? Therefore dolour would not suffer me to say: *Mother,* but, *VVoman behould thy Sonne.* God so loued the World, that for the redeeming therof, he was content to giue his only begotten *Sonne;* and the *Sonne* so loued the Father, as that for his honour he was ready to shed, & powre out his owne most precious bloud. And not being content only with the dolour of his *Passion,* he added thereto the dolour of *Compassion,* that so he might become a most abundant satisfaction for our sinnes. Therefore from hence it appeareth, that both the Father and the Sonne do commend their Charity to vs after an ineffable manner, that thereby we may not perish, but that

I 2   we

we may obtaine life euerlasting. **And**
yet mans hart doth hitherto resist so
great a Charity, & maketh choyce rather to try the wrath and indignation
of the Omnipotent liuing God, then
once to tast the sweetnes of Mercy, &
to yield to the Charity of diuine Loue.

Verily we are most vngratefull, &
worthy of all punishment, that since
Christ loued vs with such an ardēt affection, as that he was content to suffer for vs much more, then necessity
vrged. From whereas one drop of his
blould was sufficient for our Redemption, he neuertheleffe would spend it
all, and suffer innumerable other punishments besides: And yet notwithstanding all this, we are loath and for-
bearing (for his loue, and for our
owne health, and good of our soule)to
endure and suffer euen so much, as is
but needefull. The cause or source of
so great a sluggines and madnes is, in
that we do not ponder and meditate
on the *Passion* and Charity of Christ,
with that serious introuersiō of mind,
with which we ought, and that we do
not appoint, or designe times and places, sorting to so great a busines; but
only read, or heare the passion of
                                        Christ,

Chrift briefly, negligently, and curfori-
ly. Therefore the holy Prophet admo-
niſheth vs, faying *Thren.* 1. *Behould &
fee, if there be any griefe, like to my
griefe.* And the Apoſtle fayth : *Thinke
vpon him, who endured of finners fuch
contradiction againſt himfelfe, that you
be not wearied, fainting in your minds.
Hebr.* 12. But the tyme ſhall hereafter
come, when fruitlefly, and in vaine we
ſhall repent our felfs of fo great ingra-
titude towards God, and of fupine negligence of our owne Saluation.

There are many, who at the laſt
day, *repenting, and fighing for anguiſh
of fpirit, ſhall fay; The funne of Iuſtice
hath not ſhined to vs. Sap.* 5. Neither
ſhall they firſt then begin thus to lament, but before the day of Iudgmēt,
I meane, that as foone as they ſhall
ſhut and clofe the eyes of their body
by death, the eyes of their foule ſhalbe
opened to them, and then they ſhall
fee thofe things, the which when time
and oportunity was, they would not
once behould.

Of

Of the second fruite of the third Word.

CHAP. X.

AN other fruit growing from the roote of *this VVord*, may be taken from the Confideration of the miftery of the three Women, which ftoode neere vnto the Croffe of our Lord. For *Mary Magdalene* did beare the perfon of the Penitents, & therin of thofe, who did begin to ferue God. In *Mary of Cleophas* may be figured the ftate of thofe, who do go on forward and profit in Vertue. *In Mary the Mother* of Chrift and a Virgin, may be perfonated the ftate of thofe, vvho are Perfect, with whom we may deferuedly ioyne *S. Iohn*, who was a Virgin, and was vvithin a fhort tvme to become *Perfect*, if at that prefent he were not. All thefe, and only thefe are found to ftand neere vnto the *Croffe* of our Lord. for thofe, who liue in ftate of finne and neuer thinke of doing any pennance for their wicked liues, ftand far off from the *Croffe*, which is tho

scale

ſcale or ladder to Heauen.

Furthermore, all thoſe not without cauſe ſtand neere vnto the *Croſſe*, who need the ayde of him, that was crucified; for ſuch as be Penitents and Beginners in the way of Iuſtice, do wage Warre with Vices and Concupiſcences, and ſtand greatly in need of the aſsiſtance of Chriſt our Captaine, that they may be encouraged to fight, whiles they behould him combatting with the Old Serpent, and not deſcending from the Croſſe, vntill moſt happily he had triumphed ouer him. For thus doth the Apoſtle ſpeake to the Colloſsians *cap. 2. He ſpoyled the Principalities and Powers, leading them confidently in open ſhew, and triumphing ouer them in himſelfe.* And a litle before: *Faſtening to the Croſſe, the handwriting of the Decree, which was againſt vs.*

Thoſe, who do profit in the way of our Lord, ſignified by *Mary of Cleophas*, who was a Woman maried, and brought forth ſonnes, which were called the Brethren of Chriſt; do alſo need the help of the *Croſse*; leſt otherwiſe the cares and anxieties of this world, with the which they are ne

I 4

sarily entangled *do choke the good seedes;* or that they labouring by night , *do catch nothing.* Therefore such Persons ought to goe on forward in spirituall profit, and to behould Christ vpon the *Crosse;* who not satisfying himselfe with those good works (being many and great) which before he had done, would by the meanes of the *Crosse,* proceed to works of a higher Nature; from whence he would not descend, till he had ouercome, and put to fight his Enemy. For nothing is more deadly or domageable to those who are in progresse of Vertue, then to become wearie in their course, and to cease to goe forward, since as *S. Bernard* sayth *Ep. ad Garinum . In via Virtutis non progredi , regredi est ;* In the way of Vertue not to goe forward , is to goe backward; who putteth the example of the Lader of *Iacob,* vpon which all do ascend or descend , but not any doe stand still.

To conclude , those who are in state of Perfection , liuing a single and vnmaried life (especially if they be Virgins) as the *B. Virgin* the Mother of Christ, and *S. Iohn* the Disciple of rist, and beloued of him aboue o-

ther

ther in regard of his Virginity were;
thefe perfect Perfons (I fay) ftand in
great neceſsity of the aide and fuppor-
tance of Chriſt crucified; ſince ſuch, as
are placed in a more eminent & high
degree, ought greatly to feare the
blaſts of Pryde, except they be founded and rooted lowly in Humility.
For although Chriſt did often ſhew
himſelfe to be a Maiſter of Humility,
as where he ſaid: *Learne of me, becauſe
I am meeke and humble of Hart: Matth.
11.* As alſo in teaching vs, *To ſit in the
loweſt place:* & where he repeateth ſo
often: *who ſo exalteth himſelfe, ſhalbe
humbled, and who humbleth himſelfe
ſhalbe exalted. Luc. 18.* Yet he neuer
manifeſted himſelfe to be a Maiſter of
Humility in a more high degree, then
when he was ſeated in the Chayre of
his *Croſſe.* Which point the Apoſtle
will declared in thoſe words: *He humbled himſelfe, made obediēt vnto death;
euen the death of the Croſſe. Phil. 2.* For
what greater humility could be imagined, thē that he who was omnipotent,
ſhould ſuffer himſelfe to be bound, &
nayled to the Croſſe? Or that he, in
whom are all the treaſures of Wiſdome and knowledge of God, ſhould

I 5   be

be content to be reputed, as one mad
or distracted, by *Herod* and his army,
and through scorne to be cloathed
with a whyte garment ? Or lastly, that
he, *who sitteth vpon the Cherubims*,
should brooke himselfe to be crucified
in the middst of theeues ? Truly who
will seriously glasse himselfe in the
mirrour of the *Crosse*, will proue ouer
indocible, if he do not learne and confesse, that as yet he is most farre from
obtayning true Humility; howsoeuer
he may be thought to haue made
some progresse & aduancemēt therin.

Of the third fruite of the third *Word*.

CHAP. XI.

IN this third place we learne from
the Chayre of the Crosse, and from
the words of Christ spoken to his
Mother, and his Disciple, what is the
duty of God Parents towards their
Sonnes, and reciprocally of good sonnes towards their Parents . We will
begin with the first . Good Parents
ought to loue their Sonnes, yet to restraine

ſtraine and proportion their loue to them, as that it may be no impediment to the Loue of the Parents towards God. And this is that, vvhich our Saviour teacheth in the Goſpell; *He that loueth his Sonne or his daughter more then me, is not worthy of me.* Math. 10. This Precept the B. *Virgin* moſt preciſely obſerued. For ſhe ſtayed neere to the *Croſſe* with great Griefe, and with great Conſtancy. Her Griefe did witneſſe the extremity of her loue towards her Sonne, hanging vpon the Croſſe : her Conſtancy did teſtify her great obſeruance and duty towards God, reigning in Heauen. She did behould her innocent ſonne with great anxiety and care of mind (whom ſhe ſo dearely loued) ſuffering moſt bitter dolours and paines, yet did ſhe not labour either in words or action to hinder thoſe his afflictions (though ſhe could) becauſe ſhe did well know, that her Sonne was to vndergoe all thoſe totments, by the defined Counſell, & prouidence of God the Father.

Loue is the Meaſure of Griefe; therefore the Mother did much lament, to behould her ſonne to be ſo cruciated and afflicted, ſince ſhe loued

him

him much. And how could it otherwise be, but that the *Virgin* (the mother of Chrift) fhould moft ardently
loue her fonne; fince fhe was well pri-
uy, that her fonne did exceede all the
fonnes of men, in euery degree of
Prayfe, and that her fonne was in a
more ftrict bond to her, and did more
nearely belong to her, then any other
fonnes do belong vnto their Mothers.
The reafon why Women do loue
their fonnes, is accuftomed to be two-
fold. The one is, in that they bare and
brought their fonnes forth into the
World; The other in that the fonnes
become famous for their deportment
and good deferts. For otherwife there
are not Mothers wanting, who do but
litle loue, or rather hate their fonns, if
either they be of any deformity in body, or do proue wicked, or vngratefull
and vnnaturall towards their Parents,

Now the B. *Virgin* (the mother of
Chrift) loued her Sonne for both thefe
refpects in a more intenfe and high
degree, then any other Mother euer
loued her fonne. For firft , Other women alone do not generate children,
but in the generation of them they
haue their husband for their Compa-
nion

nion in that Act. But the Bleſſed Virgin alone did generate her ſonne; *Since*
a Virgin did beget , and a Virgin did
bring forth. And as Chriſt(our Lord)in
his diuine generation had a Father
without a Mother; ſo in his humane
generation he had a Mother , without
a Father. And although it may be truly
ſaid, that Chriſt was conceaued of the
Holy Ghoſt, yet the Holy Ghoſt is not
the Father of Chriſt, but the Effectour
and maker of the Body of Chriſt.
Neither did the Holy Ghoſt frame the
body of Chriſt , of his owne proper
ſubſtance, which peculiarly belongeth
to a Father; but he formed it of the
moſt pure bloud of the Virgin. Therefore the moſt *Holy Virgin* alone, without the company of a Father, did beget and bring forth her Sonne. And
ſhe alone doth challenge her Sonne, as
whole to herſelfe; and thereupon did
more loue him , then any other Mother euer loued her Oſpring.

Novv ſo far forth as belongeth to
the ſecond Reaſon: The ſonne of the
Bleſſed Virgin was, and is ſpecious, and
beautifull *aboue the ſonnes of men;* and
doth excell both men and Angels in
all manner of prayſe. Therefore it followeth,

loweth, that the *Bleſſed* Virgin, who
loued her Sonne aboue all others, did
alſo condole and deplore his death &
paſsion more, then all others. This
point is ſo vndeniable, as that S. *Bernard* is not afraid to ſay, that the
Griefe of the *B.* Virgin, conceaued touching the Paſsion of her Sône, might
be called the Martyrdome of her Hart,
according to that of *S. Simeon*; *Thy
owne ſoule ſhall a ſword pierce.* And becauſe the martyrdome of the Hart ſeemeth more intollerable, then the martyrdome of the Body; S. *Anſelme* writeth, that the dolours of the *B.* Virgin
were more ſharpe and inſufferable,
then any corporall martyrdome. Certainly our Sauiour, when praying in
the garden of *Gethſemani*, he ſuffered
his hart to be martyred, and ſtrongly
apprehending all the paines and torments which the next day he was to
vndergoe, and withall giuing (as it
were) the reines and liberty to griefe
and feare, began ſo vehemently to be
cruciated and afflicted, as that a bloudy
ſweat diſtilled from his whole Body;
The which is not read to haue fallen
out in his corporall Paſsion.

Therfore the *B.* Virgin doubtleſ-
ly

ly suffered most bitter paine, and acer-bity of affliction, through the sword of Dolour penetrating her soule. And yet in that she was most willing, that the honour and glory of God should ouer weigh the loue, which she did beare to the flesh of Christ; therefore she stood neere vnto the Crosse, full of all constancy and spirituall resolution, looking without any shew of impatience vpon her Sonne then suffering. She did not fall vpon the Earth, halfe dead (as some do imagine;) she did not teare the hayre from her Heade; she did not after a womanish manner bewaile and crye out, but she entertained & welcomed with all cauennesse and serenity of mind, what was to be tollerated, as proceeding from the good pleasure and Will of God. She greatly loued the flesh of her sonne; she more loued the honour of the Father, & saluation of the World; which two points the Sonne himselfe did more loue, then the safety and health of his owne Body. Furthermore, the assured Fayth of the Resurrection of her Sonne, to be after the third day (of the which she neuer doubted) did so animate her, and minister new spirits

of

of Constancy, as that she did not stand
in need of humane Consolation. For
she knew well, that the death of her
Sonne, was like vnto a most short
sleepe, according to that of the Prophet: *I haue slept, and haue bene at
rest, and I haue risen vp, because our
Lord hath taken me. Psal.* 3.

All good & pious Christians ought
to imitate this Example; I meane, they
ought to loue their Children; but not
to prefer them in loue before God,
who is the Father of all, and who loueth them better, and in a more perfect manner, then we know how to
loue. And first Christiãs ought to loue
their Sonnes with a manly & prudent
loue; not boulstering or encouraging
them when they do euill, but bringing
them vp in the feare of God; and cor-
recting them not only with words, but
euen with strokes, if either they offend
God, or neglect their studies, and learning. For this is the will of God, reuealed in the Holy Scriptures, as *Ecclesiasticus* speaketh, *cap.* 7. *Hast thou
children? Instruct them, and bow them
from their childhood.* And we read of
Toby, that, *he taught his Sonne from
his infancy to feare God, and to abstaine
from*

from all sinne. And the Apostle *Ephes.*
6. admonisheth Fathers, that they do
not prouoke their Children to anger,
but do bring them vp in difcipline &
correction of our Lord; that is, that
they vfe them not as feruants, but as
freemen. For thofe who beare themfelues ouer feuerely, and aufterely towards their Children, continually
checking or ftriking them for the leaft
fault, do treate them as bond flaues; fo
caufing them either to be of a bafe and
deiected difpofition, or els to fly away
from their Parents. Now thofe, who
are ouer indulgent, do make their
Children wicked; nourifhing & bringing them vp, not for the kingdome
of God, but for Hell.

The true way for the education
of Children, is, that Parents do in-
ftruct them in difcipline, fo as they
may learne willingly and promptly to
obey their Parents and maifters; and
when they do erre and offend, that
they do correct them paternally, that fo
the Sonnes may vnderftand themfelues
to be chaftized out of Loue, not out of
Hate. Furthermore, if fo it fhall pleafe
God to call any of them to the Clergy,
or to fome religious Order, let not the

K Parents

Parents refist fo good a refolution, for
feare they may refift God, who is the
firft Father of all men; but let them
fay with holy Iob, *Our Lord gaue, and
our Lord hath taken away; The name of
our Lord be bleffed*. To conclude, if
children be taken from their Parents
by vntimely death (the which thing
did chiefly happen to the *Bleffed Virgin*) let them confider & ponder the
iudgments of God; who often taketh
fome out of this World by death, to
preuent that malice and finne do not
change their good and vertuous mind,
and fo perifh eternally. Certainely if Parents did fometymes know,
vpon what counfell and inducoments,
God thus worketh, they vvould not
only not bewayle the death of their
Children, but they would euen reioyce thereat. And if the fayth & hope
of the Refurrection did feelingly, and
liuely worke in vs (as it did in our B.
Lady) we fhould no more grieue,
when any of our fonnes or friends do
dye before they arriue to old age,
then when any of them begin to fleep
before it be night, fince the death of a
faythfull and pious man is a kind of
fleepe, as the Apoftle admonifheth vs,
saying:

saying, 1. *Theff.* 4. *I will not haue you ignorant concerning them that fleep, that you be not forrowfull, as others are, that haue no* Hope. Heere he mentioneth rather Hope, then faith, becaufe he fpeaketh not of euery Refurrection, but of a bleffed and glorious Refurrection, which leadeth to true lyfe ; and fuch was the Refurrection of Chrift. That man therefore, who firmely belieueth, that there fhalbe a Refurrection of the flefh, and hopeth, that his Sonne taken away by immature death, fhall after rife to glory; hath no reafon of griefe, but rather of ioy becaufe the health of his fonnes Soule is placed in great fecurity and fafty.

I heere come to the duty of a Sonne towards Parents, the which Chrift dying, performed in a moft full and ample manner toward his Mother. It is the duty of children, *to render mutuall duty to their parents.* 1. *Tim.* 5. Now, Sonns do render mutuall duty to their parents, when they procure all things neceffary for their parents being in age : Euen as the Parents haue prouided for their children being yong, or not able to get things touching dyet or apparell, Chrift therefore did commit

mit

mit the charge of his mother (growing aged , and hauing not any one to
take care of her , after the death of
her Sonne) to *S. Iohn* , adopting him
(as it were) for her Sonne , saying to
her, *Behould thy Sonne*, & to *S. Iohn* ,
Behold thy Mother. Now heere our
Lord accomplished the function of a
Sonne most fully towards his Mother;
and this feuerall wayes . For first he
assigned to her a Sonne who being of
the same age with Chrift (or rather a
yeare yonger) was most fitting to vndergo the charge and care of the Mother of our Lord .

He furthermore out of the twelue
Apostles , made choice of him to this
incumbency and labour , whome our
Lord himselfe chiefly loued , and of
whome he alfo did know himselfe to
be greatly againe beloued; therefore
he might well repofe greater confidence and trust in him , touching his
diligence towards his Mother. Againe,
our Lord assigned him , whome he
knew was to liue very many yeares ,
and therefore without any doubt to
ouer liue his Mother . To conciude ,
our Lord was not wanting in his duty
to his Mother euen at that tyme, when
                                          his

his thoughts were to be busied, touching his owne anxieties and dolours.
For at that tyme a man might probably thinke, that his cogitations were
only fixed vpon the suffering of his
corporall dolours, and iniuries of his
enemies, and in tasting the most better
cup of his neare approching death, so
as he could not turne his thoughts to
any other affaires. Neuertheles his
charity towards his mother ouercame
him, and so litle regarding his owne
state, his care was touching the confolation and comfort of his mother; neither did the expectation of the promptitude and fidelity of S. *Iohn* deceaue
him; *for from that houre the disciple*
tooke her for his owne. Ioan. 19.

This Prouidence, which Christ had
towards his Parent, ought with greater reason to be performed by other
Sons towards their Parents. For Christ
did lesse owe to his Parent, then other
men do their Parents. Other men are
so obliged to their Parents, as that they
are neuer able to requite it. For they
owe their life to them, for which the
Sons cannot make any iust satisfaction.
Ecclesiasticus saith: *remember that thou*
hadst not beene borne, but for the. Eccl.

But Chriſt (and he alone) is exempted
from this generall rule. For he receaued life from his mother (I meane , a
humame lyfe;) but in lieu heerof he
gaue to her three liues : an *Humane
life*, when with the Father & the holy
Ghoſt he created her , the *lyfe of grace*, when preuenting her inthe Benedictions of his ſweetnes , he did iuſti-
fy her in her creation, and created her
in iuſtifying of Her : he finally gaue to
her the *lyfe of glory* , when he did ad-
uance her to eternall glory , and exalted her aboue the quyre of Angells .
Wherefore if Chriſt , who gaue more
to his mother , then he in his birth
had receaued of her , would obſerue
the law , to wit, to render mutuall duty to her , as his Parent; how much
more then are other men obliged to
performe this duty towards their Parents.

Add hereto, though in honoring of
our Parents , we performe no more
then duty tyeth vs to; Neuertheleſſe
the benignity & goodnes of God hath
added to it a reward , ſaying in the
Law: *Honour thy Father and thy Mother, that thou maiſt be long liued vpon
the Earth; Exod. 20.* And the Holy Ghoſt
addeth

addeth by *Ecclesiasticus* : He *that hono-*
reth his Father, shall haue ioy in Chil-
dren, and in the day of his Prayer, he
shalbe heard, Eccl.3 . Neither hath God
only annexed a reward to those, who
honour their Parents; but also hath adioyned a Punishment to such, that do
not honour them. For we read : *God*
fayth; He that shall curse Father or Mo-
ther, dying let him dye. Matth. 15. And
Ecclesiasticus addeth: *He, who exaspe-*
rateth his Mother, is accursed of God.
Eccl.3. And hence it appeareth, that the
Malediction, and cursing of the Parents
against their Children, hath a great
force, in that God côfirmeth the same.
Of which point no few Examples are
extant in Histories, of which, one most
notorious and remarkable is recorded
by S. *Austin*, the summe and contents
whereof is this: In *Casaria* a Citty of
Capadocia, there were ten Children
(to wit, seauen sonnes, and three
daughters :) who being accursed by
their Mother, instantly, euen by the
hãd of God, they were surprized with
such a payne and dolour, as that all of
them were horribly strooken and sha-
ken with a trembling of their Members : In which most loathsome state
they

they, not brooking the daily sight of
their owne Cittizens, wandred vp and
downe throughout the Roman Empire; Two of these at the length were
cured in the presence and sight of *S.*
Austin, by the Relicks of *S. Steuen* the
Protomartyr. *Aug. l.21. de Ciuit. c.8.*

Of the fourth fruite of the third *Word.*

CHAP. XII.

THe burden & yoake imposed by
our Lord vpon *S. Iohn*, that he
should sustaine the Care of the B. Virgin his Mother , was truly a sweet
yoake, and an easy burden. For who
would not most willingly remayne &
dwell with that mother , which did
beare nyne Monthes in her Wombe
the W*ord Incarnate* , and which did
cohabitate with him most deuoutely
and sweetly for the full space of thirty
yeares ? Or who would not enuy the
beloued of our Lord, who in the absence of the Sonne of God , enioyed
the presence of the Mother of the
Sonne of God ? But if I be not deceaued,

ued, euen we our selfes , through the
benignity of the Word Incarnate for
our fake, and through the great loue
and charity of him, who was crucified
also for our fake, may obtayne in our
prayers, that he would fay euen to vs;
Behould thy Mother; and to his mother
concerning vs; *Behould thy Sonne.*

Our mercifull Lord is no Niggard
of his fauours , fo long as we do approach to the Throne of his Grace,
with fayth, confidence, and a true and
fincere Hart. He that is defirous that
we fhould become Coheyres of the
kingdome of his Father , will not certainly difdaine to make vs Coheyres
or Competitours of the Loue of his
Mother. Neither will the moft gracious *Virgin* hardly , or difpleafingly
brooke the multitude of her Sonnes,
fince fhe hath a moft ample bofome,
and greatly coueteth , that not any of
them fhould perifh, whom her Sonne
hath redeemed with his precious
Bloud and Death . Let vs therefore
come with firme & immoueable hope
to the Throne of the Grace & Fauour
of *Chrift;* And let vs moft fuppliantly,
and euen vvith teares demaund & be-
feech him, that of euery one of vs he
L   would

would say to his Mother ; *Behould thy Sonne*; & to euery one of vs , he would say of his Mother; *Behould thy Mother.* O! how well would it be with vs, to be vnder the protection of such a Mother? Who would be of power, to draw vs from out her Bosome ? What tribulation could be so potent and strong, as to ouercome vs , confiding & trusting in the Patronage of the Mother of God, and of our Mother ?

Neither shall we be the first in the obtayning of so great a Benefit: Many haue gone before vs : Many (I say) haue cast themselfes into the armes of her Patronage and defence; and yet not any one euer returned back, confounded or frustrated of their expectation, but all cheerfull and reioycing , as securely ankering themselues vpon the assistance of so great a Mother. For of her it is written, *Gen. 2. She shall bruyse thy head in peeces.* And those, who trust in her shall fearelesly *walke vpon the Adder and Basiliske*, betrampling vnder their feete the Lyon & the Dragon. *Psal. 90.* Out of a great multitude let vs heare the testimonies and acknowledgments of some few : especially of those, who haue confidently reposed

reposed themselues in the protection
of the B. *Virgin* , the Mother of our
Lord; and then we shall credibly coniecture them to be of the number of
those, to whom it is said by our Lord:
Behould thy Mother; and of whom it is
said to the Mother, *Behould thy Sonne*.

Let S. *Ephrem* the Syrian be the
first, an ancient Father, and of so great
celebrity, as that (as S. *Ierome* witnesseth) his Bookes were publikly read
in the Churches , after the reading of
the Holy Scriptures. This Father thus
speaketh : *Intemerata , prorsus pura,
Virgo deipara &c. Intemerate, and al-
togeather pure is the Virgin Mother of
God. Serm.de laud.Deipara.* And after:
Tu portus procellis &c. Thou art the
Hauen of those ; who are tossed with
stormes, the Comfort of the World ; the
letter at liberty of those who are in Prison; the Patronesse of Orphans; thou art
the Redemption of the Captiue; the exul-
tation and Comfort of the sicke, and the
Health of All. And againe: *Sub alis tuis
&c.* Vnder thy wings keep me; and pro-
tect me, take mercy on me, who am contaminated and defiled with dirt. And
yet more after : *Non mihi alia fiducia
&c.* There is no other hope for me, O Bles-
L 2   *sed*

sed Virgin, *All hayle to thee, who art
the peace, the ioy, and health of the
World,* To this Father let vs adioyne
S *Iohn Damascene,* who was one of
the first of those, that worshipped the
most holy Virgin, and placed their
Hope in her. This Doctour thus writeth, *Orat. de Natiu. B. Virg. O Ioa-
chim & Anna, Filia & Domina &c.
Receaue the prayer of a sinner, yet ardently louing, and worshipping thee;
houlding thee, as the hope of his ioy, the
defendour of his lyfe, reducing him into fauour with thy Sonne, a firme and
earnest pledge of saluatiõ; vnloose and
dissolue the burden of my sinnes, sup-
presse my temptations, gouerne my life
piously and holily, and procure, that
(thou being my guyde) I may come to
the celestiall Beatitude.*

I will add to the former, two of
the Latin Fathers, of which S. *Anselme*
shalbe one, who thus writeth *l. de Excell. Virg. c 2. Itaque cui saltem ita con-
cessum fuerit &c.* I do coniecture, that
it is a great signe to him of obtayning
Saluateon, who with a sweet cogitation can often thinke of the B. Virgin.
And after: *Velocior est nonnumquam
salus*

salus &c. Oftentimes Health is sooner
obtained , by calling vpon the name of
the B. Virgin , then by inuocating the
name of our Lord Iesus her only Sonne.
But the reason hereof is not, because she
is greater or more powrefull then he
(for he is not great and potent by her,
but she is great and potent by him :)
Why then is health often sooner receaued by the inuocation of her, then of her
Sonne? I will shew my iudgment of this
point. Her sonne is the Lord and Iudge
of all men, discerning the merits of euery One: Therefore whyles he is inuocated (by his owne name) of euery man,
he presently heareth not , and this he
doth iustly. But the name of his Mother being inuocated and implored , if
the merits of him that inuocateth do
not deserue that he should be heard,
yet the merits of the Mother do so inter-
cede , as that he may be heard.

But S. *Bernard* doth after a wonderfull manner, describe the pious,and
indeed motherly affection of the most
Blessed Virgin towvards men deuoted
to her;as also the extraordinary and fi-
liall piety of such , who do acknowledge the *Virgin*,as their Mother and
Patronesse. Thus this Doctour sayth,

Serm.2. super Missus est. O *quisquis te intelligis &c.* O *thou, who perceauest, that in the inundation of this VVorld thou art more tossed among the stormes and tempests, then thou dost quietly walke vpon the earth, do not turne thy Eyes from the brightnes of this starre (I meane of* Mary *the star of the Sea) if so thou couetest not to be ouerwhelmed with these stormes. Yf thou be tossed with the waues of Pryde, if of Ambition, if of Detraction, if of Emulation, turne thy selfe towards this starre; and inuocate* Mary *Yf thou be afflicted with the dreadfulnes of thy owne sinnes, if thou be confounded with the guiltines of thy owne Conscience, if thou be afraid through feare of thy Iudge, if thou beginnest to be absorpt in the Hell of sadnes, and in the abisse of Desperation, thinke vpon* Mary, *in thy dangers, in thy straits, in thy necessities, meditate vpon* Mary; *inuoke* Mary; *thou following her, dost not goe abstray; thou praying to her, dost not despaire; thou thinking of her dost not erre.* And the same Father in another Booke, thus further discourseth, *Serm. de Nat. B.M. siue de aqua ductu. Altius intuemini &c. Call*

more

more deeply into mind, with what af-
fection of deuotion he, who hath placed
all plenitude of goodnes in Mary, would
haue Mary to be honeured of vs; so as if
there be any hope in vs, if any Grace, if
any health, we are to acknowledge, that
it proceeds from her. And after. *Tot is*
ergo medullis &c. With all the forces
and desires of our Harts, let vs worship
Mary, for this is the will of him, who
will haue vs to receaue all, by the me-
diation of Mary. And againe ; *Filioli,*
hac peccatorum scala &c. My Sonnes,
this (meaning the B. Virgin) is the Lad-
der of sinners, this is my greatest Confi-
dence; this is the cause of all my Hope.

To these two most holy **Fathers, I**
will annexe other two holy men, out
of the Schoole of Deuines. S. **Thomas**
Aquinas in his litle Worke of the salutation of the Angell thus sayth, *in*
opusc. 8. Benedicta ta in mulieribus &c.
She (meaning the Virgin Mary) is
blessed among all Women, *because she*
alone hath taken away Malediction, &
hath brought in Benediction, and hath
opened the Gate of Paradise. Therefore
the name of Mary (which is interpre-
ted the starre of the Sea) doth well agree
to her : for as those who are sayling, are

directed to the Port for hauen by the starre of the Sea; so Christians are directed to Glory by the help of Mary.

5. *Bonauenture* most fully discourseth of this subiect, thus writing, *in sua Pharetra l. 1. cap. 3. Sicut, O beatissima, omnis à te &c.* O most B. *Virgin, as of necessity euery one, that is in mind awerted from thee, and not respected by thee, must perish; so euery one, that is conuerted to thee, and by thee regarded, cannot possibly be damned.* The same holy Father in another of his bookes, thus writeth of the confidence of *S. Francis* in the *B. Virgin* (*in vita D. Fran.*) *Matrem Domini nostri &c. S. Francis did prosecute the Mother of our Lord Iesus Christ, with an inutterable Loue, in that she made the Lord of Maiesty to become brother to vs, and by her we haue obtained Mercy. He confiding in her next to Christ, made her his Aduocate; and in her Honour he did fast most deuoutely from the feast of the Apostles S. Peter and S. Paul, vntill the feast of her Assumption.*

To all these Holy Fathers I will range Pope *Innocentius the third*, who Was a great Worshipper of the Mother of God; and who not only in his
Sermons

Sermons did much magnify & prayse
her, but also in her Honour did buyld
a Monastery. And which is more to be
admited; He stirring the People vp
to repose their Hope in the most holy
Mother of God, as foreknowing the
euent of things to come, did vtter many things, which he after confirmed
with his owne happy experience and
triall. Thus he writeth of the *B. Virgin: Quis iacet in nocte Culpæ &c. He
who lyeth in the night of Offence and
sinne, let him behould the Moone, let
him pray to Mary that she through her
Sonne may illuminate his hart with
compunction: For who euer did inuocate her in the Night tyme, and was not
heard of Her?* Let the Reader peruse
those things, which we haue written
of *Innocentius* the third, in the second
booke and nynth Chapter, *Of the
mourning of the Doue.* Now from all
this aboue set downe, it is euidently
collected, That of the signes of Election to Glory, a singular deuotion
borne to the Mother of God, the most
B. Virgin, is not the last. For it should
seeeme, that he cannot perish eternally, of whom it is said to the *B.
Virgin,* by *Christ, Behould thy Sonne;*

L 5   So

So as that man doth not heare with a deafe eare, what *Christ* shall say to him, *Behould thy Mother.*

The End of the first Booke.

OF THE SEAVEN
WORDS OF CHRIST
ſpoken vpon the Croſſe.

THE SECOND BOOKE.

The fourth Word; to wit : Deus,
Deus meus, vt quid dereli-
quiſti me, *my God, my God,
why haſt thou forſaken me ?*
Match. 27. *is litteraly expla-
ned.*

CHAP. I.

N the former Booke we
haue explicated the *three
firſt words,* which our Lord
pronounced frō the chaire
of the *Croſſe,* about the
ſixt houre, when but a litle before he
was

was nayled to the Croſſe. We will in this ſecond Booke expound the other *foure Words*, which our ſayd Lord after the darknes of three houres, from the ſame Chayre, and moſt neere to his death, did with a great and feruerous voice pronounce. But it ſeemeth expedient, firſt briefly to declare, what kind of darknes that was, how it was occaſioned, and to what end it was directed. The mention of which darknes happened betweene the vttering of the former *three Words*, and the *foure other* Words heerafter to be diſcourſed of. For thus S. *Matthew* ſpeaketh, *cap. 27. From the ſixt houre, there was darknes made vpō the whole earth, vntill the nynth houre: And about the ninth houre*, Ieſus *cryed with a mighty voyce*; Eli, Eli, Lamma-ſabaβhani. *That is, my God, my God, why haſt thou forſaken me?* That this darknes was occaſioned through the defect & Eclips of the Sun, S. *Luke* expreſſely expreſſely obſerueth, ſaying; *Et obſcuratus eſt ſol, and the ſun was darkned.*

But now three difficulties are in this place to be diſcuſſed, and ſolued: for firſt the Sunn is accuſtomed to ſuffer Eclipſe of its light, in the New mooae,

moone, when the moone is found to
be betweene the Sunne and the earth,
the which could not be at the time of
the death of Chrift; feeing the moone
at that tyme was not in coniunction
with the Sunne, which falleth out in
the new moone; but was in the oppo-
fition which happeneth in the full
moone. For all that tyme the *Pafcha*,
or Feaſt of Eaſter was celebrated by
the Iewes, which according to the
Law, began vpon the foureteenth day
of the firſt Month. Againe admitting,
that at the Paſſió of Chriſt, the Moone
had beene in coniunction with the
Sunne; yet from hence it followeth
not, that there could be darknes for
the fpace of three houres, that is, from
the fixt houre to the nynth: fince the
Eclipfe of the Sunne cannot continue
long, efpecially if it be a full Eclipfe
and fuch as may hide the whole Body
of the Sunne, fo as the obſcurity of it
may be accounted darknes. For the
moone is more fwift in motion, then
the funne, in regard of the moones
proper motion; and confequently can
darken the funne but for a very ſhort
tyme. For the Moone inſtantly doth
begin to goe backe, and leaueth the
                                    funne

sunne free, that so it may illuminate
the Earth with its accustomed light &
splendour. To conclude, it can neuer
so fall out, that through the coniunction of the Moone, the sunne should
leaue the whole Vniuersall Earth in
darknes. For the Moone is lesser, then
the sunne, yea then the Earth, & therfore it cannot by the interposition of
its Body, so couer the whole Sunne, as
that the Vniuersall Earth should be
left in darknes.

Now if any heere should obiect &
say, that the Euangelist speaking of
the Vniuersall Earth, meaneth only of
the vniuersall Earth of *Palestines*, and
not of the vniuersall Earth absolutely.
This Obiection may easely be refelled
by the testimony of S. *Dionysius Areopagita*, who in his Epistle to S. *Poli-
carpe* testifieth, that himselfe did see
that defection of the sunne, and most
horrible darknes in the Citty of *Heliopolis*, which is in Egypt. And *Phlegon*
(a Greeke Historian, and a Gentil) cited by *Origen* and *Eusebius*, maketh
intention of this Eclips of the sunne,
saying, *lib.* 2. *Quarto anno ducentesi-
ma secunda Olympiadis &c . In the
fourth yeare of the two hundred and second*

cond Olympiade, a great and notorious defection of the Sunne, in comparison of all others which afore had hapned, was made; for the day at the sixt hower, was so turned into darknes, and to an obscure night, as that the stars in Heauen were then seene. Now this Historiographer did not write in *Iudea*, as all affirme. The same Wounder is testified by *Lucianus* the Martyr, saying: *Perquirite in Annalibus vestris &c . Reuolue your Annals, and you shall find, that the day was interrupted with darknes, in the tymes of Pilate, the sunne abandoning the Earth.* These words of *S. Lucian* are related by *Ruffinus*, *in hist. Eccl. Euseb.* In fine *Tertullian*, *Paulus Orosius,* and all others (touching this Eclypse) do speake of all the parts & coasts of the World, and not only of *Iudea*.

But these difficulties may easely be explicated. For first, where it is said in the beginning, that the Eclypse of the sunne is accustomed to be in the New moone only, & not in the full moone; this is true; when a Naturall defect of the light of the sunne happeneth. But at the death of Christ, the defect of the sunne was vniuersall and prodigious,
            which

which could be wrought only by him, who made the sunne, the Moone, Heauen, and Earth. For *S. Dionysius* writeth in the place aboue noted, that the Moone was seene by himselfe, and by *Apollophanes* about the midtyme of the day, after an vnaccustomed & most swift motion to come to the Sunne, and lying vnder it ; there remained after this manner, vntill the ninth hower, and then returned backe towards the Orient, to its owne place.

To that, which is added aboue ; to wit, that the defect of the sunnes light could not so remaine for the space of three Howers, as that during all that tyme the Earth should be in darknes; it may be answered hereto, that this is true , if we speake of a naturall and visuall defect of the sunne. But this Eclypse of the sunne was not gouerned by the lawes, or setled course of Nature, but by the Will of the Omnipotent Creatour, who as he could bring the moone after a wonderfull manner from the East , in a most rapid and swift motion to the sunne , and after three howers ended , could bring it back to its owne place in the Orient; so also was of power to cause, that the

moone

moone should remaine immoueable
vnder the sunne for those three howers ; and that it should not mooue either more slowly ormore swiftly, then the sunne it selfe.

To conclude, where aboue is added, that the Eclypse and defect of the sunne could not be obserued & seene through out the Vniuersall Earth, in regard that the Moone is lesser then the Earth, & farre more lesse in quantity then the sunne; I grant this to be most true, with reference to the interposition of the moone, only. But what the moone could not performe herein, the Creatour of the sunne & moone performed, only in not cooperating with the sunne in illustrating & lighning the Earth: For things created cannot worke or performe their functions, except the Creatour do assist & cooperate with them. And whereas some men say, that darknes might the be made throughout the whole Earth, through a condensation, and thickning of blacke and misty Cloudes; this cannot be truly auerred, since it is euident from the testimonies of the Ancients, that in the tyme of that Eclyps and darknes, the stars were seene to

M   appeare

appeare and shine in Heauen : But thicke and misty Cloudes cannot only (yea they are accustomed to) obscure the sunne, but also the moone, and the stars.

☞ Now why God would haue this signe of *Darknes* to happen at the Passion of Christ, seuerall Reasons are accustomed to be alledged, but two chiefly. The first may be to demonstrate the most great exceeation and blindnes of the Iewish People, which Reason is brought by *S. Leo Pope*, and which blindnes of theirs doth yet continue, and shall continue, according to the Prophecy of *Isay*, who thus speaketh of the beginning of the Church: *Surge, illuminare Ierusalem & c. Arise, be illuminated Ierusalem, because thy light is come, and the glory of our Lord is risen vpon thee ; because (loe) darknes shall couer the Earth, and a myst the People. Isa. 60.* To wit, most thicke and palpable darknes shall couer the Land of the Iewes, and that darknes, which is not so grosse, but may easely be dissipated and dispelled, shall couer the People of the Gentiils. The second Cause or Reason of the forsaid *darknes* at our Sauiours Passion, may be to demonstrate

monſtrate the great offence and ſinne of the Iewes, as *S. Ierome* teacheth. In former tymes wicked men did perſecute, moleſt, and trouble, yea and kill good men: But now men are arriued ro that degree of Impiety, as that they dare perſecute euen God himſelfe, inueſted with mans fleſh and nayle him to a Croſſe. In former tymes ſuites and contentions falling out among Cittizens, they fell to Words, from words to blowes, Wounds, and murther it ſelfe; But now Vaſſalls and Bonſlaues haue entred into inſurrection and rebellion againſt the King of men and Angels, nayſing, with incredible boldnes, his ſacred hands and feete with piercing Nayles to the hard wood of the Croſſe. Therefore the whole World was amazed, and through horrour of the fact trembled; And the ſunne it ſelfe as vnwilling to lend its light to the furtherance of perpetrating ſo flagitious a Crime, did withdraw in its beames, couering the whole ayre with blacke and dreadfull darknes.

But let vs now deſcend to the words of our Lord: *Eli, Eli, lammaſabacthani.* Theſe words are taken from

the beginning of the one & twentith
Pſalme, where we thus read: *Deus,*
Deus meus, reſpice in me, quare me de-
reliquiſti? O God, my God, haue reſpect
to me, why haſt thou forſaken me?
Where thoſe words, *reſpice in me,*
vvhich are in the middeſt of the Verſe,
were added by the Septuagint Inter-
preters; for in the Hebrew Text, there
are no other words, but thoſe, which
our Lord did ſpeake. In this one point
the words of the Pſalme, and of Chriſt
do differ; in that the Words of the
Pſalme are all Hebrew words, whereas
thoſe ſpoken by Chriſt, are partly *Sy-*
riach words, which kind of tongue
the Iewes did then much vſe. For thoſe
words: *Talitha cumi, id eſt, puella ſurge*
and, *Ephetha,* that is, *adaperire,* and
ſome others in the Ghoſpels, are *Sy-*
riake words, and not *Hebrew.* But to
proceed. Our Lord complaineth, that
he is forſaken of God, and he complaineth crying out with a great and vehement voyce; Both which Points are
to be explained.

This dereliction and forſaking of
Chriſt by his Father may bevnderſtood
in fiue ſeuerall ſenſes or wayes, of all
which butone is true. There were fiue
coniunctions

coniunctions of God in the Son. One
naturall and eternall ; to wit , the coniunction of the *Person* with the *Person*
of the Sonne in Essence. Another,that
is, a new coniunction of the *Diuine
nature*,with the *Humane nature* in the
Person of the Sonne ; or , which is all
one, a coniunction of the diuine *Person* of the Sonne, with the humane
Nature. The third , was the *Vnion of
Grace* and of will; for Christ being mā
was *full of grace and truth* , Ioan . 1.
And , *the things that do please God* , *he
did allwayes* , as himselfe witnesseth
in *S. Iohn. cap. 8.* And the Father more
then once said of him : *This is my beloued Sonne, in whome I am well pleased.*
Matth. 3. The fourth coniunction was
the *Vnion of Glory* ; for the soule of
Christ did see God , euen from his Cō-
ception. The fifth was the *Vnion of
Protection* , of which himselfe speaketh , when he saith : *He that sent me,
is with me , and he hath not left me a-
lone. Ioan. 8.*

Now the first Vnion is altogether
inseparable and perpetuall; becouse it
is an Vnion in *Diuine Essence*,of which
himselfe speaketh : *I and my Father are
one.* And therefore Christ did not say,

M 3   *my*

my Father , why hast thou left me ? For
the Father is not called the *God* of the
Sonne , till after the Incarnation, and
by reason of the Incarnation . The
second Vnion is neuer dissolued , neyther can it be dissolued ; for what God
once assumed , he neuer did leaue ; for
the Apostle saith: *He spared not his own
Sonn, but for vs all deliuered him. Rom.*
8. And the Apostle *Peter : Christ suffered for vs;* And, *Christ suffering in flesh,*
1. *Pet. 2. and* 4. All which sacred testimonies demonstrate , that he, who
was crucifyed , was not pure man, but
the true Sonne of God , and our Lord
Christ. The third Vnion doth in lyke
sort euer remaine , and euer shall remaine *The iust dyed for the vniust, as*
S. Peter speaketh *1. Pet.* 3. And the
death of Christ would haue profited
vs nothing, if the *Vnion of Grace* should
be dissolued. The fourth Vnion could
not be dissolued, because the Beatitude
of the Soule cannot be lost ; since it
comprehendeth an aggregation and
heaping togéther of all goods. For the
soule of Christ according to the superiour part, was truly Blessed ; of which
Point see *S. Thomas* 3. *p. q.* 45. *art.* 8.
Therefore there remaineth onely the
Vnion

vnion of Protection, which for a short tyme was broken, that the Oblation of the bloudy Sacrifice should take place, for the redemption of mankind.

True it is, that God the Father could haue protected Christ many waies, and hindred his Passion; for according heerto Christ said in his prayer, which he made in the garden: *Father, all things are possible to thee, transferre this Chalce from me; but not that which I will, but that which thou. Marc.* 14. And to *S. Peter* Christ saith: *Thinketh thou, that I cannot aske my Father; and he will giue me presently more then twelue legions of Angels?* againe, Christ might, as God, haue protected his flesh that it should not suffer; and therefore he saith, *Ioan.* 10. *No man taketh my lyfe from me, but I yield it vp of my selfe.* The which E-say prophecyed, when he said. *cap.* 53. *He was offered, because himselfe would.* To conclude, the blessed soule of Christ could haue trasmitted, and powred into its body the guift of impassibility and incorruption, but it pleased the *Father,* it pleased the Word, it pleased the *Holy Ghost* to suffer (for the execution of the common Decree) that mans

mans force should for a tyme preuaile against Christ. For this was that houre, of which our Lord spake to those, who came to take him : *This is your houre, and the power of darknes* . *Luc.* 22. In this manner therefore God did leaue his Sonne, when he suffered : that the humane flesh of his Sonne should suffer most bitter griefes without consolation.

Furthermore, Christ crying with a great voice, did manifest this dereliction , that all men thereby should acknowledge the greatnes of the pryce of the Redemption of mankind : for till that very houre he suffered all things with such incredible patience, and indifferency of mynd, as if he had wanted all sense and feeling : for synding himselfe agrieued and wronged by the Iewes, he did not charge *Pilate,* who prononced sentence against him, nor the souldiers who nayled him to the Crosse. He didnot lament, he did not bewayle , or shew any signe of dolour . Therefore when he was approching neere to his death , to the end that mankind should vnderstand, and particularly that we (his seruants) should not be vngratefull for so great

a faa fauour; and that we should magnify the pryce and worth of our Redemption, he was willing that the dolours of his Passion should publikely, and openly be knowne. Wherefore those words, *My God, why hast thou forsaken me?* are not words of accusation, or indignation, or complaint; but (as I haue said) they are words declaring with most iust reason, and in a most fit tyme, the greatnes of Christ his Passion.

Of the first fruyte of the fourth Word.

CHAP. II.

WE haue briefly expounded those things, which belong to the *fourth Word*, according to the History. Now we will gather some fruits from the tree of the Crosse. First that consideration doth present it selfe vnto vs; to wit, that Christ would drinke vp the whole Chalice of his Passion, euen to the last drop. He was to remaine vpon the Crosse three houres, from the sixt houre to the ninth.

He

He remained full three whole houres and aboue; for before the sixt houre he was nayled to the Crosse, and after the ninth houre, he gaue vp the Ghost. This point may be made euident by this Reason; the Eclyps of the Sunne began in the sixt houre, as three Euangelists do teach, *Matthew*, *Marke*, and *Luke*. And *Marke* in expresse wordes sayth: *when it was the sixt houre, there was made darknes vntil the ninth houre*. The first tree Words of our Lord were spoken vpon the Crosse, before the beginning of the darknes; the other *foure* were vttered after darknes and therefore after the ninth houre. Furthermore *S. Marke* explicateth this point more cleerly, when he saith: *And it was the third houre, and they crucifyed him &c.* And then after he subioyneth: *And when it was the sixt houre, there was made darknes*, cap. 14. Now where he saith, our Lord was crucifyed in the third houre he signifyeth, that the third houre, was not then complete, when our Lord was crucifyed, and consequently that the sixt houre was not as then begun. For *S. Marke* numbreth three principall houses, which are accustomed to con-

containe three ordinary houres . And according to this acceptance and construction the Houshoulder called the workmen to his vineyard , at the first, the third, the sixt, the ninth, and eleauenth houre. *Matth.* 20. And we doe number the Canonicall houres, to wit, the first, the third , the sixt, the ninth , and the *Vespers* , which is the eleauenth houre. Therefore in *S. Marke* our Lord is said to be crucifyed at the third houre., becaufe as then the sixt houre was not come.

From hence then it followeth that our Lord would drinke the chalice of his Passion in a most full and copious manner ; thereby to teach vs to loue better the cup of Pennance & labour , and not to loue and affect the cup of secular consolations and delights. We by the law of the flesh and the world , do desire and vvish for little Pennance and great Indulgence , small labour and much consolation , short Prayer and long chatting, or discourse . But certainly vve knovv not vvhat vve desire, since the Apostle admonisheth vs ; *euery one shall receaue his reward* , *according to his labour.* 1. *Cor.* 3. And: *He shal not be crowned, except he striue lawfully.*

N 2   *fully.*

fully .2. *Tim.* 3. Euerlasting felicity is doubtlesly worth euerlasting labour ; but becaufe , if euerlasting labour had beene abfolutly necessary thereto, we should neuer haue attained to euerlasting felicity ; therefore our mercyfull Lord was content , that onely in this life(which flyeth away like a shadow) we should labour according to our strength,in good workes , and in obsequy and obedience towards him . And therefore thofe men are without hart or courage , without vnderstanding, without iudgment , and are rather infants , and children , who confume and waft this short tyme in idlenes , and which is farre more deteftable , in grieuously offending, and prouoking Gods wrath and indignation against them . For , *if Chrift ought to fuffer , and fo to enter into his glory ?* how then can we enter into the glory of another , only by difporting, and fpending the tyme in pampering and folacing of our flesh ? If the Ghofpell vvere very intricate and obfcure , and could not be vnderftood vvithout great paines, and fatigation of mynd ; perhaps we might shadow our negligence by fome Excufe : but the Ghofpe.l

pell is cleerly expounded (as it were) &
explained frō the example of his lyfe,
who first gaue & promulgated the gospell; so as to the very blynd, it cannot
lye hidden or concealed. Neither haue
vve it explicated only by Chrift himfelfe; but there are so many cleare
Commētaries of it, which do lay open
the fenfe, as there are *Apoftles*, *Mar-*
tyrs, *Confeffours*, *Virgins*; and finally
Saints, vvhofe prayfes and triumphes,
vve celebrate almoft euery day; fince
ail thefe vvith an vnanimous cōfent cry
out, that not by pleafure, good fellovv-
fhip, andhumane delights, but, *by ma-*
tribulations, we muft enter into the
Kingdome of Heauen. Act. 14.

Of the fecond fruite of the fourth Word.

CHAP. III.

A Nother fruit may be gathered frō
the confideration of the filence
of Chrift in thofe three houres, which
was from the *fixt houre* to the *ninth*.
O *my foule*, vvhat did thy Lord in
thofe three houres? Horrour & darknes did inuolue the vniuerfall World:

And

And thy Lord did not repose himselfe
vpon a fof bed; but did hang vpon the
Crosse, naked, full of dolours, & without any comforter. Thou O *Lord*, who
only didst know, and try this, teach
thy poore Seruants, that they may vnderstand how much they are obliged
and indebted to thee; that at least they
may compassionate thee with their
teares, and learne in this their exile,
sometimes to want all consolatió for
thy Loue, if so thou shalt thinke it expedient.

Say to such: O *my Sonne*, Neuer
during the whole course of my mortall life (which was nothing, but labour and paine) did I suffer greater &
more vehement straits, desolation, &
anxiety, then during the space of those
three houres: And neuer did I tolerate
any paines with greater willingnes
and promptitude of mind, then I did
at that tyme. For then by reason of the
weight and wearines of my Body, my
wounds were more inlarged, and the
sharpnes of my griefe more increased:
Then, euen through the absence of
the heate of the sunne, the coldnes of
the ayre more insufferably augmented
the torments of my Body, being on
                                              ech

ech fyde naked . Then the very darkenes it felfe,which did take away from
myne eyes the fight of Heauen,Earth,
and all other things , forced my foule
in a fort, more vehemently & intenfly
to thinke vpon the paines and angui-
fhes of my Body: fo in regard of thefe
aggrauating Circūſtances , thofe three
Houres did feeme to me to be three
yeares. But becaufe the ardour & defires of my *Fathers* Honour (with the
which my breaſt was inflamed)and of
fulfilling my Obedience to him,and of
the procuring the health of your foules,was fo great, as that by how much
the paines of my Body were increafed, by fo much that fire of my defires
was mitigated . So as thofe three Houres (in regard of the greatnes of my
defire of fuffering) appeared to be to
me but three fmall moments of Time.

O moſt *Bleſſed Lord* , if the matter
ſtandeth thus , then are we moſt vngratefull, to whom it feemes painfull
to fpend but one fhort houre in medi-
tating of thefe thy dolours ; when to
thee it was not painfull , to hange v-
pon the Croſſe for our Redemption
three whole houres , in a horrour of
darknes, in cold , and nakednes , in

N 4　　ex-

extreme thirst, and in most bitter and cruell torments. But, O *Louer of mankind*, tell me, whether the vehemency of thy dolour, was so forcible, as to cause thee to desist in hart frō prayer, during thy long silence of those three houers? For we being in anguish and tribulation (especially if the members of our Body labour with any violent paine) cānot without great endeauour apply our mynd to pray. But I heare thee say; *Not so my Sonne*; for euen in the infirmity of my flesh, I disposed my spirit prompt to prayer; yea during those three howers, in which I spake nothing, I was still praying with the mouth of my Hart to my *Father* for you. Neither did I pray only in Hart, but euen in woundes and bloud. For behould, how many wounds there were made in my body, so many crying Voyces there were to my Father for you. And how many drops of Bloud there were, so many tongues they were, beseeching and begging Mercy for you, at the hands of my foresaid Father, and yours.

But now, O Lord, thou dost euen confound the impatience of thy Seruant, who if perhaps wearied out with labour,

labour, or griefe of Body, he do pre-
pare himselfe to Prayer, can scarsly lift
vp his Soule to God to pray for him,
or if through thy Grace he be able to
raise himselfe to so pious an Exercise;
yet he is not able to maintaine his attention therin for any long time; since
his mind is euer reflecting backe to
his labour & paine. Therfore O *pitti-
full Lord*, take mercy of thy Seruant
according to the great Mercy, that
hauing so great an Example of thy Patience set before his Eyes, he may
learne to tread thy steps, and may at
least ouercome his small troubles and
molestations in tyme of Prayer.

*Of the third fruite of the
fourth Word.*

CHAP. IV.

VV Hen our Lord crying out v-
pon the Crosse, said: *My God,
why hast thou forsaken me?* he did not
so say, as if indeed he were ignorant,
why God had left him; for what could
he not know, who knew all things?
For answerably hereto S. *Peter* answe-

N 5   red

red our Lord thus demanding : *Simon of Iohn, louest thou me?* (O Lord (sayth he) thou knowest all things; thou know-est that I loue thee. Ioan.* 2. And the A-postle S. *Paul* speaking of Christ, ad-deth : *In whom is all the treasures of wisdome and knowledge. Collos.* 2. Therfore our Lord did not demaund, therby to learne, but to coūsell vs to seeke, that by seeking and finding, we might learne many things profitable, or ra-ther necessary vnto vs. Now why God did forsake his Sonne in molestations and most bitter dolours, fiue Reasons seeme to occur to me, the which I will here produce, that I may giue occa-sion to others of greater sufficiency, to find out better Reasons of Chriſts dereliction.

1. The first then may seeme to be, the greatnes and multitude of the of-fences of mankind against God, the which the Soane did vndertake to expiate in his owne Body. S. *Peter* sayth : *Christ did beare our sinnes in his body, vpon the tree, that being dead to sinne, we might liue to Iustice; by whose stripes you are healed.* 1. *Pet.* 2. Now the Greatnes of the Offence, which Chriſt did cancell by his Paſsion, is in some respect,

respect *Infinite*, to wit, in regard of the Person offended, who is of infinite dignity and excellency. In like sort, the Person satisfying (who is the Sonne of God) is also of *infinite* Dignity and Excellency, and by reason hereof euery payne willingly endured by the Sonne of God (though it were only a drop of bloud) might be sufficient for the satisfaction. This assertion is most true; neuerthelesse that mans Redemption might be full and copious; and because it was not one Offence, but almost innumerable Offences (for the *Lambe* of *God*, who taketh away the sinnes of the world, did take vpon him not only the first sinne of *Adam*, but all the sinnes of all men) therefore it pleased God, that his Sonne should tolerate innumerable paines, and those most grieuous. And this is signified in that dereliction, of which the Sonne speaketh to the Father: *Why hast thou forsaken me?*

2. Another reason or cause was, the greatnes and multitude of the torments of Hell, the which to make more knowne and euident to vs, the Sonne of God would abate and extinguish the heate of those flames with

so

so mighty a shoure of his own paines. How great and dreadfull the fyar of Hell is, the Prophet I*say* teacheth, saying, that it is altogether intollerable : *which of you can dwell with deuouring fyre? which of you shall dwell with euerlasting heates?* Is*a*. 33. Therefore let vs render thankes to God with all our Hart and powers of our Soule , who would forsake his only begotten Sonne being in most great griefes for a time , that he might free vs from euerlasting heates of fire. In like manner, let vs render all due thankes and gratefull acknowledgment to the lābe of God, who had rarher be left of God vnder the killing sword , then that he would leaue vs vnder the teeth of the deuouring and infernall beast ; who is euer feeding , and yet is neuer with feeding satisfyed.

3.   The third cause is the greatnes of the price of the diuine grace, which is that precious pearle , the which Christ (the most wise merchant) with sale of all he had , did buy, and restore to vs , The grace of Christ, which was giuen to vs in *Adam*, & which through the sinne of *Adam* we lost, was so precious a Pearle or Margarite , as that it

did

did wonderfully adorne vs, and made vs moſt aceptable to God, and was a pledge of eternall felicity. There w)s not any, who could recouer this Pearle, being the ſumme of our riches, and taken from vs by the ſubtilty of the Serpēt, but only the ſonne of God, who through his Wiſdome ouercommeth the malice of the deuil; but this with moſt great inconuenience to himſelfe, by being expoſed to many labours and paines. Thus did the Piety and Charity of the Sonne ouercome, who committed himſelfe willingly to a moſt labourſome iourney, and moſt weariſome peregrination, thereby to redeeme the Pearle for vs.

4. The fourth Cauſe was the moſt eminent greatnes of the Kingdome of Heauen, to the which the Sonne of God opened a way, and paſſage for vs, by his immenſe labours and paines; of which point the Church of God with a gratefull remembrance thus ſpeaketh : *Tu deuicto mortis aculeo, aperuiſti credentibus regna cælorum. Thou, the ſling of death being ouercome, haſt opened to the fayethfull the kingdome of Heauen.* And that he might ouercome
the

the sting of death, it was needfull, that
he should striue, and fight in a most
cruell War with death; in which War
the Father did forsake him, that with
greater glory he might triumph.

5. The fifth Cause was the immense
Loue, with the which the Sonne did
affect his Father; for the Sonne did
wish & couet, that in the redemption
of the World, and abolition of sinne,
he might satisfy the Honour of his
eternall Father most copiouſly, and
most abundantly. But this could not
be effected, except the Father had forsaken his Sonne; that is, except the Father had suffered him to endure all
those torments, which could be exco-
gitated by the Deuill, and tolerated by
man. Therefore now if it be demaunded, why God did (as it were) abandon
his Sonne, suffering all Extremities
vpon the Croſſe? it may be anſwered,
that this was done to the end, that the
greatnes of sinne, the greatnes of Hel,
the greatnes of diuine Grace, the greatnes of Eternall life, and the greatnes
of the Charity of the Sonne of God
towards his Father, might more copiouſly and manifeſtly appeare.

From the confideration of which
                                    reasons,

reasons, another Question taketh its
solution; That is, why God to many
Martyrs did temper the Cup of their
Passions and death, with so great a-
bundance of spiritual consolation, as
that those Martyrs had rather, drinke
the Cup of their sufferings with the
mixture of those internall Comforts,
then without those comforts to want
the Cup of their Passions and Tribulations; And yet contrarywise he suffered his most beloued Sonne to drinke
vp euen to the dregs (as I may say)
his most bitter Cup, without any Consolation whatsoeuer? The reason of
the disparity of Gods proceeding herin is, in that in the holy Martyrs not
any of the former Causes did take
place, which in the Passion of Christ
we haue aboue mentioned.

Of the fourth Fruite of the fourth Word.

CHAP. V.

ANother fruite may be added to
the former, not so much proceeding from the fourth VVord, as from
the

the circumstance of the tyme, in which
it was spoken, to wit, of the horrible
darknes, which immediatly went before the prenouncing of the said *word*.
Since such *darknes* is most strong to illuminate and enlighten the Iewish nation; as also to confirme the Christiãs
themselues in true fayth, if so they wil
diligently apply their mynd to the force of the demonstration, which we
will heere set downe. The demonstration necessarily resulteth out of foure
Truths.

The first Truth is, that when Christ
was crucify'd the Sunne was so wholy
obscured that the starres were then
seene in the Heauens, as they are accustomed to be seene in the night.
This truth is warrated and confirmed
by fyue witnesses, most worthy of credit and beliefe; who being of seuerall
nations, liuing at seuerall tymes, and
in seuerall places, when they wrote
their bookes, could not write what in
those tymes happened out of any secret conuention or mutuall agreement
among themselues The first is S. *Matthew*, an Hebrew, who did write in
Iewry, & was one of those that saw the
Sunne obscured. And certainely this
man

man being graue and wife, would neuer haue written this in *Iewry* (and as
it is credible euen in the Citty of *Ierufalem*) if it had not beene moft true :
fince otherwife,in fetting downe thinges, vvhich all men did knovv to be
falfe, he might deferuedly be repre-
hended, and derided of all the inha-
bitants of *Ierufalem*, and of all *Iewry.*

The fecond vvitnes is *S. Marke,*
vvho vvrote at *Rome*; and he alfo favv
the Eclyps, becaufe then he vvas in
Iewry with other difciples of our
Lord, when it happened. The third is
S.Luke,who vvas a Grecian,and vvrote
in *Greece*; and he in like fort was an
ey-vvitnes of the Eclyps at *Antioch* in
his own Country .For vvheras *Dionyfius Areopagita* did fee the Eclyps at
Heliopolis in Egypt, *S.Luke* might more
eafily fee it at *Antioch*, as being more
neere to *Ierufalem*, then *Heliopolis*
vvas. The fourth and fifth |vvitneffes
are *S. Dionyfius*, and *Apollophanes*,
both Grecians, & at that tyme Gentils,
vvho in expreffe vvords do teftify,that
the Eclips vvas feene by them vvith a
ftupendious admiration . Thefe are
thofe fiue vvitneffes ,vvbo do vvarrant
the truth of that Eclyps, euen from
O their

their eyes, and fight thereof. To thefe
vve may adioine the Annalls of the
ancient Romans, as alfo *Phlegon* the
Hiftoriographer to Adrian the Empe-
rour, as aboue vve noted in the firft
Chapter. Therefore this firft Truth
cannot be denyed eyther by Ievves or
Pagans vvithout notorious temerity
and rafhnes. For as concerning Chriftians, this verity belongeth to the
Catholike fayth.

2. Another Truth is, that the
forfaid Eclyps cou'd not be effected,
but by the omipotency of God; and
therefore that it proceeded not in any
fort from the diuels, or from men fe-
conded vvith the ayde of diuels, but
only from the fpeciall Prouidence and
vvill of God, the Creatour and Gouer-
nour of the vvorld. This verity is thus
demonftrated. The Sunne cannot faile
in its light, but by one of thefe three
vvayes. Eyther by interpofition of the
moone betvveene the Sunne and the
Earth; or through a moft thicke and
mighty groffe cloude; or through the
retraction, vvith dravving, or extin-
ction of the beames of the Sunne. After the firft manner that interpofition
could not naturally be; becaufe at that
tyme

time (being the *Pascha* of the Iewes)
the moone was found to be opposite
to the Sunne; and therfore it fellovv-
eth, that that Eclypse vvas vvrought
vvithout any interposition of the
moone; or that through an vnvsuall
and an astonishing Miracle the moone
did moue as much in fevv houres , as
at other times it vvas to moue in fourteene dayes ; and againe that vvith the
like miracle it returned backe vvith so
great svviftnes that in the space of tree
houres it performed its motion of
fourteene dayes . Novv those euents
vvhich proceed from the Celestiall Orbes, cannot be accōplished but by God;
since the povver of the diue's is limited vnder the moone : and therefore the Apostle calleth the diuell, *The
Prince of the Power of this ayre. Eph. 2.*

The Eclypse could not be occasioned after the second manner; becaufe
(as vve haue said aboue) a thick and
grosse cloude is not of force to take
from vs the sight of the Sunne, except
vvith all it take from vs the sight of the
Starres. But it is euident from the testimony of *Phlegon* , that the Sunne
vvanting its light at the Passion of
Christ , starres vvere seene in Heauen
after

after the same manner, as they are seen in the night. Touching the third māner, it is indisputrbly most true and acknovvledged, that the beames of the Sunne could not be dravvne backe, or extinguished, but only by the Power of God, who created the sunne. From all this it then followeth, that this second Verity is no lesse irrefragable and certaine, then the first; neither can it-be impugned with lesse temerity and want of Iudgment, then the first.

3. The third Verity is, that that darknes, of which we in this place do speake, was occasioned by reason of the Crucifixion and Passion of Christ, and did proceed from the diuine Prouidence. This Truth taketh its demōstration from the tyme this darknes continued in the Ayre; for it continued as long as Christ our Lord did hang aliue vpon the Crosse, that is from the sixt hower vntill the ninth. This is witnessed by all those, who haue made mētion of this defection of the sunne. Neither can it be ascribed to chance, that this darknes (full of Miracles) could casually happen to be at the Passion of Christ; since Miracles are not wrought by chance, but by diuine Prouidence.

uidence. Neither hath there bene any Authour (that I know) that euer would attempt to ascribe this so wonderfull an Eclyps to any other cause. For those, who did know Christ, did confesse this Miracle to be wrought for his sake; and such, as did not acknowledge Christ, remayned astonished at it, confessing their ignorance of the cause thereof.

4. The fourth Verity is, that this so prodigious a darknes could intimate and signify no other thing, but that the Sentence of *Caiphas* and *Pilate* was most iniust, and that Ie*sus* was the true & proper Sonne of God, and the true *Messias* promised to the Iewes. For this was the chiefest and most vrging cause, why the *Iewes* thirsted after, and plotted the death of Christ. For in the Councell of the High Priest, Scribes, & Pharisyes, when the high Priest discerned, that the testimonies produced against Christ preuayled not, nor proued any thing, he rose vp, and said, *Matth. 26. Adiuro te per Deum viuum, &c. I adiure thee by the liuing God, that thou tell vs, if thou be Christ the Sonne of God.* But Christ consenting thereto, and confessing himselfe so to

O 3   be,

be, the high Priest , *rent his garments,
saying, He hath blasphemed, what need
we any further witnes ? Behould you
haue heard the blasphemy, what thinke
you? And they answering said: He is
guilty of death.*

And againe in the presence of Pilate, who coueted to free our Lord
from death , the High Priests and Ministers said : *we haue a law, and according to the law he ought to dye , because
he had made himselfe the Sonne of God.
Ioan. 19.* This therefore was the chiefest cause, why our Sauiour was condemned to the Crosse , Which very
Point was prophesied by *Daniel* , saying: *occidetur Christus &c.Christ shall
be slaine , and it shall not be his People
that shall deny him. Dan. 9.* And this
was the maine motiue, why God at the
Passion of Christ , did power downe
such dreadfull darknes vpõ the world,
that thereby it might be most abundantly witnessed , the High Priests to
haue erred , the People to haue erred,
Pilate to haue erred,*Herod* to haue erred , and him who hanged vpon the
Crosse , to be the true Sonne of God ,
and the *Messias* who was promised ,
The truth whereof , the *Centurion* ob-
seruing

feruing the Heauenly fignes & wounders, teſtifyed in thoſe words: *Verè filius Dei erat iſte* . *Indeed this was the Sonne of God.* Matt. 27. And againe , *Inded this man was iuſt* . *Luc.* 23. For the *Centurion* did know that thoſe celeſtiall and aſtoniſhing Prodigies were (as it were) the Voyce of God, retracting and condemning the Sentence of *Caiphas* and *Pilate* , and affirming, that that man (contrary to all Iuſtice) was deliuered ouer to death ; ſeing he was the Authoùr of Life , the true Sonne of God, and Chriſt promiſed in the Law. For what other thing could that *Darknes* , being accōpained with the cleauing of the ſtones , & renting of the veyle of the Sanctuary, import, but that God was auerted from a Peo ple (before his) & that he was highly offended; in that the *People did not know the tyme of their Viſitation* . *Luc.* 19.

Certainly if the Iewes did maturely conſider theſe things, and withall obſerue, that they are euen from that tyme diſperſed and ſcattered among many Nations, not hauing any King. or High Prieſt, or Altars, or Sacrifices or diuine Miracles, or the Anſwers of Pro-

Prophets among them, they would clerrely pereeaue themselues to be abandoned and forsaken by God, and (which is far more miserable) to be deliuered ouer into a reprobate sense; and that to be accomplished and fulfilled in them, which *Esay* did prophecy, when he introduced our Lord thus speaking : *Goe , and thou shalt tell this People: Heare you that heare , and vnderstand not: and see a Vision, and know it not. Blind the hart of this People, and make their eares heauy , and shut their eyes , lest perhaps they might see with their Eyes, and heare with their eares, and vnderstand with their Hart, and be conuerted, and I heale them.* Ifa. 6.

Of the fifth fruite of the fourth Word.

C H A P. VI.

IN the first *three words* or Senten-ces, Christ our Maister did recommend vnto vs three notable Vertues, *Charity* to our Enemies, *Mercy* to the Miserable, and *Piety* or duty to our Parents, In the *foure* following Words he

he exhorts vs to foure *Vertues*, not more worthy, then the former, but to vs no lesse necessarie, to wit, *Humility, Patience, Perseuerance*, and *Obedience*. Touching Humility. It may be truly called the Vertue of Christ (since there is no mention made thereof, in the Writings of the Wisemen of this World) for Christ throughout the whole course of his life, did really, & in his actions, practise this Vertue; and furthermore professeth himselfe to be a Maister thereof, in plaine and direct Words, saying: *Learne of me, because I am meeke, and humble of Hart, Math.* 11. But he neuer more perspicuously and clearely did commend this Vertue vnto vs (and withall *Patience*, which cannot be disioyned from *Humility*) then when he said : *My God, my God, why hast thou forsaken me?* For in these words Christ sheweth, that through the permission and sufferance of God, all his glory and excellency in the sight of men was wholy obscured, the which point also that *darkenes* or E-clyps did demonstrate. Now our Lord could not without wonderfull *Humility* and *Patience* tollerate so great an obscuration.

P The

The glory of Christ, of which S. *Iohn* speaketh in the beginning of the Gospell, when he sayth: *We saw the glory of him; glory as it were of the only begotten of his Father, full of grace and Verity. Ioan. 1.* was placed in the Power, Wisdome, Probity, Princely Maiesty, Beatitude of the soule, and in the Diuine Dignity, which he had, as he was the true and naturall Sonne of God. All this glory his Passion did cloud, and obscure, and the darkning thereof those words do plainly signify, *My God, my God, why hast thou forsaken me?* The passion did obscure his *Power*; because being nayled to the Crosse, he seemed to be of no power or ability; and therefore the chiefe Priests, souldiers, and the Thiefe did exprobate to him his impotency and weakenes, saying: *If thou be Christ, come downe from the Crosse &c.* And againe: *He saued others, himselfe he cannot saue.* Now how great *Patience*, how great *Humility* was required, that he who was truly Omnipotent, should be wholy silent to such vp-braydings?

The Passion did darken his *Wisdome*, when before the chiefest of the Priests,

Priests, before *Herod*, before *Pilate* he
answered nothing to many Interroga-
tories and Questions, as if he had bene
depriued of iudgment; by which his
silence it was occasioned, that *Herod* &
his Company contemned him, and
cloathed him in a white vestment by
way of derision. How great *Patience*,
how great *Humility* was heer also required for him to tolerate these in-
dignities, who was not only Wiser
then *Salomon*, but was the very Wisdome of God?

His *probity* and Innocency of life
the Passion obscured; who being crucified vpon the Crosse, did hang betweene two thiefes, and was repured a
seducer of the People, and Vsurper of
an other mans kingdome. And the
splendour of this his *Innocency*, that
dereliction of God, which himselfe
confessed, saying, W*hy hast thou forsaken me*, might well seeme more &
more to obscure; Since God is accustomed to forsake not pious men, but
such as be wicked. Certainly haughty
and proud men are very cautelous to
speake any thing, wherby those who
heare them, may suspect that they confesse any thing against their owne

Worth: but humble and patient men (of which fort Chrift was the King) willingly take hould of all occasion of *Humility* and *Patience* , fo as they speake nothing, which is falfe. How great *Humility*, how great *Patience* here againe is required of him to suffer thefe things, of whom the Apoftle thus fpeaketh: *It was fit, that we should haue fuch a Prieft, holy, innocent, impolluted, feparated from finners, & made higher then the Heauens. Hsb. 7.*

Furthermore the Pafsion did fo obfcure the Regall Maiefty of Chrift, as that it gaue to him , for a goulden diademe, a Crovvne of thornes; for a Tribunall, a gibbet; for Princely attendance, two Thieues. Therefore I fay againe; How great *Humility*, how great *Patience* was necessary for him , who vvas truly the king of Kings, the Lord of Lords, and the Prince of the kings of the Earth ?

Now vvhat shall I fay of the *Beatitude* of the foule, which Chrift truly had from, his Conception ? And the vvhich he was both of povver and of Will to transfuse into the Body? How vehemently did the Pafsion darken this glory, fince it made Chrift, *A man*

o,

*of sorrowes , and knowing infirmity ,
despised , and the most abiect of men.
Isa.53.* and caused him through the a-
cerbity of his sufferings , to crye out;
My God , why hast thou forsaken me?
To conclude, the Passion did so ouer-
cloud the *dignity of his* diuine Person,
as that he, vvho sitteth aboue all (not
only men, but Angels) in regard of his
Passion, said : *I am a worme , and no
man; A reproach of men, and the outcast
of the People. Psal.* 21.

To this lowest place therefore
Christ did descend in his Passion ; but
this his descending was accompanied
with great merit and exaltation. For
what our Lord did often premise in
words, saying: *Euery one, that humbleth
himselfe; shalbe exalted;* the same was
performed in his Person, as the Apostle witnesseth : *He humbled himselfe,
made obedient vnto death ; euen the
teath of the Crosse: for the which thing
God hath also exalted him, and hath
giuen him a Name , which is aboue all
Names; That in the name of Iesus, euery
knee bow, of the Celestials, terrestrials,
and Infernals. Phil.*2. Therefore he,
who was the last, is pronounced and
declared to be the first ; and a most

short

short Humiliation resolued into an e-
uerlasting Exaltation . The which
change we also find to haue happened
to all the Apostles , and to all Saints.
For *S. Paul* writeth, that the Apostles
were, *The refuse of the World, and the
drosse of all;* meaning, most base & vile
things , which are cast out by euery
one, and betrampled vpon. This was
the Humility of the Apostles ; But
what was their Exaltation, *S . Iohn
Chrysostome* teacheth (*hom. 32, in Ep.
ad Rom.*) and sheweth it , when he
sayth , that the Apostles are now in
Heauen , and do assist neere to the
Throne of Christ , where the *Cherubims* do glorify Christ, where the Se-
raphims do fly; that is, they haue their
place with the chiefest Princes of the
kingdome of Heauen, from whence
they shall neuer fall or depart . Certainly if men would attentiuely consider and ruminate, how honourable a
thing it is, to imitate the Humility of
the sonne of God heere vpon the
Earth ; and with all , would make to
themselues some coniecture, how great
that exaltation is, to the which humility it selfe aduanceth them, we should
find very few proud men. But because
most

moſt men do meaſure all things by the
falſe yard of the ſenſes of the fleſh, &
humane cogitation, therefore it is no
wonder , if *Humility* can ſo hardly
be found vpon the Earth , and that the
Multitude of proud men be infinite.

The fifth Word, Sitio *, I thirſt,
is explicated according to
the Letter.*

CHAP. VII.

THe *fifth* Word followeth, which
we read in *S. Iohn.* And indeed
it is but one Word, to wit *Sitio*, I thirſt.
But that it ſhould be truly (according
to the preſent purpoſe) vnderſtood, it
is needfull to adde the words of the
Euangeliſt, both going before and after. For thus *S. Iohn* ſpeaketh : *Poſtea
ſciens Ieſus &c. Afterward Ieſus knowing. that all things were now conſummate, that the ſcriptures might be fulfilled, he ſayth , I thirſt. A Veſſel therefore ſtood there full of Vineger; & they
putting a ſpenge full of Vineger about
Hyſope, offered it to his mouth. Ioan.*19.
Of which words this is the meaning.

P 4   Our

Our Lord would haue all things accomplished and fulfilled, which the Prophets (being full of the Holy Ghost)did foretell of his Life & death, and because all other Predictions being then already performed, this one yet remained; That is, that he should taft Vineger in his thirst, according to those words of the Prophet, *Pfal. 68. In my thirst they gaue me Vineger to drinke;* Therefore he said with a cleare voyce) *I thirst;* and those, who were present, did offer to his mouth a spōge full of Vineger, put vpon a Reede, or Cane. Thus our Lord said, *I thirst*, that the Scripture might be fulfilled. And why to the end the Scripture should be fulfilled? Why did he not say, *I thirst*, because he was really thirsty, & desired to allay his Thirst? For the Prophet did not foretell it to the end that that should fall out which he had foretould; but he did therefore foretell it, because he did foresee it after to be. And he did foresee it after to be, because the thing was truly to be, although it had not beene foreseene. Therefore foresight or prediction is not the cause of a thing after to come to passe, but the thing, which is after to be,

be, is the cause why it may be foreseene or foretould.

Now a great Myftery is in this
place reuealed. Our Lord did truly labour with extremity of thirft, euen
from the beginning of his Crucifixion;
and his thirft increafed more & more;
fo as it was one of his chiefeft torments which he fuffered vpon the
Croffe; fince fheeding of much bloud
doth drye the body, and procureth
thirft. I knew a Perfon, who being
wounded in feuerall parts of his body, from which great ftore of bloud
did flow, defired nothing but drinke;
as if his moft raging thirft had bene
the only euill or payne he then fuffered. The like is read in the life of *S.
Emmerammus* Martyr, who being tied
to a ftake, and hauing receaued many
wounds, only complayned of thirft.
(*Sur. die 22. Sept.*) Therefore how
could it otherwife be, but that Chrift
who after long wearines, had fhed
much bloud in his whipping; and after
being crucified, had opened (as it
were) foure fountaines in his body,
from which great abundance of Bloud
did for a long tyme ftreame, fhould be
cruciated and vexed with a moft bur-

ning

ning thirst ? And notwithstanding he
concealed in silence this his long torment for the space of three howers,
and could haue concealed it euen to
his death, which was present at hand:
For what other reason then did our
Lord hyde in silence (for so long a
tyme) this his vehemency of Paine, &
now being ready to dye, did manifest
it, saying, *I thirst* ; but because it was
the will of God, that all of vs should
know this torment of thirst not to be
wanting vnto Christ ? And therefore
the same heauenly Father would haue
it foretould by a Prophet in the Person of Christ, and did inspire it into
our Lord Iesus, to make this new and
most bitter paine knowne to his faithfull seruants, for an example of Patience. He said therefore, *I thirst* ; that
is, all my moisture in my flesh is spent,
my veynes are dry, my tongue is dry,
my pallate is dry, my iawes are dry, all
my invvard parts are dry; if any man
vvill comfort and refresh me, let him
giue me to drinke.

Novv let vs heare, vvhat drinke
they brought him vvho vvere present
at the Crosse : *Erat vas aceto plenum*
&c. There was a vessell full of Vineger;

and

and they putting a sponge full of Vina-
tre about Hyfope, offered it to his mouth.
O ftrang confolation and refreshment!
There vvas a veffell full of Vineger,
vvhich is pernicious and hurtfull to
wounds, and is accuftomed to haften
death , and to that end it vvas brought,
thereby to haften the death of thofe,
vvho vvere to be crucifyed. *S. Cyrill*
(cap 35. *in Ioan.*) vvith reference to
this paffage thus vvriteth : *Pro iuuante*
& *iucundo potu* &c. *For a medicinable*
and pleafant drinke, they proffered him
that , which was hurtfull and bitter.
And by reafon hereof that thing is
made more credible , vvhich S. *Luke*
vvriteth in his Gofpell : *The fouldiers*
mocked him, comming to him, and offe-
ring him Vineger. Luc. 23. And although
S. *Luke* doth write this of Chrift la-
tely nayled to the Croffe, yet it is very
credible, that the fouldiers themfelues
when they heard him crying, *I thirft,*
did giue him Vineger in a fponge vpon
a reede , the vvhich they before in a
mocking manner , had offered vnto
him. The fumme and clofure of all is,
that as in the beginning, a litle before
he vvas nailed to the Croffe, they offered him wyne mixt with gaule ; fo in
the

the end of his life they brought him
Vineger, dangerous to his wounds; so
as from the beginning to the end, the
Passion of Christ vvas a true & vehement Passion, as not accompained
with any alleuiation, or comfort at all.

Of the first fruite of the fifth Word.

CHAP. VIII.

THe Scriptures of the Old Testament are for the most part explained by the Scriptures of the Nevv.
But touching this Mystery of the *thirst*
of our Lord, the vvords of the sixty
eight *Psalme* may vvell paraphraze, &
comment the Ghospell. We do not
find clearely in the Ghospell, vvhether
those vvho offered Vineger to our
Lord thirsting, did it to gratify him, or
rather the more to afflict him; that is,
vvhether this their action proceeded
from Loue or Hate. We vvith *S. Cyrill*
do interpret in a bad sense the fact of
those vvho gaue to our Lord (suffering thirst) Vineger to drinke. But the
yvords of the *Psalme* are so cleere and
euident,

euident, as that they need not any expofition, And from thofe vve vvill gather this fruit, that vve may learne to thirft vvith Chrift after thofe things, vvhich truly and healthfully are to be thirfted after. Thefe are the Words of the Prophet : *I expected fome body, that would be grieued with me, and there was none, or that would comfort me, and I found not any. And they gaue me gaule for my meate, & in my thirft they gaue me Vineger to drinke.* *Pfal.* 68. Therefore thofe men vvho gaue to Chrift our Lord a litle before he vvas mayled to the Croffe, vvine mingled vvith gaule, and thofe vvho offered to our Lord aftervvard Vineger to drinke, vvere of that number of vvhom it is faid : *I expected fome body, that would be grieued with me, and there was none; and that would comfort me, and I found not any.*

But fome may here demaund, did not the moft *Bleffed Virgin* (the Mother of our Lord) and *Mary of Cleophas* fifter of his mother, as alfo *Mary Magdalen* vvith the Apoftle *S. Iohn,* ftanding neere vnto the Croffe, truly and from their hart grieue and lament for our Lord? In like fort, did not thofe **Women,**

Women, who weeping followed our
Lord to the Mount Caluary, truly condole vvith him? To conclude, were not
all the Apostles much agrieued . & la-
mented in the tyme of the Passion,
when as Christ himselfe foretould of
them, Ioan. 16. *The world shall reioyce,*
but you shall be gladde? All these did
truly contristate and lament; but they
did not lament together with our
Lord, in that there was not the same
reason of Griefe in Christ , and in the
others . For our Lord sayth : *I expe-*
cted some body, that would be sory with
me, and there was none; and that would
comfort me; and I found not any. Those
persons abouesayd did grieue touching the Passion and corporall death
of Christ . But Christ did not grieue
touching this point , but only for a
short tyme in the garden , to shew
himselfe to be true Man : Yea he said,
Luc. 22. With *desire I haue desired to*
eate this Pasche with you , before I suf-
fer; And in another place: *If you loued*
me, you would reioyce , because I goe to
the Father. Ioan. 4.

What cause then of griefe was
there in our Lord in which he did not
find others grieuing vvith him? To
wit,

wit, the losse of soules, for which he did suffer. And vvhat cause of Consolation, in which he had not another to comfort and reioyce with him, except the sauing of soules, after which he thirsted? This one Consolation he did seeke, this he desired, of this he was euen hungry and thirsty : but gaule is giuen to him for meate, and Vineger for drinke. For the bitternes of gaule doth signify and figure out sinne, then the which nothing is more bitter to him, that hath the sense of Tast not infected, or depraued; The acrimony or bitternes of Vinager representeth obstination in sinne: Therfore Christ deseruedly did lament, because he did see for one *Thiefe conuerted*, not only an other thiefe remayning in his obstinacy; but also many others continuing in the like peruersity of mind ; And euen then among the Apostles themselues suffering scandall, he saw *S. Peter* to haue denied him, and *Iudas* to haue despayred.

Yf therefore any man vvill comfort and bemoane Christ, oppressed vvith hunger & thirst vpon the Crosse, and from thence greatly grieuing, first let him present himselfe, as truly penitent,

nitent, and loathing all his former
sinnes. Next, let him conceaue with
Christ a great heauinesse and sorrow
in his hart, that so great a multitude of
soules do daily perish, since so easely all
men may be saued, if so they will take
the benefit of the price of mans Redemption. Doubtlesly the Apostle was
one of those , who deplored with
Christ, seing he thus sayth: *Psalm.9 Ve-*
ritatem dico in Christo &c. I speake the
Verity in Christ , I lye not , that I haue
great sadnes and continuall sorrow in
my hart: for I wished my selfe to be an
Anathema from Christ for my Bre-
thren, who are my kinsmen according to
the flesh, who are Israelits, whose is the
adoption of sonnes. The Apostle could
not more amplify & enlarge his desire
of sauing soules , then by this exagge-
ration, *of wishing himselfe to be an A-*
nathema from Christ ; For this sentence, according to the iudgment of
S. Iohn Chrysostome, is to be interpre-
ted, that the Apostle was so vehemently troubled and afflicted touching the
damnation of the Iewes, as that (if it
could haue bene) he desired to be separated from Christ , for Christ his
sake; meaning herby, he did not couet

to be separated from the Charity of
Christ, of which point he had spoken a
litle before saying, **Who shall separate
vs from the Charity of Christ** ? but to
be separated from the glory of Christ;
as making choyce rather to be depriued of the Heauenly glory, then that
Christ should be depriued of that great
fruite of his Passion, which would appeare in the conuersion of so many
thousand of Iewes. Therefore the A-
postle did truly grieue with Christ, &
did giue comfort to the griefe of
Christ.

But we haue few men in these
dayes, who are emulous, or imitatours
of him. For there are no few Pastours
of soules, who more lament, if the an-
nuall rents of their Church be dimini-
shed or lost, then if a great number of
soules vnder their charge, through
their absence or negligence do perish.
*Patientius ferimus Christi iacturam,
quàm nostram* (sayth *S. Bernard.*) *VVe
suffer with greater patience the losse of
Christ, then our owne losse , We make
great search into our daily expences. but
of the daily losses of the flocke of Christ
we rest ignorant;* Thus this holy Father *l. 4. de consid. c. 9.* It is not sufficient

Q   for

for a Prelate if himfelfe liue pioufly ,
and labour priuatly , to imitate the
Vertnes of Chrift, except withall he do
make his owne fubiects (or rather his
owne fonnes) vertuous, and by the
footefteps of Chrift, bring them to a-
ternall life. Therefore if fuch men do
couet to fuffer, and grieue with Chrift,
& to bemoane his dolours , let them
watch ouer their flock diligently , let
them not forfake their poore fheepe,
but let them direct them by Words,
and go before and leade them the
way, by good Example.

But Chrift may deferuedly complaine of priuate men, that they do not
condole with him , or with his dolours. For if Chrift hanging vpon the
Croffe, did iuftly complaine of the per-
fidy and obftinacy of the Iewes , by
whom he faw all his great labour , &
griefe to be contemned , and fo precious a medicine of his bloud to be by
them (as by fanaticall and mad men)
reiected and vilifyed; what now may
he fay, when he doth fee (not from the
Croffe , but euen from Heauen) his
owne Paffion to be valewed at no
worth, and his facred Bloud to be betrampled vpon, by thofe men who do
                                        belieue

belieue in him, or at leaſt ſay they do
belieue in him, and who offer to him,
nothing but gaule and Vineger, that is,
who do multiply their ſinnes without
conſideration of the diuine Iudgment,
or without feare of Hell? We read *in*
S. *Luke c.* 15. that *; There ſhalbe ioy in*
Heauen, vpon one ſinner, that doth
Pennance. But if that Man, who by
fayth. and Baptiſme was borne in
Chriſt, and by Pennance was recalled
from death to life, do preſently againe
dye by ſinning, is not the ioy then turned into ſorrow and griefe? and is not
the Milke changed into gaule, and the
Vine into Vinager?

Certainly, *A woman, when ſhe tra-*
uaileth hath ſorrow, (if ſhe bring forth
her child with life) *ſhe remembreth not*
the payne for ioy, that a man is borne
into the world. Ioan. 16. But if it happen
that the child do inſtantly dye, or be
borne deade, is not the mother afflicted with a double griefe? Euen ſo, many do labour and take paines in con-
feſsing their ſinnes, and perhaps put in
practiſe faſting and Almes-deeds not
without ſome difficulty; yet becauſe
through an erroneous Conſcience, or
through an vnwarrantable Ignorance,

Q 2   they

they do not arriue to perfect Pardon;
do not these men euen labour in
Child-byrth, and bring forth an Abor-
tiue, and afflict their Pastours with a
double griefe? These therfore resemble a man that is sicke, who hasteneth
his owne death by taking of most bitter Physick, from whence he hoped for
health: Or els a Husbandman, who after much labour spent in cultiuating
his Vineyard, or ground, doth through
an vnexpected Hayle showred downe,
loose all his profit, that is all his labour
and toyle. These Euills therfore ought
with great reason to be deplored with
inconsolable griefe; And who beway-
leth them, and is sory for them, he
doth condole with Christ vpon the
Crosse; And when with fortitude and
strength he laboreth to expell & driue
away these Euills, he wonderfully
compassionateth the afflictions of
Christ suffering on the Crosse, & sha'l
(in recompence thereof) reioyce with
Christ reioycing in Heauen, and raigne
with him, there reigning for euer.

Of

Of the second fruite of the fifth Word.

CHAP. IX.

VVHen attentiuely I ponder & consider the thirst of Christ hanging vpon the Crosse, another fruite (and no lesse profitable) is presented to my iudgement. For our Lord seemeth to me to haue said, *Sitio*, I *thirst*, in the same sense, when vnto the *Samaritan* woman he said, *Giue me to drinke;* for a litle after opening the mystery of this his Word, he thus subioyneth: *If thou didest know the guift of God, and who he is, that saith vnto thee, giue me to drinke; thou perhaps wouldest haue asked of him, and he would haue giuen thee liuing water.* *Iohn* 4. Now how can he thirst, who is the fountaine of liuing water? Did not our Lord speake of himself, when he said. *Ioan.* 7. *If any man thirst, let him come to me and drinke?* And is not he that Rock, of which the Apostle speaketh. 1. *Cor.* 10. *They dranke of the spirituall Rock, that followed them.*

Q 3   *and*

and the Rocke was Christ ? To conclude is not this he , who thus speaketh to the Iewes by Ieremy the Prophet *cap.* 2. They *haue forsaken me the
fountaine of liuing water ; and haue
digged to themselues Cesternes ,broken
Cesternes , that will not hould water?*
Therefore it seemes, I behould our
Lord vpon the Crosse, as vpon a high
Turret , casting his eyes vpon the
whole earth full of men, thirsting, and
languishing through thirst : who
through occasion of his owne corporall thirst, doth commiserate the common thirst of mankind , and saith : *Sitio* , that is, I am truly thirsty , since all
the humidity and moysture of my bo-
dy is already spent and dried vp ; but
this my thirst wil quickly haue an end:
Therefore I do now *thirst* that men
would beginne to know from fayth ,
me to be the true well-spring of liuing
water , and that they would come to
me and drinke, that so they need not
to thirst for all Eternity.

O how happy and blessed might
we be , if with a most attent hart, we
would heare this Sermon of the *VVord
Incarnate* . Doe not almost all men
thirst with a most burning thirst of
                                        concu-

concupiſcence, and with an inſatiable *thirſt* after the fading & troubled waters of tranſitory and floating thinges, which are vulgarly called *goods, Riches, Honours, Pleaſures*? And who is he, that drinking of this water, hath his thirſt thereby extinguiſhed? And who euer hearing Chriſt our Maiſter, did beginne to taſt and reliſh the liuing water of Heauēly wiſdom & of diuine charity, but that (the *thriſt* of terrene things being preſently aſſwaged, he begun to breath hope of eternall lyfe; and laying aſide all gnawing care of getting and heaping together earthly treaſures, did not begin to *thirſt* after Heauenly? This water of lyfe (not riſing out of the earth, but deſcending from Heauen) which our Lord (being the fountaine of the water of life, if ſo we will demand it with moſt ardent prayers, and a fountaine of teares) will giue to vs; this water (I ſay) will not only quench the thirſt of terreſtriall pleaſures, but alſo will be to vs neuer fading meate and drinke, during all the time of our Peregrination. For thus the Prophet Eſay ſpeaketh: *All you that thirſt, come vnto the waters.* Iſ*a*. 55. And to preuent that thou

maiſt

maist thinke not thinke it to be plaine
& simple water, or to be bought with
a great Price, the Prophet subioyneth:
*Make hast , come away , buy without
money , without any change , wine and
milke.* Water is said to be bought, because it is not obtained without labour , that is , without a true disposition of mynd ; but yet it is bought
without money or any exchange , because it is giuen *freely*, neyther can any
equall price for it be found. And that,
which the Prophet a litle asore called
water, he presently after termeth *wine
and milke*; since it is a most precious
and inestimeble thing , as comprehen-
ding in it selfe the perfection or vertue
of water, wyne, and milke.

This is true wisdome and charity ,
which is called *water*, because it doth
refresh and coole the heate of concu-
hiscence. It in also *wine* , in that the
mynd of man is therewith heated, and
(as it were) become drunke with a
sober ebriety; finally , it is said to be
milke, because it nourisheth with a
sweet and gentill food especially such,
who are but infants in Christ , according to those wordes of S . *Peter* the
Apostle : *As infants newly borne, desire
you*

you milke. 1, *Pet* 2. This true wisdome and Charity being incompatible with the Concupiscence of the flesh, is that sweet yoake, and light burden, the which whosoeuer willingly and humbly vndergoe, do purchace true and stable rest to their soules; so as they shall not neede to draw water from earthly and muddy Wels. This most sweet repose of mynd gaue way to solitude, to an Heremiticall lyfe, filled Monasteries, reformed the Clergy, yea reduced married Persons to no small moderation and continency.

Certainly the Pallace or Court of *Theodosius* the yonger, being Empe-rour, did much resemble a great Mo-nastery; And the House of *Elzearus* (the Earle) bare the show of a small Monastery. For in neither of these two places were to be heard any conten-tions, or disagreements, but instead thereof the singing of spirituall Hym-nes and Canticles did most frequently resound. All this we owe, as due to Christ, who hath extinguished our *thirst* with his thirst; and as a liuing fountaine, hath so watered the fields of our Harts with flowing streames, as that they need not feare any drought,

except our Harts depart from the
fountaine it selfe (which God forbid)
through the instigation of the Enemy.

Of the third fruite of the fifth Word.

CHAP. X.

THe third fruite, which may be taken from the words of Christ, is
the imitation of the Patience of the
Sonne of God. For although Humility
(conioyned with patience) did shine
in the *Fourth word*, or sentence; yet in
the *Fyfth word*, as in its proper and reserued place, the wonderfull patience
of Christ seemeth most eminently to
manifest it selfe. Patience is not only
one of the chiefe Vertues; but among
the rest it is very necessary. For thus
S. *Cyprian* speaketh, *Serm. de bono Patientia. Non inuenio inter cæteras &c.
Among the seuerall wayes of Celestiall
discipline, I do not find any thing more
necessary to mans life, or more conducing to true Glory, then that we, who labour to obserue the precept of our Lord
with feare & deuotion, should carefully
deuote*

denote our selfes to the practice of Patience. But before we difcourfe of the Necefsity of Patience, it is needfull, that we diftinguifh betweene true and falfe Patience.

Well then, that is true *Patience*, which commandeth vs to fuffer the Euill of *payne*, or punifhment, to the end we may not be forced to fuffer the Euill of *Fault*, or finne. Such was the patiëce of the Martyrs, who made choyce rather to vndergoe the torments of their Perfecutours, then to yeald vnto an abnegatiõ of their Fayth in Chrift, and to fuffer the loffe of all their temporall goods, then to exhibite worfhip and honour to falfe Gods. But counterfaite and falfe Patience is that, which perfuadeth a man to fuffer all Euills and Inconuenienccs, thereby to giue fatisfaction to the Law of Concupifcence, and to loofe euerla-fting Goods for the conferuation of temporall and momentary. Such is the Patience of the Martyrs of the Deuill (fo to ftyle them) who eafily-endure hunger, thirft, cold, heate, the loffe of their reputation and good name, and (which is more to be admired) the loffe of the Kingdome of Heauen, that

so they may increase and heape together Riches, may glut and satisfy their
owne Carnality, and aspire to certaine
steps and degrees of Honour.

Now this is incident and peculiar
to true Patience, to perfect and conserue all Vertues. And this is that,
which S. *Iames* euen preacheth in the
prayse of Patience, saying; *cap. 1. Pa-*
tience hath a perfect worke, that you
may be perfect and entire, failing in no-
thing. For other Vertues in regard of
their difficulty, except they be suppor-
ted and gouerned with Patience, cannot subsist or continue long; but when
they are accompained with Patience,
they easely commaund and ouer-rule
all opposition and resistance whatsoeuer. For Patience doth conuert,
and maketh crooked things straight,
and rough wayes plaine. Isa. 42. And
this is so indisputably true, that *S. Cy-*
prian thus discourseth of Charity the
Queene of Vertues. *Serm. de Patientia:*
Charitas fraternitatis &c. Charity is
the bond of fraternity, the founda-
tion of Peace, the knitting togeather of
Vnity; It is greater then Fayth, or
Hope; It euer goeth before martyrdome;
It shall euer remaine in vs with God in
the

the Heauenly kingdome ; Yet spoyle and deprive it of Patience, it becomes desolate, and endures not; take from it the vertue of sustaining and tolerating, and then you do pull it quite vp by the roote. The which very point (I meane the necessity of Patience) the same S. Cyprian more easily proueth to be in Chastity, Iustice, and Peace with our neighbours ; for thus he heerof discourseth: *Let thy Patience be strong & immoueable in thy hart; let not thy sanctifyed Body, and Temple of the Holy Ghost be polluted with adultery; neither let thy Innocency (deuoted to Iustice) be contaminated with any contagion of deceyt; nor after thou hast receaued the most reuerend Eucharist, let thy hand be dishonoured with the sword, or imbrued in bloud.Ibid.*Thus this Doctour; who intimateth from a contrary sense, that Chastity without the support of Patience,is not able to resist *Adultery*; nor *Iustice* can be voide of fraud, nor the taking of the *Eucharist* can free a man from *Homicide.*

This , which *S. Iames* aboue teacheth,touching the vertue of Patience, is also taught in other words by the Prophet *Dauid,*by Christ himselfe,and

R 3   by

by the Apostle. *Dauids* wordes are
these, *Psal.* 9. *The patience of the poore
shall neuer perish.* Beacuse it is a perfect
worke, and in this respect its reward
shall not consume or wast away. *Patience* also is said not to perish, because
it is recompenced for all eternity, in
regard of its fruite : after this manner
we are accustomed to say, that the labours of a Husbandman doe perish,
when they beare no fruite ; and not
perish, when they beare fruite. Now
the word, *Poore*, is heer added, because in this place it signifyeth one,
that is humble, who acknowledgeth
himselfe to be *poore*, and that he cannot eyther doe, or suffer any thing,
without the concurrency and ayde of
God ; and thus is this point expounded by S *Austin lib. de patient. cap* 15.
Neither only the poore, but the rich,
and such as do abound with affluency
of temporall wealth, may haue the
vertue of patience, so that they do not
confide and trust in their riches, but in
God ; of whome, as being truly poore
in all diuine guifts, they pray for Patience, and obtaine it.

This said point, our Lord himselfe
signifyed, when he sayd in the Ghospell

pell, *Luc.* 21. *In your patience, you shall possesse your soules* . For he onely doth truly enioy his soule, that is his lyfe, of which no man can be bereaued, who will tollerate patiently all afflictions, yea the very death of the body, so that he sinneth not againtt God. For although by dying he may seeme to loose lyfe, yet he looseth it not, but keeps, and reserues it for all Eternity. Since the death of the iust is not death, but a sleep, and a very short sleep. But those who are impatient, that so they loose not the lyfe of the Body, feare not to sinne, eyther by apostating and denying of Christ, worshipping of Idols, by becomming a prey to sensuality, or by perpetrating any wickednes whatsoeuer; these men seeme indeed for the time to preserue lyfe, but they loose eternall lyfe both of Body and soule. And as it is said of those who are truly patient : *Not one hayre of your head shall perish. Luc.* 25 . So to the impatient it may be said ; not one member of your Body shalbe free frō the incendious heats, and burning of Hell.

To conclude, this forsaid point the Apostle confirmeth, saying, *Heb.*

10. *Patience is necessary for you , that doing the will of God , you may receaue the Promise.* Where we see, that the Apostle plainly pronounceth , that Patience is wholy necessary to vs , that thereby we may alwayes do the Will of God , and by doing it may receaue the Promise, that is, *the Crowne of Glory, which God hath promised for them that loue him, and keep his Commandements, Iac. 1.* For we read , *If any loue me, he will keep my Words; He that loueth me not, keepeth not my Words.* Ioan. 14. Thus vve obserue the whole Scripture (cohering and agreing in. it selfe) to preach to all the faithfull, the necessity of Patience. And this is the Cause , why Christ going out of this life, would testify to all men his inuisible, most bitter, and most long suffering of *thirst* , that we being moued with so great an Example , should be inflamed to keep Patience in all our Afflictions. That this *thirst* of Christ was a most vehement paine, we haue aboue shewed in the explication of the word, *Sitio.* That it continued for a long tyme, it may be easily made euident.

And that we may begin from the
scour-

scourging of Christ; when Christ was
whipped, he was then already spent,
and wearied through prolixity of
Prayer, through his Agony & effusion
of bloud in the garden; Also he was
much tired with iourneys, which that
night and the day following he made;
As from the Garden to the House of
Annas, from the house of *Annas* to the
house of *Caiphas*, from the house of
Caiphas to the house of *Pilate*; from
the house of *Pilate* to the house of *Herod*; from the house of *Herod* backe
againe to the house of *Pilate*; which
seuerall iourneys contained many Mi-
les. Neither did our Lord (after his
supper the night before) taft of any
meate or drinke, or tooke any repose
and sleepe; but endured many most
grieuous afflictions in the house of
Caiphas, and then immediatly after all
these his preffures, followed the most
barbarous & cruell whipping of him;
the which was attended on with a
most vehement *Thirft*, which *Thirft*
much increased, when his whipping
was ended. After all this succeeded his
crowning with thornes, and the Iewes
mocking him to scorne; which new
vexation was also accompanied with

R 5   extre-

extremity of *thirst*, so as the same was very much increased. Then being euen wasted with so many iourneys and labours, he was next burdened with the weight of his Crosse which he bare vnto Mount *Caluary*: That iourney being ended, Wyne mingled with gaule was offered to him, the which when he began to tast, he refused to drinke therof.

Thus his iourneying to and fro receaued an end; but the *Thirst*, which vexed our Lord throughout all his trauayle and labour, doubtlesly increased. For presently his nayling to the Crosse followed, and from hence one may easily conceaue, that his *Thirst* grew greater and more vehement through the defluxion & streaming of his most precious bloud, as from foure fountaines. To conclude, during the space of three houres following (to wit, from the sixt hower to the ninth) in that horrible darknes, it can hardly be belieued, with what fyar or ardour of *thirst* that most sacred body of our Lord was consumed and wasted. And although it was Vinegre, which the Ministers of his Passion offered to him; yet because it was neither Wyne,

nor

nor Water, but Vinegre (that is, a
sharpe and vngratefull Potion) & but
small in quantity, since he was to sucke
the same by drops out of a spunge, &
was most neere vnto his death; therefore it is lawfull to affirme, that our
Blessed Redeemer euen from the beginning of his Passion to his death, did
suffer with wonderfull patience, this
dolefull and most greuious torment.
Now of what violence this torment
is, few make tryall, since they may easely find water, wherewith to quench
their thirst; but such as trauell diuers
dayes in desert places (where small or
litle water is to be found) do fully take
notice, how great a torment *Thirst* is.

    ℯ. *Curtius* writeth (*lib.* 7. *de gest.*
Alex.) that *Alexander the great* pas-
sing with his Army through a long &
tedious desart, his souldiers after much
drought and thirst came to a certaine
Riuer, of which they dranke with such
gust and greedmes, as that many of
them by losing their wynd, or breath
in drinking, did presently dye, & then
he thus concludeth : *Multòque maior*
&c The number of those, by this meanes
dying, was far greater, then euer he lost
in any one battayle. Therefore the
heate

heate of the *thirst* was so intollerable,
as that the souldiers had not that cōmand ouer themselues, as in tyme of
drinking, a litle to breath, or take their
Wind. And thus the greatest part of
Alexanders Army was extinct and pe-
rished. There haue bene some men,
who through extremity of *thirst*, haue
thought water mingled with dirt,
oyle, bloud, and other more filthy
things, to haue byn sweet and pleasant. From hence then, we may be instructed, how bitter the Passion of
Christ was, and how great Vertue of
his Patience appeared therein. And it
was Gods will, that this his Patience
should be knowne to vs, that by our
imitation of it, vve might so compassionate & suffer withChrist, as that vve
may be glorified together vvith Christ.

But it seemes to me, that I heare
diuers good and pious soules, earnestly enquiring, how they might arriue
to that height, as seriously to imitate
the Patience of Christ, and to say with
the Apostle, *I am fastned to the Crosse
with Christ*: & with the holy *Martyr*
S. *Ignatius*; *Amor meus crucifixus est.
My loue is crucifyed.* This point is not
so difficult, as many take it to be. For
it is

it is not neceſſary for all men to lye vppon the cold ground ; to diſcipline & ſcourge their body with whips vntill the drawing of bloud ; to faſt dayly with bread and water; to weare continually next to their skin a rough hayre-cloath , or iron-chayne; or to practiſe other ſuch kinds of mortification, for the taming of the body , and crucifying It, with its vices and concupiſcences: theſe actions are laudable, and alſo profitable, when they are practiſed by ſuch , whoſe bodies are able to beare them; and this by the aduice and direction of their ſpirituall Father or Inſtructour. But I in this place couet to ſhew to the pious Reader, a courſe or way of exerciſing Patience , and of imitating Chriſt, who was moſt patiēt; which courſe may agree to all men , & in which nothing is vnaccuſtomed; nothing taſting of nouelty , nothing , which may ſeeme to gaine a vulgar praiſe .

Firſt then I ſay , that one who is zealous of Patience , ought willingly to be buſyed in thoſe labours which he is aſſured are gratefull and pleaſing to the will of God, according to that of the Apoſtle , *Heb.* 10. *Patience is neceſ-*
                                          ſary

sary for you , that you doing the VVill of
God , may receaue the Promise. What
God vvould haue vs patiently to vndergoe, is not hard eyther to learne,or
to teach. Firſt experience and dayly
practiſe telleth vs,that vvhat things the
Church (our Mother) commandeth
to be done, the ſame (though hard
and difficult) are to be performed obe-
diently and patiently. But vvhat doth
the Church command vs ? to vvit , the
faſts of Lent, the Ember-dayes , and
the vigill of Saints. If theſe be performed in ſuch ſort, as they ought to be,
they then cannot be performed vvithout Patience. For if a man vpon faſting
dayes , vvill ſeeke after delicate and
curious meates ; and at one ſupper, or
dinner eate as much meate, as at other
tymes is vſuall to ſerue him both for
dinner and ſupper ; or els vvill preuent
the houre of eating before noone, and
then at night inſteed of a ſmall refection or Collation , will deuoure ſo
much, as may wel to be termed a large
and copious ſupper, certainly this Man
will not eaſily ſuffer honger or thirſt ;
neyther will he ſtand in need of Patience. But if he will conſtantly and
ſeriouſly determine with himſelfe, not

to

to anticipate the houre, except some
disease or other necessity force him;
and to content himselfe with ordinary
and meane dyet, imposed as it vvere
for pennance, and (auoyding all full
gorging) to take it in that measure &
quantity, as may seeme not to exceed
one ordinary meale; and to giue that
to the poore, vvhich should be takē at
another meale if it vvere not a day of
fast, according to S. Leo, saying (*serm.*
11. *de ieiunio* 10. *mensis:*) *Refectio P-
peris, abstinentia ieiunantis. The absti-
nence of the faster, is the refection of
the poore;* and the same Father in another place: *Esurianus paululum &c.*
*Beloued, let vs fast a litle, that we may
subtract and withdraw so much from
our custome of eating, as may relieue
the poore and needy. Serm.* 9. *de ieiunio*
7. *mensis.* and to conclude, at night to
make but a small Collation or drinking: This man (I say) hath need of
Patience to endure his hunger & thirst.
And in fasting after this manner, we
in some sort may imitate the patience
of Christ, & his crucifixion. But these
fasts are not wholy necessary, though
they be necessary for the exercise of
Patience, and for the imitation of the

,Passion

Furthermore, the Church commandeth Ecclesiasticall, or Regular Persons, to recite or sing the *seauen Canonicall Howers*; and that all the faithfull at least in prayer do read, & recite the *Lord Prayer*, and the *Salutation of the Angell*. This religious Reading and prayer, if it be performed in that sort, which it may, and ought to be, doubtlesly will stand in need of Patience. But there are many, who that they may shake of all Patience, endeauour to take away all difficulties. For they thinking, that a heauy burden is imposed vpon them, do most swiftly run all things ouer, that so in a very short space, they may dispatch themselues of the Burden. Next to this, they do not standing or kneeling, but either sitting or walking, read the Canonicall Howers, to the end that the wearisomnes of reading or praying may be mitigated by sitting or walking. I here speake of such, who read the howers in priuate, not of those who sing or say the same in the Quire. Furthermore, that they may not be forced to breake their sleep, they vse often to say their Mattins before the sunne setteth.   Tou-

Touching the attention and eleua-
tion of mind in tyme of prayer, and of
prayfing God, I fay little, fince many
thinke of nothing leffe then of that,
which they fing, or reade Therefore
taking away the difficulty of fpending
much tyme in reading, or in Prayer, &
of rifing in the night to fay their Mattins, and omitting or neglecting the labour of ftanding or kneeling ; as alfo
not regarding to put a bridle on the
mind, that it may not wander in di-
ftractions and vnneceffary thoughts,
but that it may be wholy intent vpon
that, vvhich it readeth: I fay, that once
taking avvay all thefe things, it is no
wonder, if many do not feeme to ftad
in need of Patience. But let fuch negli-
gen: men heare and obferue, with
What follicitude and care *S.Francis* did
read or recite the Canonicall howers;
and then they fhall fully fee and acknowledge, that this pious and Religious office and duty cannot be performed without the ayde and fupport
of Patience. For thus *S. Bonauenture*
writeth of him, *cap.10.vita eius. Soli-*
tus erat vir fanctus &c. The holy man
was accuftomed to pay, or performe to
God his Canonicall Howres, with no

S   *leffe*

lesse feare, then deuotion. For althogh he was afflicted with a paine in his eyes, stomacke, splene, & liuer; yet he would not as much as leane vnto the wall, when he did sing; but euer standing streight vp, and without any hood on his head, or wandring eyes he said his houres, & that sometymes not without swouning with the payne. He did, when he was in any tourney on the way, neuer omit this reuerend custome. He also was perswaded he offended highly, if in tyme of prayer he were distracted with any wandring of mynd, or vaine thoughts; and when any such thing happened, he presently cancelled the same by humble Confession: He was accustomed to say the Psalms, as if he did behould God present: And when the name of our Lord did occur therein, he was wont to licke his lips, through the sweetnes of that name pronounced by him. Thus S. Bonauenture writeth of S. Francis.

Certainly, if a man would endeauour to read his Canonicall Howers after this manner, and would rise in the night time for the saying therof, he would then find by experience, and confesse, that without labour and patience

tience he could not performe and fatisfy the diuine Office of Prayer. There are many other things, which our Mother, the Church, euen from the Will of God(manifested in the holy Scriptures)doth preſcribe to vs, the which without patience cannot be rightly performed. As for example , to diſtribute to the poore,vvhat is ſuperfluous in our riches ; to pardon ſuch as offend vs, and to make ſatisfaction to thoſe vvhom we offend or wrong ; to confeſſe all our ſinnes at leaſt once a-yeare; to communicate and receaue the moſt Bleſſed Sacrament, which requireth no ſmall preparation of mind. All theſe require great Patience for the performance therof. And thus much of theſe few things preſcribed to vs, the which I ſet downe only for an inſtance.

Another thing, in vvhich the Will of God is ſeene, and which cannot be performed on our part without Patience,is all that,which either the Deuills or men do worke , to afflict and vexe vs.For although bad men and the wicked Deuills,when they do exerciſe their malice againſt vs , do intend no good ; notwithſtanding God (without vvhoſe permiſſion they can do nothing)

S 2   thing)

thing) would not permit that their
vexation, except he iudged it might be
profitab e to vs. Therefore affliction is
to be receaued as from the hand of
God, and is in this respect to be suffered patiently and vvillingly. So *Iob*
(being a plaine & vpright man) vvas
not ignorant, that those Calamities
which he suffered, did proceed from
the malice of the Deuill; to wit, when
in one day, he lost all his riches, all his
sonnes, and the health of his Body;
Notvvithstanding he said : *Our Lord
gaue, and our Lord hath taken away;
the name of our Lord be blessed;* because
he did knovv, that these Calamities
could not haue fallen vpon him, vvithout the vvill of God. I do not speake
this, as if I vvould counsell men, vvho
are afflicted either by men or Deuils,
that they cannot, or ought not to re-
paire their losses, to seeke to cure their
Body by medicins or physicke, or to
defend themselues and their states:
But only this I do admonish, that men
do not study reuenge against wicked
men, nor render Euill for Euill; but
that they do patiently suffer, what God
will haue them to suffer; that so doing
the will and pleasure of God, they may
                                    receaue

receaue the *Promise.*

The laſt way of practiſing Patience conſiſteth, in that we do vnderſtand & conceaue, that all thoſe things, which may ſeeme to happen either by chance or fortune, as much drought of Weather, ouer much rayne, peſtilence, Penury, and the like, do not come without the Prouidence and will of God; & that therefore we ought not to complaine of the Elements, or of God; but that we acknowledge the puniſhment of God for our ſinnes, that thus being ſubiect to God, we may patiently beare all aduerſities with true Humility. For by doing ſo, it will come to paſſe, that God being appeaſed, will leaue to vs behind him his Benediction, and chaſtize vs (as his Sonnes) with a paternall correction, and not depriue vs (as baſtards and adulterate) of our heauenly Inheritance. I will here adioyne one Fxāple out of S. *Gregory,* from whence we may gather, how great the reward allotted to Patience, is. He relateth (*hom.* 35. *ſuper Euang.*) that a certaine man called *Steuen,* was ſo patient, as that he reputed thē his chiefeſt friēds, vvho had beene moſt troubleſome vnto him; giuing them thanks for their

contu-

contumelies, and esteeming the losses
and detriments offered to him, to be
his chiefest gaine and benefit; thus
numbering and ranging his Aduersa-
ries amōg his Benefactours. This man
the vvorld (no doubt) would repute,
as mad or foolish; but he listened to
the Apostle of Christ not with a deafe
eare, saying. 1. *Cor.* 3. *Yf any man seeme
to be wise among you in this world, let
him become a foole, that he may be wise.*
For as S. *Gregory* vvriteth in the place
aboue alledged, many Angels were
seene to be present at the instant of his
death, who did carry his soule directly
into Heauen, And the holy Father feared not to range this *Steuen* among
the Blessed Martyrs, in regard of his
wonderful Patience.

Of the fourth fruite of the fifth Word.

CHAP. XI.

AS yet remaineth one fruite behind (and this most sweet) which
may be gathered from the word) *Sitio, I thirst.* For *S. Austin* expounding
the

the said word saith, That by this word
was not signified only the desire of
corporall drinke ; but a desire with
which Christ did burne for the health
and saluation of his Enemies. But now
taking occasion from the sentence of
S. *Austin*, we may ascend a litle higher,
and say; that Christ did *thirst* after the
glory of God , and the saluation of
men;and that we ought to *thirst* after
the glory of God , the honour of
Christ, our owne health, & the health
of our Brethren. That Christ was euen
thirsty of the glory of God,& health of
soules, cannot be doubted; since all his
vvorks,all his Sermons or speaches,all
his sufferings , and all his miracles do
euen preach, and proclaime the truth
hereof. Therefore to vs it rather belongeth to thinke, (to shevv our grate-
fulnes to so great a Benefactour) by
vvhat meanes vve may be inflamed, as
truly to *thirst* after the honour of
God, *VVho, so loued the VVorld, as that
he gaue his only begotten Sonne.* Ioan 3.
and withall after the honour of Christ
truly and ardently , *whe loued vs , and
deliuered himselfe for vs an oblation &
host to God, in an odour of sweetnes .
Ephes. 5.)* As also that vve may so truly
com-

compassionate vvith our Brethren, as
most vehemently to *thirst* after their
health & saluation. But this one thing
is chiefly and principally incumbent
vnto vs, to wit, that vve do so truly, in-
tensly, and from the bottome of our
Hart *thirst* after our owne proper
health and saluation, as that our *thirst*
thereof may force vs, according to our
strength and povver, to thinke, speake,
and do euery thing, vvhich may con-
duce vnto the purchasing therof For if
we do not *thirst* after the honour of
God, nor the glory of Christ, nor the
health of our Neighbours, it followeth
not, that God shall therefore want his
due honour; or Christ be depriued of
his glory, or cur Neyghbours shall
not obtaine their saluation; but it fol-
lovveth, that vve our selfes shall perish
eternally, if vve neglect to *thirst* after
our ovvne peculiar health and Saluation.

From the consideration of vvhich
point, a strong admiration possesseth
me, to vvit, from vvhēce it proceedeth,
that vve knovving Christ so ardently
to haue *thirsted* after our Health and
Well-fayre, and acknovvledging him
to be the Wisdome of God, are neuerthelesse

theieſſe litle moued to imitate him in
ſo great a matter, vvhich to vs is aboue
all things moſt neceſſary. Neither doe I
leſſe vvonder to obſerue, hovv greedily our ſelfes do *thirſt* after temporall Goods, as if they vvere eternall,
and yet do ſo negligently ſleight our
eternall ſaluation, and ſo litle *thirſt* after it, as if it were a thing momentary
and light. We may adde hereto, that
temporall Goods are not pure goods,
but mixed with many euils and incon-
ueniences, yet neuertheles are moſt
ſollicitouſly & painfully ſought-after,
vvhereas Eternall ſaluation is exempted from being accompanied with
any Euill, and yet it is ſo neglected, &
ſo faintly coueted, as if it had in it
ſelfe no vvorth, ſolidity, or firmneſſe.
O *Bleſſed Lord*, ſo illuminate my inte-
riour eyes, that I may at length fynd
the Cauſe of this ſo blind and dangerous an Ignorance.

Certainly Loue begetteth a deſire,
and deſire, when it beginneth vehemently to burne, is called a *Thirſt*. But
who cannot loue his owne ſaluation,
eſpecially being to remaine for all E-
ternity, and voyd of all Euill? And if ſo
great a matter cannot be but beloued,

     T   why

why is it not vehemētly desired? Why
is not ardently *thirsted* after? Why is it
not procured vvith all endeauour and
force? Perhaps the reason hereof is, in
that , Eternall saluation doth not fall
vnder our sense, & therefore we haue
no experiment thereof, as we haue of
our Corporall health and prosperity;
and therefore this we *thirst* after, that
we but couldly desire. But if this were
the reason of so great an Ignorance,
from whence then did it spring , that
Dauid (being a mortall man) did so
ardently *thirst* after the Vision of God,
in which Vision eternall health consisteth, as that he cried out, *Psal.*41.*Euen
as the Hart desireth after the fountaines of* Waters, *so doth my soule desire after thee* , O God. *My soule hath
thissted after God, the strong* , *and liuing; when shall* I *come, and appeare before the face of God* ? Where we see,
the Prophet as yet remaining here v-
pon earth , did most burningly *thirst*
after the Vision of God, which is eternall health it selfe. And this desire did
not happen to *Dauid* alone , but to
many other men, eminent for sancti-
ty; to vvhom all earthly matters seemed sordide, base, and vnsauory; and
vvho

vvho moſt greedily, & withall ſweetnes did reliſh, and taſt the remembrance or recordation of God.

Therefore the Cauſe is not, why
vve do not earneſtly *thirſt* after eternall Beatitude, in that it falleth not
vnder our ſenſe, but by reaſon it is nor
thought vpon attentiuely, daily, and
with a full fayth . Now, it is not
thought vpon, as it ought to be , becauſe we are not ſpirituall, but ſenſuall : *The ſenſuall man perceaueth not*
thoſe things which are of the ſpirit of
God. 1. Cor. 2. Wherefore O *my Soule,*
if thou doſt couet to *thirſt* after thy
ovvne health, & the health of others,
and much more after the honour of
God, and Glory of Chriſt , heare then
S. *Iames* ſaying *Cap. 1. Yf any of you*
lacke Wiſdome, let him aske of God,
who giueth to all men abundantly , and
vpbraideth not, and it ſhalbe giuen him.
This wiſdome (being ſo high & perfect) is not found in the ſchooles of
this world, but only in the Auditory of
the ſpirit of God ; which ſpirit turneth
a ſenſuall man, into a ſpirituall. And it
is not ſufficient to demand, or pray for
this wiſdome once, or twyce, and
coldly; but we ought euen to beſiege

the eares of God with our inceſſant petitions, and inutterable lamentations. For if a Carnall Father be not accuſtomed to deny his little child moaning, and asking ſome bread, *How much more (ſayth our Lord) will your Father from Heauen giue the good ſpirit to them that aske him? Luc. 11.*

The ſixt Word : Conſummatum eſt, *It is conſummate,* Ioan. 15. *literally expounded.*

CHAP. XII.

THe *ſixt Word* pronounced by our Lord vpon the Croſſe, is related by the foreſaid *S. Iohn,* as almoſt conioyned with the *fifth.* For preſently after our Lord had ſaid, I *thirſt,* & had taſted vinegre brought vnto him, S. Iohn thus addeth : *When Ieſus therefore had taken the Vinegre, he ſaid,* It is *conſummate.* Io. 19. And truly according to the letter, the word *Conſummatum eſt,* ſignifieth nothing, but that the worke of Chriſts Paſsion was then conſummate, perfected, and ended. For two works or labours the Father
did

did enioyne vpon his Sonne; One was
the preaching of the Gospell; The o-
ther, his suffering for mankind. Of the
first Worke our Lord did spake in *S.*
Iohn c. 17. *I haue consummated the*
worke, which thou gauest me to doe; I
haue manifested thy name to men.
This our Lord spake after his last and
longest Sermon, made to his Disciples
after his last supper. Thus he had finished then his *first VVorke*, imposed
by his Father. The *second VVorke* concerned his drinking the Cupp of his
Passion, of which himselfe sayth :
Can you drinke of the Cup, which I
shall drinke of ? Matth. 20. and againe :
O Father, if it be possible, let this Cup
passe from me, Matth. 26 and yet more :
The Cup, which my Father hath giuen
me, shall I not drinke it ? Io. 18. Therefore of this worke of his Passion, our
Lord being most neare to his death,
said; *Consummatum est,* It is consummate, and finished; I haue drunke vp
this whole cup, euen to the dregs, nothing is now remaining but to depart
out of this life : *And so bowing his head,*
he gaue vp the Ghost. Ioan. 19.

But because neyther our Lord himselfe, nor *S. Iohn* (as affecting breui-

ty) did explaine and fet downe, what
that was, which was *confumate*, and
finished, occasion thereby is giuen to
vs to apply that *confummatum eft*, to
diuers myfteries, and this not without iu't reafon and fruite. Firft then
S. *Auftin* referreth the word *confummatum eft*, to the fullfilling of the Pro-
phecies which were deliuered of our
Sauiour; for thus he writeth *in Comment. huius loci*. *Our Lord knowing,
that all things were confummate, that
the Scripture fhould be confummated &
accomplifhed faid, I thrift*. And taking
the vinegre, he faid, *It is confummate.*
That is, *that is now fullfilled which did
remaine to be fullfilled*. From whence
we gather, that our Lords meaning
was; that all thofe things are now cõ-
fummate and finifhed, which the Prophets had foretould of his lyfe and
death: For example, His *Conception* in
thofe words, *Behould a virgin fhall cõ-
ceãue. Ifa. 7.* His *Natiuity* in Bethleem:
*And thou Bethleem, the land of Iuda,
out of thee fhal come forth my Captaine,
which fhall rule my People of Ifrael, Mi-
cheas 5.* The *Apparitiõ of the new Star,
A ftarre fhall rife out of Iuda. Num. 24.*
The *adoration of the Kings* : *The Kings*
of

of Tharsis, and the Ilands shall offer pre-
sents. Psal. 71. The Preaching of the
Ghospell: The Spirit of the Lord is vpon
me , to preach to the poore he sent me.
Isa. 61. Christ *Miracles.* Isa. 35. *God him-*
selfe will come , and saue vs ; then shall
the eyes of the blind be opened , and the
eares of the deafe opened: then shall the
lame leape as an Hart , and the tongue
of the dumbe shalbe opened. His riding
vpon an Asse , or coult of an Asse :
Zach. 9. *Behould thy king will come to*
thee , the Iust and Sauiour ; himselfe
poore and riding vpon an Asse, and vpon
a Colt, *the fole of an Asse.* To conclude,
the Scene of his whole Passion by
parts , is described by *Dauid* in his
Psalms, by *Esay, Ieremy, Zachary*, and o-
thers as abouesayd. And this is that,
which our Lord going towards his
Passion, said: *Behould, we go vp to Ieru-*
salem , and all things shalbe consum-
mate , which were written by the Pro-
phets of the Sonne of Man. Luc. 18. Of
those things therefore, which were to
be *consummate,* our Lord now sayth,
consummatum est ; that is to say, all is
now *consummate* and finished , which
the Prophets foretould of me , that so
they may be found to be true Prophets.

Fur-

Furthermore, according to the sentence of S. *Iohn Chryſoſtome*, the vvord *conſummatum eſt*, ſignifieth, that all the power permitted to men and the Deuils againſt Chriſt, was *conſummated* and ended in the Paſſion of Chriſt, of which povver Chriſt himſelfe ſpake to the chiefe of the Phariſees, Prieſts, or Officers of the Temple: *This is your hower, and the power of darknes.* Luc. 22. Therfore this hower, and whole tyme, during the which (God permitting) the wicked had power ouer Chriſt, was ended, when our Lord ſaid, *Conſummatum eſt.* For then the peregrination of the Sonne of God among men, receaued its end; which peregrination, *Baruch* the Prophet foretould, when he ſaid *cap.3. This is our God, and there ſhall none other be eſteemed againſt him. He found out all the way of diſcipline, and deliuered it to Iacob his ſeruant, and to Iſrael his beloued; After theſe things he was ſeene vpon the Earth, and was conuerſant with men.* And the Condition of his mortall life, (according to which he was hungry, did thirſt, did ſleepe, was ſpent out with iniuries, whipping, wounds, and ſubiect to death) did take

its

i:s end together with his peregrinatiō.

Therefore when Christ said vpon the Crosse , *consummatum est* , these words imply, that that iourney was finished ; of which he saith in another place : *I came forth from the Father, & came into the world ; againe I leaue the world , and go to the Father.* Iob . 16. That laborious and painefull peregrinatiō is finished, of which Ieremy speaketh. *cap.* 14. O *expectation of Israel, the Saniour thereof in the time of tribulation ; why wilt thou be a seiourner in the Land, & a wayfaring man, turning in to lodge ?* The mortality of Chtists humanity is *consummate* and ended ; the power of all his Enemies against him is *consummate* ; finally the sacrifice (greatst of al sacrifices) is *consumate*, to which all the Sacrifices of the old Law, (as being but types & shadowes) had necessary relation, as to a true and solid sacrifice. For thus S. *Leo* speaketh *Serm.* 8. *de pass. Dom. Traxisti Domine omnia ad te &c.* O Lord thou hast *drawne all things to thee , because the veyle of the Temple being cut a sunder , the Holy of Holyes departed from the vnworthy Priests ; that so the figure might be turned into the Truth,* Prophe-

T 5   *cy*

cy *into manifestation or clearenes,and*
the Law *into the Ghospell.*

And a litle after : *Now the variety
of Carnall Sacrifices ceasing, one Oblation of thy Body and Bloud , doth fill vp
and include all the differences of hosts.*
Thus he. For in this Sacrifice the *Priest*
vvas God and man ; the *Altar* the
Crosse; The *sacrifice* the Lābe of God;
the *fire* of the *Holocaust*, Charity ; the
fruite of the sacrifice, the Redemption
of the World. I say the Priest was *God*
as *man* , then whome not any can be
imagined to be greater : *Thou art a
priest for euer according to the Order of
Melchisedech.* Psal. 109. And truly according to the *Order of Melchisedech,*
for *Melchisedech* is read in the Scripture so be vvithout Father, without
mother, without genealogy, & Christ
vvas without Father vpon earth, without Mother in Heauen, without Genealogy, For *who shall shew his generation?* He was be gotten *before the Day-
star* ; and *his comming forth from the
beginning , from the dayes of Eternity.*
Mich. 5.

The *Altar* of this great Sacrifice
was (as aboue I said) the *Crosse* ; the
vvhich by hovv much it was more vile
and

and bafe, before Chrift vvas crucified
thereon, by fo much it was after made
more illuftrious, and more ennobled;
and in the laft day it fhall appeare in
Heauen more bright and fhyning then
the funne. For the Church interpreteth
that of the *Croffe*, which is faid in the
Gofpell, *Matth. 24.* *Then fhall the figne
of the fonne of man appeare in Heauen.*
In like fort the Church thus fingeth:
*This figne fhalbe in Heauen, when our
Lord fhall come to iudge.* The which
point is alfo confirmed by *S. Chryfo-
ftome* ; who further affirmeth, that
vvhen the funne fhalbe obfcured, and
the Moone not giue her light, then
fhall the *Croffe* be more fplendid and
radiane then the Sunne.

Furthermore the *Sacrifice* fhalbe
the *Lambe of God*, altogether innocent
and immaculate, of whom *Efay* thus
fpeaketh: *cap. 55. Euen as a fheepe to the
flaughter fhall he be led; and as a lambe
before his fhearer he fhalbe dumbe, and
fhall not open his mouth.* And the *Fore-
runner* of our Lord fayth: *Behould the
Lambe of God, behould who taketh a-
way the finnes of the World.* *Ioan. 1.*
And the Apoftle *S. Peter: Not with corruptible things, gould or filuer, are you
redeemed*

*redeemed, but with the precious bloud of
an immaculate and vnspotted Lambe,
Christ:* Who alfo is called in the Apocalyps, *cap. 13. The Lambe slaine from
the beginning of the World*, Becaufe
his Price being forefeene of God, did
profit thofe who vvent before the times of Chrift. The *fyar* burning the
Holocauft, and perfecting the Sacrifice,
is Charity in a high degree, being as it
were, a furnace fet on fire, vvhich did
burne in the hart of the Sonne of God,
vvhich fire many waters of his Paffion vvere not able to extinguifh. To
conclude, the *fruite of this Sacrifice*
vvas the expiation of all the finnes of
the Sonnes of *Adam*, and the reconciliation of the whole World. For thus
S. Iohn fpeaketh, *1. Ioan. 2. He is the
propitiation for our finnes; and not for
ours only, but alfo for the whole World.*
Which very thing is fignified by the
words of *S. Iohn Baptift* : *Agnus Dei,
Ecce, qui tollit peccata mundi.*

But heere arifeth a doubt, vvhich
is, Hovv could Chrift be both Prieft &
Sacrifice, fince it is the function of the
Prieft to flaughter that, vvhich is to be
facrifized? But Chrift did not flay himfelfe, neither could he lawfully fo doe;
fince

since then he should haue rather perpetrated sacriledge, then offered vp Sacrifice. It is true, that Christ did not slay himselfe; neuertheleffe he truly offered vp sacrifice, becaufe willingly and freely he offered himfelfe to be slaine for the glory of God, and expiation of sinne, For neither could the souldiers & other Ministers haue euer apprehended and taken him; neither could the nayles haue pierced his hands and feete; nor death could haue seized vpon him (though faftened to the Crofse)except himfelfe had bene willing thereto. Therefore *Efay* moft truly sayth : *He was offered, becaufe himfelfe would.* And our Lord himfelfe sayth. Io. 10. *I yield my lyfe ; no man ta-keth it away from me, but* I *yield my felfe.* And the Apostle *S. Paul* moft euidently : *Chrift loued vs, and deliuered himfelfe for vs, an oblation, and hoft to God, in an odour of fweetnes. Eph.* 3 :

Now what euill or sinne, or rather atrocity vvas in the Pafsion of Chrift, all that belonged to *Iudas*, the *Iewes*, to *Pilate*, and the souldiers ; for thefe men did not offer vp Sacrifice, but did commit muft horrible facriledge, deferuing the name not of Priefts, but

of

of sacrilegious Persons. But vvhat in the same Passion was good, religious, and pious, streamed from Christ, who out of the affluency and abundance of his Charity, offered himselfe as a Sacrifice to God, not in slaying himselfe, but in tollerating most patiëtly death; to wit, the death of the Crosse; and this to the end he might appease the wrath of God, reconcile the vvorld to God, satisfy the diuine Iustice, that so mankind should not perish . Which point S. *Leo* expresseth in most few words, saying: *He suffered at the hands of furious men, who whiles they were busied about their wickednes, they became seruiceable to our Redeemer.*

Fourthly, a Great War betweene Christ and the Prince of this world is *consummate*, and finished in the death of Christ; of which warre our Lord thus speaketh in *Iohn cap.12. Now is the iudgment of the world, now the Prince of this World shalbe cast forth, And when I shall be exalted from the Earth, I will draw all things to my selfe.* This warre was iudiciall, not military: It is like to the war of those, who contend in Suites and Causes, not of souldiers who fight in the field. For
the

the Deuill did contend with the Sonne
of God, touching the pofsefsion of the
World, that is, of mankind. The deuill for a long tyme had intruded himfelfe into the Pofsefsion of the World,
becaufe he had ouercome the *firſt*
man, and had made him (with all his
ofspring) his feruant, or bondflaue.
Therefore S. *Paul* himfelfe calleth the
Deuils, the *Princes and Potentates of*
this VVorld, and the Gouernours of this
darknes. Eph. 6. And Chrift himfelfe
(as aboue we haue ſhewed)calleth the
Deuill, *the Prince of this* World. The
Deuill would not be content to be reputed the *Prince of the world* , but alfo
to be accounted *a God* , according to
that in the Pfalmes : *The diuels are the*
Gods of the Gentils. P*fal.* 95 . For the
diuell was commonly adored by the
Gentils in engrauen Idols,& was worſhipped with the facrifice of Rams,
and Calfes.

Now on the other fyde the Sonne
of God (as lawful heere of all things)
did challenge to himfelfe the principality of the world. Therfore this warre
was in the end *confummate,* and ended
vpon the Croffe, and the feptencе was
giuen in behalfe of our Lord Iefus-
Chriſt,

Christ : becaufe our Lord had moft a-
bondantly fatisfyed the diuine Iuftice
vpon the Croffe, for the offence of the
firft Man , and of all the faithfull . For
the Obedience exhibited to God , by
the Sonne , was greater then the difobedience of the feruant to his Lord ;
And the Sonne of God was more hū-
bled , euen to death , for the honour
of his Father then the feruāt was puf-
fed vp in pryde , through his iniury of
God. Therefore God being reconciled to mankind by the mediation of
his Sonne, did violently take mankind
out of the Power of the diuell ; and ,
*did tranflate vs into the Kingdome of
the Sonne of his Loue. Coloff.* 1.

There is another reafon, which S.
Leo is accuftomed to bring , which I
will relate in his owne words: *Si cru-
delis & fuperbus inimicus &c . Yf the
proud & cruel Enemy could haue known
the reafon of the mercy of God;he would
rather haue ftudied to tēper with gent-
leues the minds of the Iewes , for feare of
loofing the feruitude of all his Captines,
whiles he did perfecute the liberty of
him , who was not owing to him in any
thing. Serm* 10. *de paff.* Certainly a
moft forcible reafon. For it was reafonable,

fonable, that the diuell fhould loofe
his empire or command ouer all thofe
whome he had conquered vnto him
by finne; becaufe he was not afrayd to
ftretch out his arme euen vnto death,
againft Chrift, who was not his feruant, and whome he could not induce
to finne.

But if the matter ftand thus: If the
warre be *confummate* and ended, if
the victory be in the power of the Son
of God, and he willeth, *That all men*
may be faued. 1, *Tim.* 2. how then
commeth it to paffe that fo many men
do remaine euen to this day flaues to
the diuell in this lyfe, and in the next
lyfe are fent to the torment of Hell?
I anfwere this in one word: becaufe
themfelues will fo. For Chrift returning from the warre victorious, performed two moft great benefits to ma-
kind. The one, that he did open the
gate of Paradife to the iuft; which frō
the fall of the *firft man,* was euer fhut
euen to that day. And in that very day
of his victory, he fayd to the Thiefe
who was iuftifyed by Fayth, Hope, &
Charity throgh the merit of the bloud
of the fame Chrift: *To day thou fhalt*
by with me in Paradife; and heerupon

V the

the Church exulting singeth: *The sting
of death being ouercome, thou didst open
the Kingdome of Heauen to beleeuers.*
The other benefit; that he did insti-
tute the holy Sacramnts, which should
haue power of remitting sinne, and
confirming grace, and did send forth
publishers thereof into all parts of the
world, who with loud voice did pro-
clame & preach, *He that shall beleeue,
and be baptized, shalbe saued.* Therefore our Lord being victour in this
Warre, did open the way to all men
for the enioying the liberty of the glory, belonging to the Sonnes of God.
Now if any forbeare to enter into this
way, they perish through their owne
default; not through the impotency,
weaknes, or negligence of the Redeemer.

Fifthly to conclude, the Word, *consummatum est*, may rightly be vnderstood of the *consummation* of the edifice, which is the Church. That the
Perfection of a building, may be called
the *consummation of it*, Christ himselfe
our Maister, doth warrant, saying:
*This man began to build, but he could
not consummate or finish it.* Luc. 14.
Now S. *Epiphanius*, S. *Austin* and o-
ther-

ther holy Fathers do teach, that , that
Church was confummate and perfected in the Paffion of Chrift , which
was begun in his Baptifme. They further teach , that *Eue* being buit or
made of the ribbe of *Adam* fleeping ,
was a figure of the Church , which is
built out of the fide of Chrift , whiles
he began to fleep by death . And they
alfo note, that the Scripture fayd not
without fome myftery , that *Eua* was
edificata , non formata , built, not fra-
med .

Now that the Church did beginne
to be built from the Baptifme of Chrift
S. Auftin proueth , expounding that
place of *Pfal. 71. He fhall rule from
fea to fea , and from the Riuers , euen
to the ends of the VVorld.* For the Kingdome of Chrift in which is his Church
began from the Baptifme of Chrift ;
in which he receauing the Baptifme of
S. Iohn , did confecrate the water, and
did inftitute his Baptifme, which is the
Gate of the Church. Which point manifeftly appeared from the voyce of
the Father, heard from Heauē. *Matth.
3. This is my beloued Sonne , in whome
I am well pleafed ; heare him.* And frō
that time , our Lord began to preach ,

and to assemble disciples togeather ,
who were the first that came vnto the
Church . For although the opening of
the side of Christ was made after his
death, and then bloud and water came
from thence , which signified two
chiefe Sacraments of the Church , to
wit , *Baptisme*, and *Eucharist* ; Neuertheles all the Sacraments receaue their
vertue from the Passion of Christ ; and
the flowing of bloud and water from
the side of Christ being then dead was
a declaration of the mysteries , not an
institution. Therefore most truly the
consummation of the edifice of the
Church was then said to be , when
Christ speake this Word , *Consummatum est*, *It is consummate*: because then
nothing was remayning to be effected,
but his death , which instantly did follow, and which did *consummate* and
perfect the price of our Redemption.

Of the firſt fruite of the ſixt Word.

CHAP. XIII.

THey are not few fruits, which may be gathered from the *ſixt Word*, if the aboundance thereof be attently conſidered. And firſt frō that which aboue we ſaid, to wit, that by *Conſummatum eſt*, may be vnderſtood the fulfilling of the Propheſies concerning Chriſt. *S. Auſtin* draweth a moſt profitable doctrine. For as we are acertained, from the euent of things, that thoſe points were true, which the holy Prophets ſo long afore did foretell; ſo we ought be aſſured, that thoſe things ſhall infallibly come to paſſe, which the ſame men did propheſy herafter to be, though as yet they be not accompliſhed. For the Prophets did ſpeake not out of humane Witt, but from the Holy Ghoſt inſpiring them: and ſince the Holy Ghoſt is God, and that it is impoſſible, that God ſhould eyther be deceaued, or lye; therefore it demonſtratiuely followeth, that all

V 3   thoſe

those predictions are to be heerafter
fullfilled, which were foretould by the
Prophets in after tymes to fall out ,, &
yet are not fullfilled . *Sicut vsque ad*
hodiernum diem (saith *S. Augustin in*
*Psal.*76) *Euen as to this day all forwar-*
nings , and speaches of the Prophets haue
had their Euent ; so also those , which
yet remaine vnaccomplished , shall heer-
after haue. Let vs then feare the day of
Iudgement . Our Lord is to come ; He
came in humility, he shall come in splen-
dour and glory . Thus he,

But we haue more forcible argu-
ments, then the ancients had , that we
should not rest doubtfull of the Euent
of future things. Those men , who
went before the tymes of Christ, were
obliged to belieue many things without any experiment aforhand , but we
from the accomplishing and fullfilling
of things , which already haue happened, may easily belieue , that the rest
yet remaining , shalbe also fullfilled .
Those who liued in the dayes of *Noë,*
and did beare that the generall deluge
was after to be , *(Noë* being the Prophet of God and foretelling this very
thing, not only by word , but by causing with such labour the Arke to be
                                            made)

made) could not easily be induced to
belieue any such future inundation to
be, because they neuer saw any such
deluge before; & therefore the wrath
of God descended vpon them suddenly.
But we knowing that to haue beene
already fullfilled, which the Prophet
Noë did foretell, why may we not
with facility belieue, that a deluge of
of fyre shall heerafter come, in which
all those things shalbe destroyed, which
we now esteeme and prize at so high a
rate? And yet neuerthelesse there are
very few, who so belieue these things
to be, as to withdraw their desire from
such matters, as are heerafter to perish,
and to fix their minds, where there are
true and euerlasting Ioyes.

But this very Point is prophesied of
our Lord himselfe, that such men may
rest inexcusable, who from the accom-
plishment of things past, can not be
drawne to belieue that thinges future
shalbe fulfilled. For thus our Lord speaketh. *Matth. 24. And as in the dayes of
Noë, so also shall be the comming of the Son
of man: for as they were in the dayes before the floud, eating and drinking, wedding and giuen to mariage euen vnto
that day, in which Noë entred into the
Arke,*

Arke, and knew not till the floud came, and ouer tooke them all : so also shall the comming of the Sonne of man be. VVatch therefore, because you know not at what houre the Sonne of man will come. And the Apostle S. *Peter* sayth : *The day of our Lord shall come as a thiefe, in which the Heauens shall passe with great violence, but the elements shallbe resolued with heate, and the earth, & the works which are in it, shalbe burned.* 2. Pet. 3. But men, who sleight these thinges, say : these are farre off, and of great distance from vs. Be it, that they are farre of from vs, yet thy death is not farre of from thee, and the houre of it is vncertaine ; And yet it is certayne, that we must giue an account of euery idle word in the particular iudgment, which is not farre off. And if an account must be rendred of euery idle word, what reckoning must be made for false & pernicious words, for periury & blasphemy which is so familiar & ordinary to many? & if of words, what account then is to be giuen of deeds? of Adulteries ? of deceits in buying & selling? of murders and other grieuous sinnes ? Therefore it followeth, that the predictions of the Prophets being already

allready fulfilled make vs inexcusable,
except we may certainly belieue, that
all things which remaine, are also fulfilled .

Neyther it is sufficient to belieue,
what things Fayth teacheth vs to be
practized, or to be auoyded, except
our fayth doth stirre vs vp efficaciously
to the practizing or auoyding thereof.
If an Architect should say ; Such a
house is ruinous, and will instantly fall
downe , and they within the House
make shew to belieue the Architect ,
yet wil not come out of the house, but
suffer themselues to be oppressed with
the ruine and fall of the house ; what
credit do these men giue to the words
of the Architect ? Which errour the
Apostle chargeth other lyke men with
saying , *Tit. 1. They say they know God,
but in deeds they deny him.* And if the
Physitian shal command, that the sicke
Patient drinke no wyne ; and he is
persuaded, that the Physitian prescri-
beth profitably & healthfully for him ;
but in the meane tyme he demandeth
for wine, and is angry if it be not giuen to him : what shall we heere say?
Certainly that the sicke man is eyther
depriued of his wit and senses, or that
                    X   he

he giueth no credit to his. Physitians directions. O would to God, there were not many among Christians, who say, , that they do beleue the future Iudgment of God, and diuers other mysteries of Christian fayth; but deny them in their deeds, and conuersation.

Of the second fruite of the sixt Word.

CHAP. XIV.

ANother fruite may be gathered from the second explication of the words of Christ, *Consummatum est* For we said aboue with *S. Chryso stome* that the laboursome iourney of the peregrination of Christ himselfe was *consummate*, and finished in the death of Christ; which iourney of his cannot be denyed, but to haue beene most painefull aboue all measure: yet the asperity of it is recompensed with the shortnes of the tyme, with the fruit, with the glory and honour proceeding from thence. It continued thirty three yeares; but how can a labour

bour of thirty three yeares be compa-
rid to a repofe and reft for all eternity?
Our Lord did labour with hunger ,
with thirft , with many dolours , and
innumerable iniuries; with ftripes ,
with wounds, with death its felf; but
now he drinketh of a *Torrent of pleafure*, which pleafure fhall neuer ceafe,
but be interminab'e.

To conclude , our Lord *is humbled,
is made the reproach of men , and the
out-caft of the People.* Pfal. 21 . but in
recompence heerof we read of him
thus: *God hath exalted him , and ha.h
giuen him a Name , which is aboue all
Names , that in the Name of IESVS
euery knee bow , of things in Heauen,in
Earth, & vnder the Earth* . Philip. 2.
But now to caft our Eye on the contrary fide : the perfidious Iewes reioyced til the houre of Chrifts Paffion; *Iudas* (being become a flaue to coue-
toufnes) reioyced, till he had gayned
fome few pecces of filuer; *Pilate* reioyced till that houre of Chrifts Paffiő,
becaufe he loft not thereby the fauour
and grace of *Auguftus* , and had reco-
uered the friendfhip of King *Herod* .
But now all thefe haue beene already
tormented in Hell for the fpace of fix-

teeene hundred veares almost, and the
smoke of their flames shall arise and
ascend vp for all Eternity.

From hence let all the seruants of
the *Crosse* learne to be humble, gentle,
patient, and let them ackowledge how
good & happy a thing it is for a man
to take vp his owne Crosse in this present lyfe, and to follow Christ his
Captaine: neither let them enuy those
who seeme in the Eye of this worrld
to be happy. For the lyfe of Christ, of
the holy Apostles, and the Martyrs is
a most true Comentary of the words
of him, who is the Maister of all Mai-
sters : *Blessed are the poore in spirit, for
theirs is the Kingdome of Heauen: Blessed are the meeke, blessed are they that
mourne; biessed are they that suffer per-
cutiõ for Iustice, for theirs is the Kingdome of Heauen.* Matth. 5 But on the
contrary side : Wee *be to you that are
rich; because you haue your consolation:
woe to you that are filled, because you
shalbe hingry : woe to you that now do
laugh, because you shall mourne and lament.* Luc. 6 And although not only
the words of Christ, but also the life
and death of Christ (I meane, not only the Text, but the Comment also) be
vnder-

vnderstood of few, and that this doctrine is banished out of the Schooles
of this world; neuertheles if a man
would in soule goe out of this world,
and vse a serious introuersion vpon
himselfe, and say to himselfe: *I will
heare, what our Lord God will speake
in me.* Psal. 84. And withall would
with humble prayer and lamentation,
beate at the Fares of our Heauenly
Maister (who is both the *Text*, and
the *Comment*) he then would not with
difficulty vnderstand the Truth, and
the Truth would free him from all er-
rours; so as that should not seeme hard
to him, which afore seemed impossible.

Of the third fruite of the sixt Word.

CHAP. XV.

NOw the third fruite, which we
may gather from the sixt woads,
is that our selfs may learne, as being
spirituall Priests, to offer to God spirituall Hoasts, as *S. Peter* speaketh, 1.
Pet. 3. Or as the Apostle *S. Paul* teach-

eth vs : *To exhibe our Bodies , a liuing.
Hoast , holy , pleasing God, our reasonable seruice.* For if those words , *consummatum est ,* did signify , that the
sacrifice of the Chiefe Priest was perfected vpon the Crosse ; then it is iust,
that the disciples of him that was crucifyed , as coueting to imitate their
maister to their small hability , should
also offer vp sacrifice to God. And certainly the Apostle *S. Peter* teacheth
that all Christians are Priests; meaning , not such as those are , who are
created by Bishops in the Catholicke
Church to offer vp the Sacrifice of the
Body of Christ; but spirituall *Priests ,*
that is as himselfe expoundeth , to offer vp *spirituall Hoasts ;* nor Hoasts
properly called , such as were in the
Old Testament, as *sheep, oxen, turtles,
doues ,* and in the new Testament, the
Body of Christ in the *Eucharist :* but
mysticall Hoasts , which may be exhibited by all men , as Prayers, laudes,
good workes , fasting , Almesdeeds
&c. Of which S. *Paul* thus speaketh
Heb. 13. *By him therefore let vi offer al-
waies the Hoast of prayer to God , that
is to say, the fruite of the lips confessing
his Name.* But the same Apostle teach-

eth

eth vs in his Epistle to the *Romans*,
most accurately, to offer a mysticall sacrifice to God, euen from the consideration of our Bodies : for there were
foure lawes or necessary conditions of
Sacrifices . The first, that an Hoast be
present in the sacrifice, that is, a thing
dedicated to God, the which was impiety to conuert to any prophane vse.
Another was . that it should be a liuing thing, as a sheep, a Goate, a
Calfe. The third, that it should be
holy, that is, cleane : for among the
Hebrews some were accounted cleane
Creatures, others vncleane . The
cleane liuing Creatures were sheep,
Oxen, Goates, Turtles, sparrowes, doues; and the rest were taken as im
pure and vncleane, as Horses, Lions,
Foxes, Birds liuing by pray, Crowes,
and the like . The fourth, that the
Hoast should be enkindled and set on
fire, that so it might send forth an o-
dour of sweetnes. And all these the
Apostle doth reckon, when he saith :
I beseech you exhibit your bodies, a li-
uing Hoast, holy, pleasing God, & then
addeth, *your reasonable seruice*; to the
end we may vnderstand him, not to
counsell vs to a sacrifice properly cal-

led, as if he did meane, that our Bodies (like vnto sheep sacrificed) should
be truly slaine, and burned, but to ex
hort vs to a mysticall sacrifice and ra-
tionall; to a sacrifice only by resem-
blance, not proper; spirituall, not corporall. Therefore the Apostle, per-
suadeth vs, that as Christ for our
health, did offer vp the Sacrifice of his
owne Body vpon the Crosse, by a true
and reall death; so ought we to offer
vp our Bodies to his honour, as a certaine Hoast, liuing, holy, and perfect,
and therin pleasing to God; the which
Hoast after a certaine spirituall manner, may be said to be slaine, & burned.

Let vs explicate in order the seuerall conditions. First our Bodies ought
to be Hoasts, that is, things consecrated to God; the which, not as our own
but as the things of God, we are to
vse to the glory of God; to whome
we are consecrated by Baptisme; and
who bought vs with a great price, as
the same Apostle saith, 1. Cor. 6. Neyther ought vve to be an Hoast of God,
but vvithall a liuing Hoast through the
lyfe of grace, and the Holy Ghost. For
those men, vvho are dead through
sinne, are not the Hoasts of God,
but

but of the Deuill, who mortifieth their
soules, and much glorieth therein. But
our God, who euer liueth, and is the
fountaine of life, will not haue stin-
king Carcasses to be offered to him,
which are profitable for nothing, but
to be cast out to the Beasts: Therefore
it is necessary, that we conserue the
life of the soule with all diligence,
that by this meanes we may exhibit
to our Lord our *Reasonable Seruice.*

Neither is it required only, that the
Hoast be liuing, but also it must be *holy*,
as the Apostle sayth: *liuing, & holy.* The
Hoast is said to be holy, when it is offered of *cleane* liuing Creatures, not
of *vncleane.* Now the cleane Creatures, which are fourefooted, as aboue
we said, were *sheepe, Goates, Oxen,* of
Birds, *Turtles, sparrowes, Doues.* The
first sort of these liuing Creatures do
figure out an Actiue life; the second a
Contemplatiue. Therefore those men,
who do lead an Actiue life among the
faythfull, if so they will exhibit themselues a holy sacrifice or Hoast to God,
they ought to imitate the simplicity
and gentlenes of the *Lambe*, which is
ignorant how to hurt its fellow. In like
sort they are to imitate the labours &

paines of the *Oxe*, which is not idle, nor wandreth here and there, but bearing his yoake, and drawing after him the plow, laboreth continually in tilling the ground. To conclude the promptitude and agility of the *Goate*, in clyming of mountaines, and the sharpnes of eyes in beholding things afar of

Neither those men, who lead an Actiue life in the Church of God, ought to content themselues with meeknes, and iust labours, but it behoueth them also by their often iterated and multiplied prayers, to ascend high, and to fixe their eyes vpon those things, which be aboue. For how shall they refer their works to the glory of God, and send vp the incense of their sacrifice, if seldome or neuer they thinke on God? If through Contemplation they do not burne in loue towards him? For the Actiue life of Christians ought not to be wholy disioyned, and separated from the Contemplatiue life, nor the Contemplatiue from the Actiue, as presently hereafter we will shew. Therefore those men, who do not imitate *Sheepe*, *Oxen*, *Goates*, *Doues*, and the like, which are daily

serui-

feruiceable and profitable to their
owner or maifter, but purfue & hunt
after temporall benefits; thefe men
cannot offer vp to God a holy Hoaft,
but they beare themfelues like to ra-
uenous Beafts feeding vpon flefh, as
VVolues Dogs, Beares, Gleads, Vulturs,
Crowes, who pamper their Bellyes, &
follow that Lyon, *which roaring goeth*
about, feeking whom he may deuoure.
1. Pet. 3.

Now Chriftian men, who haue
chofen to themfelues a Contemplatiue
life, and who endeauour to exhibit to
God a liuing and holy Sacrifice, are to
imitate the folitude and lonelines of
the *Turtle,* the purity of the *Doue,* and
the prudence of the *Sparrow.* The folitude of the *Turtle* chiefly belongeth
to Monkes and Hermits, who labour
not to communicate with fecular men,
but wholy deuote themfelfes to Contemplation, and to the prayfes of God.
The Purity of the *Doue,* conioyned
with fecundity, is neceffary for Bifhops
and Clergy men, who negotiate with
men, and whofe function is to beget
fpirituall Children, and to nourifh and
breed them vp. Which men, except
they do often by Contemplation fly

vp

vp to the supernall Countrey, as also
through Charity to descend downe to
the Necessities of men; can hard'y
coople and ioyne purity with fecundity, but either as being giuen to Contemplation only, they shal beccme ste-
rill and barren; or otherwise being
wholy bused in the procreation of
Children, they shalbe contaminated
and defiled, with terrene dyrt & filth;
And thus while they couet to gaine o-
thers, perhaps (which God forbid)
they loose themselues.

Furthermore to both sorts of these
men, whether they giue themselues
ouer to a Contemplation life, or to an
Actiue, the Prudence of the *Sparrow*
may very much aduantage and benefit them. There are sparrows, which
are bred in the Mountaines; others a-
bout Houses. The Mountaine Sparrowes do with an incredible industry
auoyd and flie the snares or nets of
them, that secke to take them. The do-
mesticke sparrowes do make their
nests about the caues of howses; but
they so conuerse and liue nere men, as
that they loue not the sight of them,
nor will easely suffer themselfes to be
caught by them: Euen so the prudence
of

of Sparrowes is necessary to all Christians, but especially to the Clergy & Monks; that they may be cautelous in auoyding the deceites and snares of the Deuill, and that they so do conuerse with men, as they may profit them; but let them auoyde ouermuch familiarity & acquaintance with them, especially with Women. Let them also eschew all Confabulations, & ouer much tattle, as also immoderate eating and drinking; Let them not be spectatours of common Playes, and other publick sights, except they couet to be ensnared by the Deuill.

There remaineth the last law or Condition of sacrifices, to wit, That they be Hoasts, not only liuing & holy, but also *well pleasing*, that is, sending vp a most sweet Odour and smell. This point the Scripture signifieth, when it sayth, *Gen. 8. Our Lord smelled a sweet sauour*; As also when it speaketh of our Lord: *Christ deliuered himselfe for vs, an oblation and Hoast to God, in an odour of sweetnes. Eph. 5.* Now that an Hoast may send forth a most gratefull sauour vnto God, it is necessary, that it be killed and burned. This also is performed in a mysticall and reasonable

Sacri-

Sacrifice, of which we speake with the Apostle, to wit, when Carnall Concupiscence is truly mortified, and burnt away with the fire of Charity. For there is nothing, which doth mortify a mans Carnall Concupiscence more efficaciously, speedily, & perfectly, thē a sincere Loue of God: for it is the King and Lord of all the Affections of the Hart; and all of them are gouerned, and depend of it, whether it be Feare, Hope, Desire, Hate, Anger or any other perturbation of the mind. Novv loue it selfe doth not giue place, except it be to a greater loue; And therefore when diuine loue doth inwardly possesse and inflame the hart of man, then at the length do carnall Concupiscences giue place, and being mortified, rest quiet. Thereupon fiery desires and most pure Prayers do ascend vp to God, like to aromaticall wood in an odour of sweetnes. This then is that Sacrifice, the vvhich God requireth from vs, and the which most promptly and diligently to performe the Apostle exhorteth vs.

But because this Oblation is a thing hard, and fraught with difficulty, therefore *S. Paul* vseth a most efficacious

cacious Argument to perswade vs to
it, The argumēt lyeth in these Words:
*I beseech you by the mercy of God, that
you will exhibit your bodies &c. Rom.
12.* But which be they, and how many
are the Mercies, by which the Apostle
beseecheth vs? First, is our Creation, by
the which he made vs to be somç-
thing, vvhereas afore we were nothing. The second, when he made as
his scruants, he not hauing any need of
vs, but only that he might be benefi-
ciall vnto vs. The third, when he
made vs to his Image, and thereby
made vs capable of our knowing of
him and of his friendship. The fourth,
When he adopted vs his Sonnes
through Christ, and made vs Coheires
with his only begotten Sonne. The
fifth, when he made vs members of
his spouse, and of his Body, of both
which he is the Head. To conclude,
The sixt, in that he offered himselfe v-
pon the Crosse, an oblation and Hoast
to God, in an odour of sweetnes, that
he might redeeme vs from seruitude,
and wash away all our spots, and that
he might exhibit to himselfe, *A glorious Church, not hauing any spot or
wrinkle, Eph. 5.* These are the Mercies
of

of God, by which the Apostle beseecheth vs. As if he would say; Our Lord hath conferred vpon you so great benefits, you neither deseruing nor asking them; Why then should it be thought greiuous to you, if you offer your selfs, a liuing, holy, and well pleasing sacrifice to God? Doubtlessly if one would attentiuely ponder and consider these points, it would not be thought heauy and burdensome, but light and easy, yea pleasant to serue so good and bountifull a Lord with your whole hart and strength, throughout the whole tyme of your life; and to the imitation and example of him, to offer your selues, as an Hoast, or Oblation, yea an *Holocaust* in an odour of sweetnes.

Of the fourth fruite of the sixt VVord.

CHAP. XVI.

THE *Fourth Fruite* may be taken from the fourth explication of the Word, *Consummatum est*: For if it be true (as it is infallibly most true) that
Christ

Chrift through the iuft iudgement of
God did transfer and bring vs from the
feruitude of the diuell, to the future
fruition of the Kingdome of Heauen;
we are then diligently to fearch, & not
to defift, till we fynd, what is the caufe
that fo great a number of men make
choice, rather to deliuer themfelues
vp againe to the enemy of Mankind,
that with him they may eternally burn
in the fornace of Hellfire, rather then
to ferue Chrift, being a moft benigne
Lord, yea moft happily and vndoub-
tedly to reigne with him? I fynd no
other reafon heerof, then becaufe in
the feruice of Chrift, the beginning is
to be taken from the *Croffe*; and that
it is moft neceffarily incumbent vpon
vs, to crucify the flefh, with its vices
and concupifcences. This bitter Potion, or cup of wormewood of its
owne nature is moft vnpleafing to a
ficke Man; and often is the caufe, why
he had rather continue in his ficknes,
then to be cured after this manner.
Truly if a man were not a *Man*, but a
Beaft, or els a man depriued wholy of
his fenfes and wit, it might be more
pardonable for him, to feeke to be gouerned only by fenfuality and corpo-
X   rall

rall delights: but seeing man is partaker of reason; he vnderstandeth or ought to vnderstãd, that he who commãdeth the flesh to be crucifyed with its vices & cõcupiscences, is not ready only to command. but also to help, yea to preuent with the ayde of his grace; and also to direct, that the skilfull Physitian may know, how to temper this bitter cup, as that it may be taken & deunke vp without any fastidious difficulty.

Furthermore, if euery one of vs were the first to whome it was sayd: *Take vp the Crosse, & follow me. Math. 16.* Perhaps we might distrust of our owne force, and not be willing to touch the Crosse, as fearing we could not be able to support it. But seeing many before vs, not only men of full age, but euen children, and yong virgins, haue with great fortitude taken vp the Crosse of Christ, and haue borne it constantly, and haue crucified their flesh with their vices and concupiscences; why should we be afrayd? why should we be disanimated & dismayed thereat? S. *Austin* being ouerborne in iudgement with this argumét, did maister & ouerrule his carnall

con-

concupiſcence, which for a long tyme
he thought impoſſible to conquer. For
he propoſed to himſelfe beſore the
eyes of his mynd, many both men and
Women recorded in hiſtory, as moſt
continent and chaſt, and then in the
ſecret of his ſoule, he ſaid to himſelfe:
Cur non poteris, &c. Why art thou not
*able to performe, what theſe men and
women haue performed? They were not
able through their owne force, but
through the aſſiſtance of their Lord
God. Lib.*8 *Confeſſ c.* 11. And vvhat is
here ſpoken of the Concupiſcence of
the fleſh, the ſame may be ſaid of the
Concupiſcence of the *Eyes* (which is
couetouſnes or auarice) and of *Pryde
of lyfe:* ſince there is no Vice, which
may not be crucified and mortified;
through the help and ayde of God.
Neither is there any danger of the
want of Gods good concurrency therin, ſeing as S. *Leo* ſayth: *Iuſtè inſtat
præcepto &c. He may iuſtly command
that, which he furthereth with his
owne aſſiſtance. Serm.* 16. *de paſſ. Dom.*
They truly are miſerable (I may well
ſay, mad and fooliſh) who, when it is
in their povver to vndergoe the ſweet
& light yoake of Chriſt, & therby find

in this life rest to the Soule, and in
the next, reigne with the same
Christ; rather will subiect themselues
to the yoake of Oxen, at the command
of the Deuill, and to be thrall to flesh
and sensuality, and finally to be tormented in Hell (with their Lord the
Deuill) for all Eternity.

Of the fifth fruite of the sixt Word.

CHAP. XVII.

THe fifth fruit is to be collected
out of the foresaid Words, *Consummatum est*; as they do signify the
edification & building of the Church,
to be consummate and perfected vpon
the Crosse; & that the Church it selfe
did proceed from the syde of Christ
dying, as another *Eue* from the rib of
Adam sleeping. This Mistery teacheth
vs, that we reuerence the *Crosse*, that
vve honour the *Crosse*, that we prosecute the *Crosse* with all loue and affection. For who is he, that loueth not
the place, from whence his mother
came

came out? Certainly all good Catho-
likes are wōderfully affected towards
the most sacred House of *Loreto*, because in it the *B. Virgin*, Mother of
God, was borne; and because in it also
Iesus Christ, our Lord and God, was
borne, not out, but in the Virginall
Wombe. For thus the Angel speaketh
to *Ioseph: That which is borne in her, is
of the Holy Ghost. Matth. 1.* And here-
vpon the Church it selfe, being mind-
full of her owne birth or Natiuity,
doth paint and place the *Crosse* in euery place, on the fore-front, of Churches, &in houses; neither doth she mi-
nifier any Sacrament without the signe
of the *Crosse*; nor doth she sanctify or
blesse any Creature without the *Crosse*.

But we then especially do manifest
our great loue to the *Crosse*, when we
patiently suffer aduersity for the loue
of him, who was nayled, and dyed vpon the *Crosse*. For this is to glory in the
Crosse; to wit, to do that, which the
Apostles did, *They went from the sight
of the Councell, reioycing, because they
were accounted worthy to suffer reproach
for the Name of Iesus. Act. 5.* And the
Apostle *S. Paul* explicateth, what it is
to glory in the *Crosse*, when he saith,

Y 3 *Rom.*

Rom. 5. VVe glory in tribulations, know-
ing that tribulations worketh Patience;
Patience , *Probation ; and probation ,*
Hope: And Hope confoundeth not , be-
cause the Charity of God is powred forth
in our Harts , by the Holy Ghost , which
is giuen vs . And from hence it is, that
S.Paul writing to the *Galathians* thus
concludeth, *cap. 6. God forbid , that I*
should glory , sauing in the Crosse of our
Lord Iesus Christ, by whom the world is
crucified to me , and I to the World.
This is the triumph of *the Crosse*, if the
world with all its delights be (as it
were) deade to a Christian soule , louing Christ crucified ; and the Christian soule it selfe become deade to
the world, louing tribulation and contempt (which the World hateth) and
prosecuting with contempt carnall
pleasures, and temporall glory, which
the vvorld much loueth and admireth;
And thus it is brought to passe , that
the seruant of God is *consummated* &
perfected; so as it may be said of him
also, *Consummatus est .*

Of the sixt fruite of the sixt Word.

CHAP. XVIII.

THe last fruite remayning, is to be gathered from the Example of the Perseuerance of our Lord vpon the *Crosse*; since from that word, *Consummatum est*, we gather, that our Lord had consummated and finished the whole Worke of his Passion, euen from the beginning to the End; so as nothing more thereto could be desired or wished, *The works of God* (sayth *Moyses*) *are perfect. Deut.* 32. And euen as the Father, did perfect in the sixt day the vvorke of mans Creation, and vpon the seauenth did rest, So the Sonne in the sixt day did *consummate* the worke of mans Redemption, and vpon the seauenth did also rest. In vayne did the Iewes cry out before the *Crosse, If he be the king of Israell, let him now come downe from the Crosse.* But *S. Bernard* sayth more aptly *Serm.* 1 *de Resurrect.* Immò, quia Rex Israel est, &c. Yea because he is the King of Israel,

let

let him not loose the title of his King-
dome. And a litle after : *Non tibi dabis*
occasionem &c. Christ *will not giue oc-*
casion of depriuing thee of perseuerance,
which alone is crowned . He *will not*
cause the tongues to be silent of Prea-
chers , perswading and comforting the
faint harted and weake, and saying to
euery of them : Looke *thou doest not*
forsake thy Place or Station ; the which
doubtlesly would follow , if they might
reply , Christ *hath forsaken his Place.*
Christ therefore perseuered vpon the
Crosse , till the end of his life , that he
might so *consummat*, and perfect his
owne Worke, as that nothing should
be wanting thereto and that he might
leaue after him a most admirable
Example of Perseuerance.

Truly it is an easy matter to perseuer and continue in sweet places, and
in doing pleasing Actions; but to perseuer, and constantly to remaine long
in labour and dolour, is most difficult.
But if we did know , what induced
Christ to perseuer vpon the *Crosse*, perhaps our selues would learne to beare
our *Crosse* perseuerantly, yea if it were
lawfull to hang vpon it euen vntill
death. If a man do cast his eyes only
vpon

vpon the *Crosse*, the Instrument of so
lamentable a death (being but seene)
it cannot but beget an horrour in his
hart. But if he looke vp with the eyes,
not so much of his body, as of his
soule, towards him who commandeth
vs to beare the *Crosse*, and towards
the place, whither the *Crosse* leadeth,
and to the fruit or benefit, which the
said *Crosse* produceth; then it is not a
thing hard or vngratefull, but easy &
pleasant to perseuer in kissing of the
Crosse, and perseuerantly to hang v-
pon the *Crosse*.

What therefore moued Christ so
incessantly , without complaining ,
to hang vpon the Crosse euen vntill
death ? The first cause heerof was the
loue towards his Father : *The cup ,*
which my Father hath giuen me (sayth
he) *wilt not thou, that I do drinke it ?*
Ioan. 18. Christ did loue his Father
with an ineffable loue; and with the
lyke loue was beloued of him. Therefore when Christ did see that cup to be
prepared for him , by his most good &
louing Father , he could not in any sort
suspect , but that it was giuen to him
for a most happy end, and to him most
glorious . Was it then any strange
thing

thing if he did drinke vp all the cup
most willingly : Furthermore , the Father made a mariadge for his Sonne ,
and espoused to him the Church , but
then bespotted , and wrinkled ; the
which neuerthelesse if he would diligently wash in the hoate bath of his
bloud, he should easily make it to be
glorious , *Not hauing eyther spot* , *or
wrinkle .Ephes.* 5. Therefore Christ loued his spouse giuen to him by his Father ; in regard whereof it was not
painefull to him , to wash away all
her spots with his bloud , that so she
might appeare beautifull and glorious

For if *Iacob* for the loue of *Rachel*
laboured seauen yeares in looking vnto the flooke and sheep of *Laban,* so as
he was almost confumed away with
heate and frost , and want of sleep ,
and if those so many yeares seemed to
him , but a few dayes in respect of the
greatnes of his loue, *Gen.* 2. I say if *Iacob* litle prized the labour and toyle
of seauen yeares for one *Rachel* ; what
wonder then is it , if the Sonne of
God would perseuer & continue three
houres vpon the Crosse for his Spouse
(the Church)) which was to become mother of many thousand holy
SONNES

Stanes of God? To conclude, Christ
did not respect only the loue of his Father, and of his Spouse, when he was
ready to drinke the cup of his Passion;
but also he had a regard to that most
eminent glory, and greatnes of Ioy neuer to be ended, to the which he was
to ascend by the meanes and instrumēt
of the *Crosse*, according to that sentence of his Apostle, *Philip. 2. He humbled himselfe, made obedient to death,
euen the death of the Crosse, For the
which thing God also hath exalted him,
and hath giuen him a Name, which
is aboue all Names; that in the Name of
Iesus euery knee shall bow, of things in
Heauen, in earth, and vnder the Earth,*

We may adioyne to the Example
of Christ the Example of the Apostles. *Saint Paul* reckoning the Crosses
of himselfe, and of the other Apost-
postles, thus contesteth: *Rom. 8. Who
then shall separate vs from the Charity
of Christ? Tribulation? or distresse? or
Famine? or Nakednes? or Danger? or
Persecution? or the Sword? As it is written, for we are killed for thy sake all the
day; we are esteemed as sheepe for the
slaughter.* And then the Apostle answereth: *But in all these things we haue*

Z 2 *ouer-*

ouercome, because of him, that hath loued vs. Thus the Apostles during their
continuing in their punishments, had
not their eyes so much fixed vpon the
punishments, as vpon the loue of God,
who loued vs, and gaue his Sonne for
vs. In like sort they had respect to
Christ himselfe, *Who loued vs, & gaue
himselfe for vs* The same Apostle writing to the *Corinthians* sayth : *I am replenished with consolation; I do exceedingly abound in ioy, in all our Tribulation. 2. Cor. 7.* But from whence commeth so great cōsolation, from whence
so great ioy, as that it almost taketh a-
way the sense and feeling of Tribulation? The Apostle answereth to this
demaund in an other place, saying :
*Because, that our tribulation, which is
momentary and light, worketh aboue
measure, exceedingly an eternall weight
of glory in vs 2. Cor. 4.* Therefore the
Contemplation of eternall glory,
which he did place before the eyes of
his mynd, was the cause, why tribulation did appeare to him to be but momentary and light. *Has cogitationes
&c.* (sayth S. *Cyprian*) VVhat persecution can ouercome these thoughts? what
torments are able to daunt them? l. &
mart.

mart. To all this may be referred the Example of *S. Andrew*, who beheld the *Croße* (whereupon he hanged two daies)not as an vnpleasant *Croße*, but saluted it, as a friend. And when the People endeauoured to take him off frem thence, he would not in any case suffer them, but continued hanging thereupon till death;Neither was this man imprudent and foolish, but most wyse,and full of the Holy Ghost.

Now from these examples of Christ, and his Apostles, all Christians may learne, bew they ought to beare themselues, when they cannot descend from their *Croße* ; that is, when they cannot be freed of their Tribulation without sinne. In the number of these are first Regular Persons, whose life being tyed to the vowes of *Pouerty*, *Chastity*,and *Obedience*, is reputed like vnto Martyrdome. In like sort married Persons, when through diuine Prouidence the husband hath gotten a harsh,cholerick,vnquiet (and almost intollerable) wyse: or the wyse hath a husband of a fierce, & rough disposition; and such was the husband of *S. Monica*, as *S. Austin* witnesseth. Againe,those that are slaues, condem-

ned

ned to perpetuall prison, or to the
Gallyes. In like sort, sicke Persons who
labour with some incurable disease.
And poore men, vvho cannot aspire to
riches but by stealth and thieuery. All
these (and such others in like case) if
they desire to suffer their *Crosse*, with
spirituall ioy, and great reward, let
them not looke vpon the *Crosse*, but
vpon him who hath layed the *Crosse*
vpon their shoulders. But he doubtlessly was God, who is our most louing
Father, and without whose Prouidence
nothing in this world is done. Now
the pleasure and will of God is best,
& ought to be most gratefull vnto vs.

Furthermore, all men ought to say
with Christ, *The Cup which my Father
hath giuen me, wilt thou not, that I
should drinke?* And with the Apostle
*In all these things we ouercome for his
sake, who loued vs.* Moreouer all men
ought, and may consider who cannot
depose and lay aside their *Crosse* without sinne, not so much the present labour, as the future reward, which
doubtlesly doth surmount all labour
and griefe of this present life, the A-
postle saying: *Rom. 8. The sufferings of
this time are not condigne to the glory to
come,*

come, that shalbe reuealed in vs. Who
speaking of *Moyses* in an other place,
thus writeth : *Moyses esteemed the re-*
proach of Christ greater riches, then the
treasure of the Egyptians ; for he looked
into the remuneration. Hebr. 11.

To conclude, we may produce for
the comfort of those men who are
constrained to vndergoe a heauy *Crosse*
for a long tyme , the example of two
men, who did lose their perseuerance,
and thereupon did fynd incomparably a farre greater *Crosse* . *Iudas* the
Betrayer of Christ, when he reflected
vpon himselfe, did detest his sinne of
Treachery, and not enduring the confusion and shame which he must suffer, if he would conuerse with the A-
postles and Disciples , did hang himselfe. So as he changed only , but a-
uoyded not the *Crosse* of the Confusion , which he did flie ; Since greater
Confusion shall follow him at the day
of iudgment , in the presence & sight
of all the Angels, and of men, when he
shalbe declared to be not only the
Betrayer of Christ , but withall his
owne Homicide or Butcher. And how
great blindnes then was it in him , to
auoyde a small confusion among a few

per-

persons; who being the Disciples of
Christ, were mild and gentle, & who
euer would haue beene ready to ex-
hort him to hope well of the Mercy
of the Sauiour of the world; but no:
to auoyde the infamy and confusion
of his betraying of Christ, & hanging
himselfe in the Theater and eye of all
men and Angels?

The second example may be ta-
ken out of the Oration of *S. Basill in*
40. Mart. The summe whereof is this.
In the persecution of *Licinius* the Emperour, fourty souldiers being resolued
to continue in the Fayth of Christ,
were condemned, that openly in the
ayre, without any shelter, in a most
cold tyme and place, they should spend
the whole night, and so through a
most long and sharp Martyrdome,
should perish through cold and frost.
There was prepared neere vnto the
place when they were, a hoat & comfortable Bath, to receaue such of the
souldiers, as would deny their Fayth.
Of the whole number of the souldiers thirty and nyne, setting before
their eyes not so much the present
punishment of being frozen to death
(which would in a short tyme be
ended)

ended) as the Eternity of glory and
happines, perseuered in their Fayth, &
receaued from the hands and bounty
of our Lord, most glorious Crownes.
Our souldier, who had his mind fixed
only vpon the present torment, could
not perseuere in his Christian fayth,
did thereupon leape into the warme
Bath. But he had no sooner gotten
thereinto, but that seuerall parts of
his flesh being already congealed, did
fall asunder, and the poore wretch
breathed out his Soule, and as denier
of Christ, descended into Hell and to
perpetuall torments. Thus he flying
death, he found death, and changed a
short and light *Crosse* or tribulation,
for an euerlasting and most grieuous
Crosse.

Now, all those do imitate these
two most vnhappy men who do forsake the *Crosse* of a religious Courfe
of life; who do cast off a sweet yoake
and easy burden, and when they least
thinke therof, they do find themselfes
to be tyed to a farre more grieuous
yoake of diuers Concupiscences and
Passions, which they can neuer satisfy,
and thus being pressed downe with
the most heauy weight of their sinnes,

Z 3   they

they are not able to breath, or take
wynd. The like reason is of all those,
who refuse to beare their *Crosse* with
Christ, and yet through sinning are
forced to beare a far more grieuous
Crosse with the Deuil!.

The seauenth Word; to wit, Pater,
  in manus tuas commendo Spiritum meum : *Father, into thy
  hands, I commend my Spirit.*
  Luke 23. *is litterally explained.*

CHAP. XIX.

VVE are now come the *last
Word* or Sentence of Christ,
which being ready to dye vpon the
Crosse he spake, not without great
clamour, saying : *Pater in manus tuas
cōmendo spiritum meū,* Father into thy
hands I commend my spirit. We will
explicate in order euery word. *Pater,*
he deseruedly calleth him *Father*, because himselfe was an obedient Sonne
to him, euen to death ; and therefore
most worthy that he should be heard.

In

In manus tuas , into *thy Hands.* The
Hands of God in the Scriptures are
said to be his *Intelligence* and *Will,* or
VVisdome and *Power* ; Or (which is
coincident herewith) the *Vnderstanding of God* knowing all things, and his
Will, being able to performe or do all
thinhs: For with these two, God as not
wanting Instruments otherwise, doth
all things ; because as S. *Leo* speaketh:
In Deo Voluntas, Potentia est : In God
his Will is his Power. *Serm.* 2 *de Natiu.* Therfore with God, *to will* a thing
is *to doe* a thing, according to that : *He
hath done all things , whatsoeuer he
would. Psal.* 113. *Commendo,* That is, I
do commend or deliuer vp in pledge,
that it may be restored with trust,
when the tyme of restitution shall
come.

Spiritum meum , Touching this
word, how it is here to be taken, there
is no small Controuersy. The word,
Spiritus, is accustomed to be taken for
the *Soule,* vvhich is the substantiall
forme of the Body , as also it is taken
for life it selfe : and the reason hereof
is, because breathing is a signe of lyfe;
and who do breath, do liue ; and who
ceafe to breath, do dye. And certainly
if

if by the word *Spirit*, vve vnderstand
in this place the *Soule* of Christ, we
are to take heed, that no man should
imagine there were any danger for
that soule to goe out of its body: As
when other men are in dying, their
soule is accustcmed to be commended
to God, through many Prayers, and
great Care, in that it goeth to the Tribunall of the Iudge, ready to receaue
for its good, or wicked works, Glory,
or Punishment. Such a Comenda-
tion as this, the soule of Christ did not
need; both in that it was blessed from
the beginning of its Creation; as also
becaufe it was ioyned in *Person* with
the Sonne of God, and might be called, the *Soule of God:* and lastly by reafon, as victorious and triumphing. it
went out of its Body, and was a terrour to all the Deuills, but they could
be no terrour to it. Therefore if the
Spirit be taken in this place for the
Soule, then these words of our Lord,
Commendo spiritum meum, do signify,
that the Soule of Christ, which vvas in
its Body, as in a Tabernaele, was to be
in the hands of the Father, as *in depo-
fito*, vntill it did returne to the Body,
according to that, *Sap. 3. The soules of*
the

the lust are in the hands of God.

But it is much more credible, that
by the word *Spirit*, in this place *corpo-*
rall life is vnderstood, so as the sense is
to be this: I do now deliuer vp the spirit of my life, and therein I cease to
breath and to liue: But this *spirit*, this
life (*O Father*) I commend to thee,
that within a short tyme thou mayst
restore it to my Body: For to thee nothing is lost, but all things do liue to
thee, who in calling out that which
is not, makest it be; and in calling
out that, which doth not liue, makest
it to liue. That this is the true meaning
of this place, may first be gathered out
of the 30. *Psalme*, from whence our
Lord did take this Prayer. For thus
Dauid doth there pray: *Thou wilt bring*
me out of this snare which they haue hid
for me, because thou art my Protectour;
Into thy hands I commend my spirit. In
which place the Prophet by the *spirit*,
most euidently vnderstandeth *lyfe*; for
he prayeth to God, that he will not
suffer him to be slayne by his Enemies
but that he will preserue his lyfe. Furthermore the same point is deduced
as true, euen from this place of the
Gospell. For after our Lord had said;

Father,

Father, into thy hands I do commend my
spirit, the Euangelist did subioyne :
And saying this, he gaue vp the Ghost;
For *to giue vp the Ghost* signifieth to
cease to draw spirit or wynd, which is
proper to those Creatures which are
liuing; the vvhich thing cannot be
said of the soule, the substantiall forme
of the Body; but it is said of the ayre
which vve *breath*, vvhilst we liue; and
we do cease to *breath*, vvhen we dye.

Last'y the foresaid exposition is gathered from those words of the Apostle, *Hebr.* 5. *Who in the dayes of his*
flesh, with a strong cry and teares, offe-
ring prayers and supplications to him,
that could saue him from death, was
heard for his reuerence. This place
some do vnderstand of the prayer,
which our Lord made in the garden,
saying : *Father, if it be possible, trans-*
ferre this Chalice from me, Mar. 14.
But in that place our Lord did not pray
with a strong cry, neither was he
heard, neither would he haue beene
heard, that he should be free & exempted from the death. For he prayed
that the Chalice of his Passion might
passe from him, thereby to shew a naturall desire of not dying, and himselfe
to

to be true man, whose nature doth abhorre death: But he added; *Not that which I will, but that which thou, let thy Will be done*. Thus we see, that the prayer of Christ in the garden cannot be that Prayer, of which the Apostle speaketh to the Hebrews.

Others maintaine, that that prayer of Christ mentioned by *S. Paul*, is the same, vvhich our Lord made for his Crucifiers vpon the Crosse, saying: *Father forgiue them, for they do not know what they doe. Luc.23.* But at that time our Lord did not vse any strong crye, neither did he pray for himselfe, that he might be saued from death; both which two points are euidently expressed by the Apostle to the Hebrews. For being vpon the *Crosse*, he prayed for his Crucifiers, that that most grieuous and heauy sinne might be pardoned to them. Therefore it remaineth, that those words of the Apostle be vnderstoode of that last prayer, which our Lord made vpon the Crosse, saying, *Father into thy hands I commend my spirit*; the which prayer he made with a strong crye, *S. Luke* saying: *And Iesus crying with a loud voice, said &c.* Where vve see, that *S. Paul* and *S. Luke* do do clearely herein agree tog ather.

Furthermore our Lord prayed, that he might be saued from death, as S. *Paul* doth witnesse, but the meaning hereof cannot be that he should not dye vpon the *Crosse*; for therein he vvas not heard, & yet S. *Paul* testifieth that he was heard; but the meaning is, that he prayed, that he might not be vvholy absorpt vp by death, but only might tast death, and presently returne to life; For thus much is implied in those words: *He offered vp prayers to him, that could saue him.* For our Lord could not be ignorant, but that he was to dye, especially being then most neare to death; but he coueted to be safe from death, in this sense; to wit, that he might not be detayned long by death; which was nothing else, but to pray for a speedy Resurrection; in which his prayer he was fully heard, since he did rise most gloriously the third day. This explication of the testimony of S. *Paul* euidently conuinceth, that when our Lord said, *Into thy hands I command my spirit*, the *spirit* is taken for *Lyfe*, not for the *Soule*. For he was not sollicitous of his soule, the vvhich he did knovv to be in safety, since it

was

was most blessed, and did see God face to face euen from its Creation ; but he was sollicitous and carefull of his Body, which he savv vvas to be depriued of lyfe through death ; and therefore he prayed, that his Body might not long remaine in death, the vvhich petition (as aboue we said) he in a most full manner obtayned.

The first fruite of the seauenth Word.

CHAP. XX.

NOw according to our former Method, I wil gather some fruits from this Last word of Christ, & from his death presently ensuing. And first, euen from that thing, which seemeth to be most full of infirmity, weaknes, and simplicity, the great Power, Wisdome, and Charity of God is demonstrated. For in that our Lord gaue vp the Ghost, crying with a great Voyce, his Power and strength is manifestly discerned; since from this vve may gather, that it vvas in his povver not to dye, and that he dyed willingly. For

A a those

those men, vvho dye naturally, do lose
by degrees their force and voyce, and
in their last agony & fight vvith death,
they are not able to cry out with anʸ
great and vehement speach or Voyce.
Therefore not without cause the *Centurion* seeing, that Iesus after so much
profusion of Bloud, vvith a great and
loyvd voyce dyed, said: *Certainly, this
was the Sonne of God. Mar.* 15. Chrift is
a great Lord, vvho euen dying sheweth his povver, not only by crying
out with a great Voyce at his last breathing; but also in cleauing the Earth,
cutting a sunder the stones, opening
the Monuments, and in rending the
Veyle of the Temple, all vvhich things
to haue fallen out euen at the very
tyme, vvhen Chrift dyed, the Euangelist witnesseth.

Furthermore all these strange Euents haue their mistery, by vvhich the
Wisdome of Chrift is manifested. For
the concussion of the Earth, as also the
cleauing of the stones did signify, that
by the Passion and death of Chrift,
men vvere móued and stirred vp to
pennance, and the harts of the obstinate vvere euen cut a sunder, vvhich
Effects at that very time to haue happened,

pened, *S. Luke* writeth, when he
fayth, that many returning from that
fpectacle and fight, *did knock their
breafts*. The opening of the graues &
fepulchers doth defigne the glorious
Refurrection of the dead to fucceed
after that of Chrift. The tearing or rending of the Veyle (whereby was dif-
couered the *Sancta Sanctorum*) was a
figne that through the merits of the
death of Chrift, the Celeftiall Sanctuary was to be opened, and that all the
Saints were after to be admitted to
fee the face of God. Neither only in the
fignification of thefe Myfteries did
Chrift fhow his Wifdome; but alfo in
that he did produce & draw life from
death, in figure whereof *Moyfes* caufed
water to flow out of a ftone. And
Chrift himfelfe for the fame Caufe
faid, he refembled a graine of wheate,
in that by dying, he brought forth
much fruite. For as a graine of wheate
by being corrupted, doth bud forth an
eare of liuing Corne ; fo Chrift by dying vpon the Croffe, enriched multi-
tudes of Natiõs with the life of Grace,
& *S. Peter* moft manifeftly thus fpeaketh of Chrift: *He fwallowing death,
that we might be made heyres of life*

enfu-

euerlasting. 1. *Pet*. 3. As if he would
haue said; The *First man* swallowing
the forbidden sweet apple, condemned all his posterity to death; But the
second Man swallowing downe the
bitter apple of death, brought all those
to eterna l life, who were borne a-
gaine of him.

To conclude, Christ manifested &
opened his Wisdome in dying, because he made the *Crosse*, (then the
which nothing was before more des-
picable and contemptible) most honourable and glorious ; so as euen
Kings themselues do account it an honour to signe their Foreheads there-
vvith. Neither is the *Crosse* made only
honourable, but also svveet to the lo-
uers of Christ; Whereupon the Chutch
thus singeth: *Dulce lignum, dulces cla-
uos, dulce pondus sustinxit*. The which
very point S. *Andrew* demonstrated
by his ovvne example , when behoul-
ding the *Crosse*, vnto vvhich he was to
be fastened said : *Salue Crux preciosa
&c. All haile*, O *precious Crosse, which
hath receaued honour and beauty from
the members of our Lord; Thou art long
desired, and carefully sought after; thou
art loued without any intermission, and*
                                        comes

cemes prepared to a willing mind. I approach *to thee with security and ioy, that thou exulting mayst receaue me, being the disciple of my Maister Iesus Christ, who did hang vpon thee.*

Now what shall we speake of Charity? The sentence of our Lord is this: *Greater Charity then this no man hath, that a man yield his life for his friends.* Ioan. 15. This Christ performed vpon the Crosse, since no man could against his Will, depriue him of life. For himselfe thus sayth hereof: *No man taketh my life from me, but I yield it of my selfe.* Ioan. 10. Therefore as aboue is said no man hath greater Charity, then he, that yieldeth his life for his friēds, because nothing can be found more precious, and to be beloued, then Life, it being the foundation of all goods. *For what doth it proffit a man* (sayth our Lord) *if he gaine the whole world, and sustaine the domage of his soule,* that is, of his *lyfe?* And from hence it is, that all things labour to resist with all their strength (yea aboue their strength) those, who do endeauour to take away their lyfe. And we read in Iob: *Skinne for skinne, and all things, which a man hath, he will giue for his*

A a 3   *lyfe.*

lyfe. But these passages are generall, vve vvill descend to particulars.

Chrift did ineffably fhew by many meaacs to all mankind, and to euery one of vs , his Charity by dying vpon the *Croffe.* First becaufe his life vvas the most precious of all liues ; as being the *lyfe* of man, vvho vvas God, the *lyfe* of the most potent King of Kings, *the lyfe* of the most wifeft of all the Doctours . Furthermore he gaue his *lyfe* for his Enemies , for wicked men, for vngratefull men; Againe , he laid dovvne *his lyfe*, that he might deliuer thefe his Enemies, wicked & vngratefull men, from the burnings, and torments of Hell , to the which they vvere already condemned. Laftly , he gaue *his lyfe*, that he might make thefe men to become his Brethren and Coheyres, and moft happily place them in the kingdome of Heauen for all E-ternity. And is there any man of that flinty, or fauage nature, who from this tyme vvill not loue Chrift Iefus with all his Harts, and will not fuffer any aduerfity for his fake? O *mercifull God*, auerr and turne fuch à ftony and iron hart, not ohly from our Brethren, but from all men whofoeuer , either Infidels, or Atheifts.   *The.*

The second fruite of the seauenth Word.

CHAP. XXI.

A N other fruite (and that moſt profitable) is, if we learne to vſe frequently that prayer, which our Lord taught vs, when being ready to goe to his Father, he ſaid: *Into thy hāds I commend my ſpirit.* But becauſe he was not preſſed and vrged with that Neceſſity, with the which we are vrged, ſince he was the Sonne, and Holy, we but ſeruants and ſinners : Therefore our Mother and Miſtreſſe (the Church) inſtructeth vs to frequent, and often vſe it, but as it is entire and whole in the Pſalme of Dauid, and not diuided, as our Lord pronounced it . In the Pſalme it is thus read: *Into thy hands I commit my ſpirit : Thou haſt redeemed me*, O *Lord God of Truth.* Pſal. 30. Chriſt did omit the later part , becauſe himſelfe was the Redeemer , and not the party redeemed, but we, who are redeemed with his moſt precious bloud, ought not to pretermit this part of the

the Pfalme. Chrift alfo prayed to his Father, as his only begotten fonne, We pray to Chrift, as our Redeemer: therfore we fay not, *Father into thy hands I commend my spirit* ; But, *into thy häds O Lord I commend my spirit, thou haft redeemed me O Lord God of Truth.* According to which manner of fpeach *S. Steuen* (the firft Martyr) being ready to dye, faid : *Lord Iefus receaue my spirit. Act.* 7.

Furthermore our Mother (the holy Church) teacheth vs to fay this Prayer at three feuerall tymes . Firft, euery day at the *Complyme*, as thofe vvell knovv vvho read the Canonicall Howers. Againe, when we approach to the moft holy Eucharift, after thofe words are faid : *Domine non fum dignus,* The Prieft firft for himfelte, and atter for the Communicants doth fay : *in manus tuas commendo spiritum meum.* Laftly at our departure out of this lyfe, all the faithfull are admonifhed, that they fay, *In manus tuas commendo spiritum meum.* As concerning the Complyme, it is not to be doubted, but that there is faid , *In manus tuas Domine &c.* becaufe the *Complime* is accuftomed to be read tovvards the

end

end of the day; and as S. *Basill* speaketh, *Primis se intendentibus tenebris &c. Assoone as darknes commeth: & because it may so fall out, that in the night tyme vnexpectedly death may surprize vs; therefore we commend our soule to our Lord, that if so sudden death might happen to vs, it might not happen to vs vnforseene, in Reg. fusius explic.q. 37.* That at the tyme of receauing the most Blessed Eucharist, is said: *In manus tuas commendo &c.* the reason is, because that action is very dangerous, and withall very necessary, so as without perill it cannot often be frequented or intermitted: *For he, that eateth the Body of our Lord vnworthily, eateth iudgment to himselfe.* 1. *Cor.* 11. That is, he eateth condemnation to himselfe. And againe, *He that eateth not the body of our Lord, eateth not the bread of lyfe, and life it selfe. Ioan.* 9. Thus vve are brought to straits on ech syde; being partly like to those men, who suffer extremity of hunger, and yet are vncertaine, whether that which is brought to them to eate, be meate or poyson. Therefore with iust reason we say with feare and trembling: *O Lord, I am not worthy that*

B b   *thou*

thou shouldest enter into my house, except out of thy ineffable goodnes thou wilt make me worthy; therefore, *say the word, and my soule shalbe healed.* But because of this I also doubt, whether thou wilt vouchsafe to cure my **wounds**, *I commend my spirit into thy hands*, that so in this terrible busines thou mayst be present to my soule, which thou *hast redeemed with thy precious Bloud.*

Yf men would ponder these things maturely, they would not so greedily approach to receaue Priesthood, that by daily celebrating they might maintaine their corporal state; For such men are not accustomed to be much carefull (as they ought to be) whether they come with due preparation, since their End is rather the meate of the Body, then the meate of the Soule. There are also many, who attend vpon Prelats and Princes, who perhaps do not come rightly prepared to this dreadfull table; yet they approach to it, as drawne through a humane feare, least they may displease their Prince or Prelate, if at the appointed, and accustomed tyme, they be not present among, and one of those who are to commu-

communicate. What therefore is to be
done? It may be, it were more profitable to come to that table more rarely.
Yea but it is more profitable often to
frequent that table, so it be with reuerence & due preparation: For by how
much one commeth more rarely, by so
much he is made lesse apt to participate of that Heauenly Table, as *S. Cy-
ril* hath wisely admonished. *lib.* 4, *in
loan c.* 17.

There now remaineth the tyme
of neare approaching or imminent
death, at what time it is necessary with
great feruour of mind, frequently and
often to repeate and say: *Into thy hāds
I commend my Spirit; thou hast redemed me, O Lord God of truth.* That is
the tyme, in which the chiefest busines
of all is hādled : for if it should so happen, that the soule departing out of
the Body, commeth into the hands of
the Deuill, there is no hope left of Saluation. And contrariwise, if it haue its
passage to the paternall Hands of God,
no povver of mans Ghostly Enemy is
after to be feared. Therefore with an
inutterable moaning , vvith true and
perfect Contrition, with a strong fayth
and confidence in the infinite mercy

of God, it is againe, and againe to be
iterated and repeated; Into thy hands,
O Lord, I commend my spirit: And because at that instant of tyme, those
vvho haue led a negligent and care-
lesse life, do suffer no greater temptation, then of despayre, as if the tyme
of Pennance and repentance were then
past; Let such oppose against this temptation the buckler of Fayth, since it is
written : In what day soeuer the sinner
shall repent, I will not remember his sinnes: Ezech. 33. Let them also take the
Helmet of Hope, which trusteth in the
boundles Mercy of God, and let them
often repeate : Into thy hands, I commend my spirit; neither is that reason,
which is the foundation of our Hope,
to be omitted; to wit, Because thou hast
redeemed me, O Lord God of Truth. For
who vvill restore to Christ his innocēt
bloud? who vvi'l repay backe to him
the price with which he bought vs? For
so S. Austin speaketh, teaching vs in
those words, to confide much in our
Redemption, which is in Iesus Christ;
which cannot be in vayne, and fruit-
les, except our selues do put a barre or
hindrance therto, through Impeni-
tency, or Desperation.

The

The third fruite of the
seauenth Word.

CHAP. XXII.

THe third fruit is placed, in that
we may learne, that death neare
approaching, we are not much to confide in the Almes-deeds, Fastings, or
the prayers of our kinred & friends.
For there are many, vvho during the
vvhole course of their lyfe, are wholy
forgetfull of their soule; busiyng their
mynds with nothing els, but how to
leaue their wife, children, and K ns-
folks rich, & of great estate. But when
themselfes come to dye, then (& not
before) they begin to thinke of their
ovvne soule; And becaufe they haue
distributed and deuided their goods
& faculties among their forsaid friends
they commend the charge of their soules to them, that by their meanes their
soules might be helped with Almes-
deeds, Prayers, masses, and other good
workes. Christ did not teach vs this by
his example, since he commended his
soule not to his kinsmen, but to his
Bb 3   Father.

Father. Neyther doth *S. Peter* admonish vs; that we should commend our soules to our Children, or kinsfolkes, *but to the faythfull Createur , by good deedes* 1.Pet.4.

I do not say this, as reprehending those who either procure , or desire Almes-deedes,or sacrifices of the holy masse to be offered vp for them after their death : But I much blame those; vvho repose too much trust in their Children and kinsfolkes; since daily experience teacheth , that they quickly forget their dead Ancestours. I further reprehend them , because in a matter of so great importance , they will not prouide for themselues , and that they will not giue and performe the Workes of Charity , and Almesdeeds ,by which they may purchase many friends,by whose meanes as we read in the Gospell, *they may be receaued into the Eternall Tabernacles.* Luc, 16. I also greatly blame them, who do not obey the Prince of the Apostles, commanding vs,as is aboue said , *to commend our soules to our faythfull Createur,* and to commend them not only in words ,but also *in good Workes:* Since good works sent before to God, are

are thofe, which efficacioufly and truly
commend the foules of Chriftians to
God.

Let vs heare, what voyce founded
from Heauen to S. *Iohn,* *Apoc.*4. *I heard
a voyce from Heauen , faying to me,*
Write: *Bleffed are the dead, which dye
in our Lord: from hence now , fayth the
fpirit, that they reft from their labours,
for their works follow them.* Therefore
good works performed by our felfes,
whilft we liue (and not to be done
after our death by our Children , or
kinsfolkes) are thofe, which certainly
do follow vs: efpecially if thofe works
be of their owne nature not onely
good, but as *S. Peter,* not without miftery hath expreffed: for thus he fpeaketh,
*In bene factis commendent animas fuas
fideli Creatori* : *let them commendent
their foules to their fayth full Creatour,
by good deeds* ; meaning in works well
done. For there are many , who can
number many good Works by them
done, as many Sermons preached, many Maffes daily celebrated, their howers of prayers for many yeares , their
faft of Lent continued in like fort for
many yeares, their Almes-deeds, and
thofe not in number few . But when

these come to the diuine ballacing &
examination , and are precisely to be
discussed , whether they were well
done ; to wit , with right intentions,
with due attention, in fitting tyme and
place, proceeding from a man gratefull to God ; O how many things,
which did appeare to be gaines to the
soule, will rather be accounted , as losses and detriments vnto it ! And how
many things , which seemed in mans
iudgment to be gould, siluer, and precious stones , built vpon the founda-
tiō of fayth, will be found to be wood
& straw, which the fire will instantly
consume !

The consideration of this point
doth not a litle terrify me , & by how
much I draw more neare to my end
(for as the Apostle speaketh , *Heb. 8.*
That which groweth ancient, and wa-
xeth old , is nigh vnto vtter decay) so
much the more euidently I see , that
the admonition and Counsell of *S.*
Iohn Chrysostome is necessary to me ;
who councels vs , not to weigh and
prize to much our owne good works;
because if they be good works indeed
(that is, works vvell & piously done)
they are registred by God in his booke
of

of Accounts , and there is no danger,
that they shalbe defrauded of their
due reward : but let vs daily thinke
(sayth he) of our euill & bad works,
and labour vvith a contrite hart and
spirit, vvith many teares , and serious
pennance, to wash them away. For
such men , vvho performe his aduise
herein, shall say at the close and end of
their life vvith great confidence and
Hope : *Into thy hands I commend my*
spirit, thou hast redeemed me, O Lord
God of Truth.

Of the fourth fruite of the
seauen VVord.

CHAP. XXIII.

THere followeth the fourth fruite,
which may be gathered from the
most happy hearing of the prayer of
our Lord , that from so comfortable
an Euent all of vs may be much auima-
ted and encouraged to commend our
spirits to God with greater vehemency and ardour of deuotion. For the A-
postle did most truly write , that our
Lord *Iesus* Christ was heard , *for his*

Bb 5 *reue-*

reuerence. Heb. 5. Our Lord prayed to his Father for a speedy Resurrection of his Body, as aboue we haue shewed. His prayer was heard, so as his Resurrection was no longer delayed, then it was needfull to proue, that his Body was truly dead. For except it could be infallibly demonstrated, that his Body did truly depart out of this lyfe, both the Resurrection, as also the whole Christian Fayth might be doubted of, and called into question. Therefore our Sauiour was to remaine in the graue for the space at least of fourty houres; especially seeing the figure of *Ionas* the Prophet was to be accomplished, which (as our Lord himselfe taught in the Ghospell) was to premonstrate and foreshew his death.

But to the end, that the Resurrection of Christ might be accelerated & hastened so farre forth, as it was conuenient; and that it might be more manifestly proued, that the prayer of Christ was heard, the diuine Proui-dēce would, that the three dayes and three nights, during which tyme *Ionas* was in the Belly of the Whale, should be reduced in the Resurrection of Christ, to one entire and whole day, and two

parts

parts of two dayes; which time not
properly (but by the figure *intellectio*)
might be said to contayne three dayes
& three nights. Neither did the Father heare the prayer of Christ only
in shortning the tyme of his Resurrection, but also in restoring incomparably a better lyfe, then before he
enioyed. Since the lyfe of Christ before his death, was mortall, but it is
restored to him immortall: *Christ ri-*
sing againe from the dead, now dieth
no more; death shall no more haue do-
minion ouer him, as the Apostle speaketh. *Rom.*6. The lyfe of Christ before
his death, was passible, that is, subiect
to hunger, thirst, wearines, wounds;
but being restored impassible, it stāds
not obnoxious to any iniury. The Body of Christ was before death *Ani-*
male; but after the resurrection it became *spiritale*; that is, so subiect to
the *spirit*, as that in a twinkling of an
Eye, it might be caryed into any place,
where the spirit it selfe would.

Novv the reason, why the Prayer
of Christ was so easily heard, is subioy-
ned by the Apostle, when he sayth,
pro sua reuerentia, for his reuerence.
The Greeke word here vsed, (to
wit,

wit , ευλαβία) signifieth *a reuerentiall feare* , vvhich was most eminent
in Chrift tovvards his father. Therefore *Esay* describing the guifts of the
Holy Ghoft, which were in the soule
of Chrift, of other guifts thus sayth :
*The spirit of wisdome and Vnderstan-
ding shall rest vpon him : the spirit of
Counsell and Strength : the spirit of
Knowledge and Piety* ; but of *reuerentiall Feare* , the said Prophet thus
speaketh : *And the spirit of the Feare
of our Lord shall replenish him.* Isa. 11.
Novv becaufe the soule of Chrift was
moft full of *reuerentiall Feare* towards
his Father , therefore the Father did
take moft great pleafure in him , according to that we'read in *S. Matthew* :
*This is my beloued sonne, in whom I am
well pleafed.* Matth. 3. & 17. And euen
as the Sonne did euer reuerence the
Father in a moft high degree, so did the
Father euer heare him praying , and
granted whatfoeuer he desired.

Novv from hence may we learne,
that, if vve expect euer to be heard by
our heauenly Father , and to obtaine
whatfoeuer we demaund of him , we
ought to imitate Chrift herin , in pro-
fecuting our said heauenly Father with
                                    fupreme

supreme Reuerence, and in preferring nothing before his honour. For so it wilbe effected, that whatsoeuer we pray for, we shall obtaine, and peculiarly, that, in which consisteth the chiefest good of our state; I meane, that vvhen death shall approach, God may receaue our sou'e passing out of the Body, commended vnto him, vvhen the roaring Lyon standeth neere vnto vs, as being ready for a prey. Neither let any man thinke, that *Reuerence* is exhibited to God only in genuflection, or in bovving of the knee, in vncouering of the Head, or in any other worship and honour of such like nature. The word ευλαβϊα, or *timor reuerentialis*, doth not signify only this externall honour; but it chiefly denotes a great feare of offending of God, and an invvard & continua! horrour of sinne, and this not through dread of punishment; but through loue of our Celestiall Father. He is truly indued with *reuerentiall Feare*, who dare not thinke of offence or sinne, especially mortall sinne: *Blessed is that man* (sayth *Dauid*) *who feareth our Lord; He shall haue great delight in his Commandements:* That is, he truly fea-

reth

reth God (and in that respect may be called *Blessed*) who with all bent of Will and Endeauour, studies to keep all the Commandement of God. And from hence it proceeded, that that holy widdow *Iudith*, *timebat Dominum valde*, as we reade in her Booke *cap.* 8. For she being but a yong Woman, and of great beauty, and very rich, lest she should (after the death of her husband) either giue or take any occasion of sinning, did remaine shut vp with her maids in a secret chamber, and wearing a haire-cloath about her body, fasting all dayes, excepting the feasts of the house of *Israel*. Behould here with what great zeale euen in the old Law (which permitted far more liberty, then the Ghospell doth)a yōg, rich and beautifull Woman did take heed of Carnall sinnes, for no other reason, then that she *greatly feared our Lord*.

The sacred Scripture doth mention and commend the same thing in Holy *Iob*. For he made a couenant with his eyes, that he would not so much as thinke of a Virgin; that is, he vvould not look vpon a Virgin, to preuent therby that no vnchast thought

i might

might creep into his mind. And why did *Iob* so warily and diligently auoid such allurements? Becaule he greatly *feared our Lord :* for thus it there followeth: *For what part should God from aboue haue in me?* that is, if an vncleane cogitation should in any fort defile my mind, I should not be Gods portion, nor God should be my Portion. There were no end, if I should insist in examples of Saints during the tyme of the New Testament. This therefore is the *Fesre*, wherewith the Saints were endued, of which if our selfes were full, there were nothing, the which we could not most eafily obtaine of our Heauenly Father.

The last fruite of the seauenth Word.

CHAP. XXIV.

THere remaineth the laft fruite, which is gathered from the confideration of the Obedience of Chrift, manifefted in his laft words, and in death it felfe. For wheras the Apoftle fayth: *He humbled himfelfe, made obedient*

dient vnto death, euen the death of the Crosse.Philip.2. This was chiefly performed, when our Lord pronouncing those Words, *Father into thy hands,I commend my spirit*, did presently giue vp the Ghost. But it will be conuenient to repeate, & ponder more deeply what may be said of the Obediēce of Christ; that so we may gather a most precious fruite from the tree of the holy *Crosse*. Therefore Christ (our Maister and Lord of all Vertues) did exhibit such Obedience to God his Father, that a greater cannot be conceaued or imagined.

First, the Obedience of Christ tooke its beginning from his Conception, and continued without intermission euen to his death;Thus the whole life of our Lord Iesus Christ was but one Act, or Course of a continuated, and vninterrupted Obedience. Truly the soule of Christ euen in the first moment of its Creation, had the vse of freewill, and withall was replenished with Grace and Wisdome; and therefore euen from that first momēt, Christ being as yet inclosed in the wombe of his mother, began to exercise Obedience. Where we read in the

39. Pfalme, in which it is faid in the Perfon of Chrift: *In the head of the booke it is written of me , that I should do thy will: my God, I would , and thy law in the middeft of my Hart.* That: , *in the head of the booke* , fignifieth no other thing, but in the fumme of the diuine Scripture that is , throughout the whole Scripture, it is chiefly preached of me, that I am peculiarly chofen and fent to this end, that I fhould do thy Will. I, my God, will, & I haue moft willingly accepted thereof, and *thy law* , that is thy commandement I haue placed in *the middeft of my hart*, that I might euer thinke thereof, and might moft diligently performe and execute it.

And hither alfo thofe words of our faid Lord haue reference : *My meate is to do the will of him that fent me, to perfect his worke.* Ioan. 4. For as meate is not taken once or twice through a mans life , but is taken daily & with pleafure : fo our Lord himfelf did continually , and with a willing mind practice all Obedience to his Father. And hereupon he faid : *I defcended from Heauen , not to doe my owne will, but the will of him , that fent me.*

C c *Ioan.*

Ioan. 6. And more cleareiy in another place : *He that sent me, is with me, and he hath not left me alone, because the things that please him , I do alwayes.* *Ioan.* 8. And because Obedience is the most excellent Sacrifice of all Sactifices, according to the iudgment of *Samuel,* therefore it followeth, that how many works Christ did. all the tymo, that he. liued as Pilgrime vpon the Earth, so many Sacrifices did he offer vp, and those most gratefull to God. This therefore is the first Prerogatiue of the Obedience of Christ; to wit, in that it endured from his Conception, to the end of his sife.

Furthermore the Obedience of Christ was not determinable to any one kind of worke, as we commonly see it is among men, but it was extended to all those things, vvhich it should please God his Father to command him. And from hence so great variety is seene in the life of Christ our Lord, as that one vvhile he would stay in the desert, neither eating nor drinking, & perhaps not sleeping, but liuing with beasts, as *S. Marke* noteth. *c.* 1. At another tyme he vvas in the frequency & sight of men , eating and drinking :

Then,

Then, he remained obscure and secret at home, and that for no few, yeares. At an other tyme appearing excellent for wisdome and Eloquence, working most great and stupendious Miracles: Novv, with great authority casting buyers and sellers out of the Temple; At an other tyme latent, & (as it were) weake, declining from the multitude and company of men; All which things require and exact a mind, free from all proper free will. For neither would our Lord haue said: *Math.* 16. *He that will come after me, let him deny himselfe*; that is, let him renounce his proper will, and proper iudgment: Neither except Christ himselfe had performed it before, he wou'd haue persuaded his disciples to the perfection of Obedience, when he said: *Luc.* 14. *If any man commeth to me, and hateth not his Father and mother, and wife, & childen, and brethren and sisters, yea and his owne life besides, he cannot be my Disciple*. Thus according hereto did Christ himselfe forsake all things, which are accustomed to be so ardently beloued, yea his owne life; the which he was so prepared to lose, as if he did hate it.

Cc 2   This

This is the true roote and Mother of Obedience, vvhich shyned most admirably in Christ our Lord. And who want this, shall hardly euer come to the revvard of Obedience. For how is it possible, that one should promptly obey an other mans Will, who is wholy deuoted to his ovvne will, and his owne iudgment? This is the Cause why the Celestiall Orbes do not resist or withstad the Angels mouing them, vvhether they be caried towards the East, or West; because they haue not any peculiar and proper propension either to one part, or to the other. And the same reason is, why the Angels themselfes stand at a becke obedient vnto God, as holy *Dauid* singeth in the 102. Psalme. To wit, because they haue no proper Will, repugnant and refractary to the will of God; but being most happely conioyned vvith God, they are one spirit vvith him.

Furthermore, the Obedience of Christ is not only largely on ech syde diffused; but withall by how much it is depressed downe by Patience and Humility, by so much, through the excellency of its merits, it is eleuated and aduanced on high. Therefore the

third

third Propriety of the Obedience of
Chrift is , that it defcendeth to an incredible Patience and Humility. Chrift
being an Infant, to fulfill the Obediēce
of his Father , began (though full of
knowledge and prudence) to inha-
bite in a darke prifon. Other Infants,
who want Reafon in their mothers
Wombe , fuffer no griefe or molefta-
tion : But Chrift enioying in his mothers wombe the vfe of Reafon, would
haue had no doubt a horrour to remaine in that ftraite Prifon nyne
Months , had not the obedience towards his Father, and loue to mankind
caufed him for the fetting vs at liberty (as the Church fingeth) *that he did
not abhor the wombe of the Virgin,*

To proceed , no fmall Patience &
Humility was neceffary , that Chrift
during all the time of his Infancy(who
then was more wife then *Salomon*,
fince in him *were all the treafures of
VVifdome and Knowledge*) fhould ac-
commodate and apply himfelfe to the
manners & weakenes of Infants : But
that Continency , Modefty , Patience,
and Humility was altogether moft admirable, that during the fpace of eigh-
teene yeares (to wit, from the twelfth

yeare, to the thirtith) he by the command of his Father, remained so obscurely in *S. Iosephs* bowse , as that he
was reputed but the Sonne of a Car-
penter, ignorant in learning, and perhaps indocible; when notwithstanding
he did transcend all men and Angels in
wisdome. I may here next alledge his
great glory, rising from his preaching
and working of miracles , but yet accompained with extreme pouerty and
daily labours : *The foxes haue their holes,*
and the foules of the ayre nests ; but the
Sonne of man hath not where to repose
his head. Luc 9 And he being wearied
through iourneying , did sometimes
rest himselfe by sitting vpon the side
of a fountaine ; and preaching the
kingdome of Heauen, went on foote
to Cityes and Castells : Yet notwithstanding it had beene most easy, for
him (it so it had stood with his Obedience to his Father) to abound with
all things, through the help and ministery of men or Angels.

What shall I now speake of Christs
persecutions, of his reproaches, and
maledictiōs, spittings, buffeting, whipping , and finally of his sufferings and
paines vpon the Crosse ? For in all
                              these

thefe his humble Obedience did
take fuch deepe roote, as that it may
plainly feeme to be in-imitable. But
yet there remaineth a greater profundity and depth of his Obedience,
which concerned the laft of all terrible
things; & to this *Abyfmall* profundity
the Obedience of Chrift defcended,
whē crying with a loud voyce, he faid:
Eather into thy hands I commend my fpi-
rit ; and faying this, he gaue vp the
Ghoft. Luc. 23. The Sonne of God may
be thought and fuppofed to fpeake to
his Father in this fort. O *Father* I haue
receaued commandement from **you**,
that I fhould lay downe my lyfe ; and
after receaue it ; now the tyme commeth, that I accomplifh this your laft
command. And although the difiun-
ction of my foule from my flefh (both
which euen from the beginning of
their vnion to this houre haue remained together in great peace and charity) be moft bitter ; and alfo although
death, introduced through the Enuy
of the diuell, be very aduerfe to nature, and the laft of all terrible thinges ;
notwithftanding your commandment
being moft deeply into the middft of
my hart, doth ouerballance all other
things.

things. Therefore I now stand prepared euen to swallow downe death, and
to exhaust & drinke vp this most bitter
chalice giuen to me by you. And because your commandement was, that
I should after resume & take it againe;
therefore into your hands I commend
my spirit, that you may restore it to
me in the next conueniency of tyme.
And thus licence of departing being
taken of his Father, his head being
enclined to obedience, he gaue vp the
Ghost. Thus Obedience became victorious & triumphant. Neyther did it receaue a most ample reward onely in
Christ himselfe, that he, who descended lower then any man, and obeyed
all men for his loue towards his Father should ascend aboue all, and command ouer all: But it also obtayned,
that all men, who would imitate his
obedience and humility, should themselues ascend aboue all the Heauens, &
should be committed and placed ouer
the goods of their Lord, and in the end
should be made partaker of the Celestiall Throne and Kingdome. To conclude, Christ did take so remarkable
a Triumph ouer the rebellious, diso-
bedient, and most proude Spirits, as
that

that all of them do stand affrighted, and flye at the very signe of the *Crosse.*

All those, who couet to aspire to true glory, and to the rest and peace of their soule, ought to behould and imitate this exemple. Neyther only Regular men, who through the vow of obedience to their Superiours (who preside in the place of God,) but also all men, who labour to be the disciples and Brethren of Christ, ought to aspire to the prize and rewatd of this most worthy victory, except they will rather make choyce to bewaile and lament for all eternity, with the proud dicels, vnder the feete of the Saincts. For Obedience, which is due by diuine precepts, and which God himselfe comandeth to be giuen to those who rule vpon Earth, is most necessary to all men. For Christ said to all: *Take vp my yoake vpon you. Matth.* 11. And the Apostle preacheth to all, saying: *Obey your Prelats, and be subiect to them. Heb.* 13. And *Samuel* instructeth heerein all Kings, when he sayth: *Will our Lord haue Holocausts and Victimes, and not rather that the voyce of our Lord be obeyed? Better is obedience then Victimes.* 1. *Reg.* 15. And then he addeth to sh-

D d

the greatnes of the Sinne of disobe-
dience , *Because it is* (as it were) *the
Sinne of enchantement , to resist* ; meaning to resist the commandements of
our Lord , and of those , who do gouerne in the place of our Lord.

But for the benefit of those , who
willingly subiect themselues vnder the
Obedience of their superiours , I will
here adde some few points touching
their happy state; and this not out of
my priuate Iudgment , but from the
words of *Ieremy* the Prophet , who
guyded by the Holy Ghost, thus sayth:
*It is good for a man when he beareth the
yoake from his youth: He shall sit solitary and hould his peace , because he hath
lifted himselfe aboue himselfe.* Thren.3.
Certainly a wonderfull felicity is signified by that word , *It is good for a
man* : since from the words following
it euidently is gathered, that *Good*, in
this place, is taken for that , which is
profitable, honourable, pleasant, and
on ech syde blessed. For he that shall
accustome himselfe to beare the yoke
of Obedience from his youth , shalbe
free during all his life from a most
heauy and seruile yoake of Carnall Cu-
litics and desires. S. *Austin* deposeth
the

the truth of this point, shewing in his
8. Booke of *Confessions*, how difficult
a matter it is, to cast of the yoake of
Concupiscence from ones selfe, who
for diuers yeares hath beene enthral-
led to the law of the flesh; as on the
contrary, how pleasant and easy it is, to
beare the yoke of our Lord, before the
soule hath bene defiled, or ensnared
with Vice.

Furthermore, how great a gaine is
it, to merit in euery worke in the sight
of God? For he, who doth nothing out
of his owne proper will, but from O-
bedience to his Prelate and superiour,
this man in euery worke performed
by him, sacrifizeth to God a most gratefull Sacrifice, because as *Samuel* speaketh; *Obedience is better, then Sacrifice*
1. *Reg.* 15. And *S. Gregory* giueth a reason of this disparity, saying: *By bloudy
Sacrifices the flesh of an other, by Obedience the proper will is immolated and
offered vp l.* 35. *mor. cap.* 10. Adde hereto, as a thing most admirable, that if so
be the Prelate should fortune to sinne
in commaunding, the subiect sinneth
not, but meriteth in obeying, so that
that which is commanded be not a
manifest and euident sinne. The Pro-

phet *Ieremy* doth adde : *He shall sit so-litary, and should his peace.* What sig-nifieth here , *he shall sit* , but that he shall remaine quiet , because he shall find the rest of his soule? For whosoe-uer abandoneth his owne will, deuo-ting himselfe wholy to fulfill the will of God, coueteth nothing , seeketh af-ter nothing, is ambitious of nothing, but remaynes free from all Cares, and sitteth with *Mary Magdalen* , at our Lords feete, *hearing his word*; Luc. 10. And indeed he sitteth truly solitary, both because he doth conuerse with those, who are *one Hart*, *and one Soule*; as also in that he affecteth no mā with a priuate and peculiar Loue, but loueth all in Christ, and for Christ. And hence it is, that he is quiet, as not conten-ding with any one, or hauing any pe-culiar negotiation or busines with o-thers. And the reason of so great a tranquillity and quietnes is , because, *he hath lifted himselfe aboue himselfe*; that is , he hath transcended and pas-sed from the Order of men , to the Order of Angels.

There are many men, who *do cast themselues vnder themselfs* , and des-cend to the Order of Beasts ; To wit, those

those men, vvho euen breath nothing
but earthly matters, and prize nothing
but what is gratefull to the flesh, and
senses of the Body, And these are Co-
uetous men, lasciuious, and euen en-
slaued to good cheere, felowship, and
drunkennes. There are others, vvho
liue *the life of men*, and after a certaine manner remaine in themselues,
such are *Philosophers*, vvho either
search the secrets of Nature, or deliuer
precepts touching manners. To conclude, there are some others, who do
lift themselfs aboue themselfs, and this
not vvithout a peculiar priuiledge and
assistance of God, leading not an humane, but Angelicall life. These are
those, who renouncing all things,
vvhich the vvorld affords, and denying their ovvne will, can say vvith the
Apostle: *Our conuersation is in Hea-
uen.Phil.3.*For the Angels are not defiled with any filth of sinne, and they
do euer contemplate the face of the
Father which is in Heauen, and omitting all other affayres, they are wholy
busied, and intent in executing the
Commandements of God, according
to that of the 102. Psalme: *Blesse our
Lord all yee his Angels, doing his word*,

This is the felicity of a Regular life, the which if it do seriously imitate the purity and Obedience of the Angels, will doubtlesly participate of their Glory in Heauen; especially if they follow Christ their Captaine and mayster, *Who humbled himselfe, made obedient vnto death; euen the death of the Crosse. Phil. 2. And when as he was the Sonne of God, learned obedience from those things he suffered. Heb. 5.* That is, he experimentally learned, that true Obedience was tryed by Patience; And thus he did not only teach Obedience by his owne Example, but withall taught the principles and foundation of true and perfect Obedience, vvhich are Humility and Patience. For who freely and willingly obeyeth his superiour, commanding honourable and pleasing things to be done, may be much doubted of, whether the vertue of Obedience, or some other Allectiue draweth him to obey: But he, who vvith all alacrity and cheresulnes of mynd obeyeth in things vile and laborious (where Humility and Patience are necessary) declareth that as a true Disciple of Christ, he hath learned perfect Obedience.   *S. Gre.*

S. *Gregory* notably sheweth the
difference betvvene true and forged
Obedience, vvho thus speaketh, *l.* 35.
mor. c. 10. *Quia nonnunquam nobis
&c.* Because sometymes things pleasing
to this world, at other tymes things displeasing are commanded to be done,
therefore we are chiefly to knowe, that
sometimes Obedience, if it haue nothing
of it selfe in it, is no obedience; And sometymes except it hath something of it
selfe, it is lesse. For example, when pleasing things of this world are commanded, when the higher and more worthy
place is commanded to be taken, he, who
obeyeth these Commands, euacuateth
and frustrateth in himselfe the vertue
of Obedience, if out of a secret desire he
affecteth them. For he suffereth not himselfe to be gouerned by Obedience, who
in vndertaking the prosperous things of
his life, serueth his owne humour of Ambition. Againe, When aduerse and distastfull matters are commanded, when
it is commanded to receaue obloquies,
and contumelies; except the mind of it
selfe doth desire these things, the merit of
obedience is lessened; because he descen-
deth vnwillingly to such things, as are

Dd 4   abiect

abiect and vile in this life. For Obe-
dience suffereth detriment, when no de-
sires of any part do accompany the mind,
prepared to receaue disgraces or contu-
melies. Therefore Obedience touching
things aduerse and displeasant, ought to
haue something of it selfe ; and againe
touching things prosperous and grate-
full, it ought to haue nothing of it selfe.
And Obedience, when the subiect of it, is
a thing displeasing, is so much the more
glorious and worthy, by how much the
desire of him that obeyeth is more firm-
ly contayned to the diuine will ; As on
the contrary, where the subiect is plea-
sant and sweet, Obedience is so much
the more true, by how much the mind is
estranged from all vayne and humane
complacency.

But the weight of this Vertue of
Obedience, we may more clearely bal-
lance, if we call to mind the memorable
Acts of two men, now reigning in Hea-
uen. Moyses, when he fed sheep in the
desert, was called by our Lord speaking
to him, by the ministery of an Angell in
the fiery Bush, that he should gouerne
ouer all the multitude of the Israelits.
Exod. 3. But because he was humble and
                                    lowly

*lowly in himselfe, he was afraid of the
profered glory of so great a gouerment;
saying: I beseech thee, O Lord I am not
eloquent from yesterday, and the day
before, and since thou hast spoken to thy
seruant, I haue more impediment and
slownes of tongue &c. I beseech thee, O
Lord, send whom thou wilt send. Behould
heere, how* Moyses *discourseth and de-
bateth with the Authour of the Tongue; and acknowledged himselfe to be of
imperf. speach, that thereby he might
auoyde the power of so great a soueraignty and gouerment. In like sort,* S.
Paul *was admonished from Heauen (as
himselfe testifieth in his* 2. Epistle to the
Galathians *) that he ought to ascend to*
Ierusalem; *Who meeting with the Prophet* Agabus *in his iourney, was aduer-
tized, how great aduersity and trouble
did expect and wayte for him in* Ierusalem. *For it is thus written:* Agabus
taoke Paules girdle, & binding his owne
hands and feete, he said: Thus the man
whose girdle this is, so shall the Iewes
binde in Ierusalem. Act. 22. But S. Paul
instantly answered: I am ready not only
to be bound, but to dye also in Ierusalem,
for the name of Iesus.

E e   Thus

Thus S. Paul through a command
of diuine Reuelation going towards Ierusalem, knoweth afore hand, what
vexations were there to afflict him; ne-
uerthles he willingly desireth them: He
heareth of troubles, of which he might
wellbe afraid; yet he coueteth with all
endeauour oo aspire to them. Thus Moyses hath no part of his owne desire touching his command; and therefore he
partly laboureth against the coommand,
thereby to eschew his gouernment ouer
the Israelites. But S. Paul is drawne to
vndergoe aduersities out of his owne desire; who foreseeing imminent euills,
boyleth in deuotion of spirit to sustaine
farre greater. The former man was willing to decline the glory of present Power, though God commanded him to
accept thereof: This later (God preparing for him asperity and molestations)
thirsteth after more violent afflictions,
yea euen death it selfe. Now from the
immoueable Vertue of these two worthy
Captaines leading vs the way, we may
be instructed, that if we desire earnestly
to ghine the palme and reward of Obedience, we must play the souldiers, in
performing things prosperous only by cō-
maxi

mand, though with some reluctation of our owne Nature, but things aduerse & distastfull, to execute euen out of our owne deuotion and Zeale.

Thus farre *S. Gregory* Which doctrine Christ our Lord & Maister, euen from his owne example most cleerly approued. For when he knew the multitude would come and take him, that they might make him a King, we read; *That he fled into the moūtaine, himselfe alone.* But whē he saw that the Iewes & the souldiers with *Iudas*, were to come to apprehēd him, & draw him to punishmēt, then according to the command, which he receaued from his Father, he of his owne accord did presently meete them, and suffered himselfe to be taken and bound. Therefore Christ not in words did vaunt of Obedience; but in workes, and in earnest, exhibited Obedience vnto his Father, grounded in true Patience and Humility. Vpon this example of the most noble vertue of Obedience, all those ought to haue their eyes fixed, who aspire to the high reward, due for a voluntary abnegation of ones proper Will, and *imitation of Christ.*

THE

THE TABLE

The first Booke.

The second Booke.

FINIS.